BIG NIGHT IN

CHRONICLE BOOKS
SAN FRANCISCO

BY DOMENICA MARCHETTI

BIG NIGHT IN

More Than 100 Wonderful Recipes for Feeding
Family and Friends Italian Style

PHOTOGRAPHS BY SUSIE CUSHNER

Library of Congress Cataloging-in-Publication Data:

Marchetti, Domenica.
    Big night in : more than 100 wonderful recipes for feeding family
and friends Italian-style / by Domenica Marchetti : photographs by Susie
Cushner.
        p. cm.
    ISBN 978-0-8118-5929-5 (alk. paper)
    1. Cookery, Italian. 2. Menus. I. Cushner, Susie. II. Title.
TX723.M3265 2008
641.5945—dc22

                            2007042022

Manufactured in China.

Prop styling Jennifer Gotch
Food styling Rori Trovato
Design and typesetting by Katie Heit

THE PHOTOGRAPHER WISHES TO THANK:
Heath Ceramics
400 Gate Five Road, Sausalito CA 94965
415.332.3732
www.heathceramics.com

Soule Studio
542 Sparkes Road, Sebastopol, CA 95472
www.soulestudio.com

Alex Marshall Studios
3632 Houghton Ave., Corning, CA 96021
530.824.3800
www.alexmarshallstudios.com

Maison Midi
148 S. La Brea Ave., Los Angeles, CA 90036
www.maison-midi.com

Luna Garcia
201 San Juan Ave.,Venice, CA 90291
www.lunagarcia.com
෴෴෴෴෴

10 9 8 7 6 5 4 3 2 1

Chronicle Books LLC
680 Second Street
San Francisco, California 94107

www.chroniclebooks.com

❦ ACKNOWLEDGMENTS ❧

I wish to gratefully acknowledge the people who helped to make this book come true:

Chronicle Books editor Bill LeBlond, who enthusiastically supported this project from the beginning; and Amy Treadwell, project editor, who deftly steered it through the entire process.

Lisa Ekus-Saffer, for embracing *Big Night In* when it was scarcely an idea, and for her caring, guidance, and sound advice. Thanks also to Jane Falla and everyone at the Lisa Ekus Group for their hard work and support.

Photographer Susie Cushner and food stylist Rori Trovato, who captured not only my recipes but also the spirit of this book in each delectable photo.

At Chronicle Books I would also like to thank those who have worked so hard on my behalf, including Peter Perez, copy editor Michelle Starika Asakawa; designers Jay Peter Salvas and Katie Heit.

Chef John Coletta, for generously sharing his recipe for Calabrian Fennel Salad with Red Finger Chiles.

My sister, Maria Marchetti, who contributed recipes, creative input, and so much more in the way of support.

A huge thank you also to those who took the time to test and taste, offered invaluable feedback and tips, and expressed their support and friendship in countless other ways: Diane Morgan, Michelle Andonian, Kelly Dolan, Anne and John Burling, Kimberley Ferlazzo-Ricci, Susie Gordon, Dana Jones, Janice Rivera, and the Uncles. (Special thanks to Anne and Kimberley for brightening up my much-neglected garden as I raced to meet my deadline.)

My parents, Frank Marchetti and Gabriella Marchetti (whose unsurpassed skills as a cook and a hostess continue to inspire me), for all their years of unwavering support and encouragement.

Most of all, I wish to thank my family, Scott, Nick, and Adriana, without whom there would be no BNIs.

CONTENTS

Introduction

Remember when our most memorable meals were the ones we occasionally splurged on in fancy restaurants? These days, more of us are finding that the meals we remember and savor the most are those we share with family and friends around our dining room or kitchen tables, or on our backyard patios. The hours spent at the table seem like minutes because the food and company are both so good.

Americans are more accomplished and ambitious in the kitchen than we used to be. We have discovered the joy of recreational cooking and entertaining. Italians mastered this art long ago; they possess an enviable quality to make their guests feel at once special and like family by feeding them well and generously. When I was a girl, my parents often had people over. Whether hosting a small sit-down dinner or a buffet, my Italian-born mother always made everyone feel right at home with her warm, open personality, and with her homemade ravioli, lasagne alla Bolognese, roasts, tortes, and other delights.

I have many fond memories of the lavish dinners that my uncle Emilio used to organize every summer at his farmhouse in the hills of Abruzzo, where a staff of cooks—wives of the farmers he employed—would turn out overflowing dishes of homemade egg noodles in a rich ragu, baby lamb seasoned with fresh herbs and roasted in a great big stone fireplace, and platters of crispy roasted potatoes and sautéed greens. These dinners often would begin with house-cured prosciutto and sheep's milk cheeses and end with hot shots of espresso and a sweet, crumbly jam tart. After the meal, the kids would run around the grounds while the adults stayed at the table, drinking wine and laughing as my uncle told "grown up" jokes (we kids were not allowed to hear these jokes until we were well into our teens).

At my home in northern Virginia, I possess one standard range with an oven and four burners, and alas, no staff of farmers' wives. I'm not even good at telling jokes. But I can still turn out a memorable meal for my friends and family, and I do it often. That is what this book is all about—capturing the same spirit of generosity, openness, and simplicity that characterize the Italian way of entertaining.

Big Night In is, first and foremost, a collection of my favorite recipes to cook and serve when I am having people over. This is not everyday Italian food. The recipes are creative and generous, and some are downright indulgent. Simply put, this is a book of great party food.

But it is also a helpful guide. *Big Night In* simplifies the feat of welcoming guests and making them feel special. Here you will find tips and advice for organizing a "Big Night In" without a big fuss, from planning and making the meal to creating just the right atmosphere in which to serve it.

The chapters are arranged logically, the same way that a meal typically unfolds: Appetizers and Antipasti; Soups and Salads; Pasta, Rice, and Savory Tortes; Main Courses; Vegetables and Side Dishes; and Desserts. The chapter on main courses is further divided by cooking technique—from the grill, from the oven, from the stove top—to simplify things even more. If I know a roast is going to be occupying my oven for two hours, I may want to serve it with a salad and a stove-top side dish rather than a baked gratin.

Within that conventional framework, however, there is lots of room for improvisation. For instance, many of the recipes in the Pasta, Rice, and Savory Tortes chapter make great party centerpieces. Pasta Timballo (page 99), stuffed with little meatballs, ragu, hard-boiled eggs, and lots of cheese, is practically a meal in itself. Three-Cheese-Stuffed Red and Yellow Peppers (page 141), from the Main Courses chapter, make a fine vegetarian entrée for a casual dinner, but are also great buffet fare and would make a swell side dish to serve with Beef Tenderloin alla Bandiera Italiana (page 133). For a refreshing luncheon entrée, you can't beat my Zia Gilda's Insalata di Riso (cold rice salad; page 69), which also doubles as a perfect side dish for the Mixed Grill Platter of Steaks, Chops, Thighs, and Sausages (page 113).

In the Desserts chapter you'll find a wide-ranging selection of sweets, from a refreshing, icy Blood Orange Granita (page 183) to a rich Chestnut-Cognac Bavarese (page 190). I adore *crostate,* rustic Italian tarts. They are easy to make, beautiful to look at, and versatile. I've included three of my favorites: a luscious Lemon Crostata (page 201), a gorgeous lattice-top Harvest Crostata (page 202) with a pear and apple filling, and a creamy Toasted Coconut Crostata (page 204), in honor of my sister, the coconut lover.

Be sure to read the Cook's Notes and Do Ahead notes that accompany the recipes. They provide time-saving tips, information on ingredients and substitutions, and—most important—what you can do in advance to minimize last-minute cooking—and stress! In the Main Courses chapter you will also find, under the heading Goes With, recommendations for what side dishes to serve with your entrées.

A bonus chapter titled Buon Giorno offers a creative brunch menu for a "Big Morning In." I guarantee you have never tasted anything as light as the Heavenly Eggs made with mascarpone cheese (page 211).

Finally, *Big Night In* provides a dozen suggested menus for a variety of gatherings. Menus are personal, and I hesitated to even include them here. But they are also useful roadmaps, and fun to read and consider. You can follow them to the letter or just use them as a jumping-off point.

This is truly a great time to be in the kitchen. Farmers' markets abound, offering an ever-growing selection of fresh local produce—tender baby vegetables, heirloom tomatoes, hearty greens, and more. Farm Stand Sauté (page 159) and Tomato and Cheese Tart (page 170) are just two of many recipes in this book that rely on the best of what's in season.

But we also have access to a world of imported goods, including an amazing array of cheeses. In this book you will find recipes that call for Italian cheeses that only a few years ago would have been hard to find—robiola and cacio di Roma to name just two. When I was growing up, my mother would buy dozens of tins of imported Rizzoli brand *alici in salsa piccante* (anchovies in a piquant sauce; see page 16) on every visit to Italy, and then stuff them into our suitcases for the trip home. I wouldn't dream of making my Caesar Salad (page 62) without them. Now those same anchovies are just a click away on the Internet.

All of these ingredients serve to enhance the pleasure of cooking for those of us who love to be in the kitchen. Cooking gives me immeasurable joy; I don't spend an afternoon rolling out pasta and making ravioli so that people will *ooh* and *aah* over it. I do it because it gives me great satisfaction. But it gives me even greater satisfaction to share what I make with my family and my friends. That is what it really comes down to: the treasured experience of sharing a meal with those we love.

Tips for Planning a Big Night In

Let us first dispense with the fallacy that so many books on entertaining feel compelled to perpetuate: there is no such thing as stress-free entertaining. Even if you have your party catered, hire a valet to park cars, a bartender to mix drinks, and an army of wait staff, you will still feel some stress. If you care about your guests you will want to make sure they are having a good time, that they are relaxed and socializing, that their glasses are filled, and that there is enough food to go around. Maybe you will worry about how your house looks, or how you look, or whether the kids are trashing the downstairs, but you will worry about something.

Having said that, let me also add that there is plenty you can do to turn down the level of stress considerably and turn up the enjoyment—for your guests and yourself. Over the years I have collected numerous invaluable pieces of advice that I rely on when I'm planning a gathering, whether it's a dinner for six or a backyard barbecue for twenty. Follow these ten tips and I assure you that you will be well on your way to a low-stress, highly entertaining Big Night In.

1. KNOW YOUR PARTY.

Since this is a book about casual entertaining, I won't remind you to polish your silver and iron your hand-wrought lace tablecloth. (My mother almost always used her silver when she entertained, but I hardly ever do.) If you enjoy these things, you should incorporate them into your party. Are you having a sit-down dinner in which you expect to have intense discussions? Or are you inviting the neighborhood to an open house? Do your guests have adventurous palates, or would they prefer a simply grilled steak? Having a clear idea of whom you are cooking for can help you determine the other factors, including the type of gathering, the menu, the seating (or standing) arrangements, and such.

2. PLAN AHEAD.

It sounds like a no-brainer, but many of us have a tendency to let things slide till the last minute. Decide on your menu well in advance of your party. If there are any unusual or hard-to-find ingredients in any of your recipes, make sure you give yourself enough time to search them out or special-order them. If you are going to be roasting whole beef tenderloin or a capon, make sure you have a butcher or meat department that you can count on to provide such ingredients for you.

Make a detailed grocery list. Buy as much as you can in advance, but leave the most perishable items—meat, fresh vegetables, cheese, and the like—until shortly before you plan to cook or set them out. Stock up on useful pantry items, such as crackers and chips, olives, and other condiments. I almost always have two or three cheeses in the refrigerator that I can set out with crackers and olives if I need a last-minute appetizer.

Do you have all the equipment you need? Many of the recipes in this book call for large oven-proof baking dishes that can be brought straight to the table. Lasagne made in a disposable aluminum pan will taste just as good as one made in a ceramic dish, but the one in the ceramic dish will look a lot more appealing on your buffet table. Consider investing in a couple of round and rectangular dishes of different sizes that you can use over and over again. If you are making fresh pasta for the first time, consider borrowing a pasta-rolling machine from a friend before buying your own. Once you've tried it and decided you like it, then you can decide whether to purchase your own.

Dinnerware and barware. Most of the time we can get by with what we already own. But suddenly, when we start setting the buffet table we realize we don't have enough soup plates or ice cream bowls or wine glasses. For large parties, I have used sturdy, attractive paper plates. But they never seem to hold up as well as I would like, and they generate a lot of trash. This is a good time to remember rental places, which were created for just this sort of situation. Cookouts aside, most people would rather eat on china than paper. If you are serving mixed drinks, you will need barware. If it is wine you are pouring, make sure you have many more wine glasses than guests, as they will invariably set them down and forget where they put them. For some reason people like to give me those decorative wine "charms" that fasten to the stem of the glass so I have lots of them, and since I like things that sparkle I use them.

3. SET THE TABLE.

It is a good idea to do this the day or night before your party, especially if you are having a lot of people over. For a buffet, set out the platters, bowls, and utensils that you plan to use. This will give you the opportunity to think about where on the table you plan to put your various dishes. Remember to position the individual plates at the beginning of the buffet, but the utensils and napkins at the end. It is not easy to negotiate a buffet table with a plate in one hand and your fork, knife, and napkin (not to mention a drink) in the other. For brunch, remember to set up a station, whether in the dining room or the kitchen, where guests can help themselves to coffee and other beverages.

Don't be afraid to mix colors and patterns on the table. I have plenty of ceramic dishes, platters, and bowls, but they don't all match. I use them anyway—they add color and variety to the table. Think about height as well. Place two or three cake stands one atop another with the largest on the bottom, and arrange a different finger food on each tier.

For a sit-down gathering, a set table is a cue that you are organized and ready. After all, you don't want to be setting out forks and knives and plates while you are attending to last-minute cooking details *and* trying to make your guests feel welcomed and relaxed. On the other hand, when it comes to family gatherings and dinners with close friends I usually let this rule fly out the window and have them set the table.

If you like to place a centerpiece on your table, choose one that won't interfere with the interaction at the table. When my daughter did a third-grade science project on what liquid keeps flowers freshest we purchased four short rectangular glass vases at a craft store. Now I use that quartet of vases on my dining-room table. Sometimes I put stones and votive candles in them, and sometimes I fill them with short bouquets of flowers.

4. SPRUCE IT UP.

Even if all of the beds upstairs are unmade, make sure that the areas where your guests are going to congregate are cleaned and tidied. Vacuum the carpet, fluff the pillows, and set out a vase or two of fresh flowers. Clean the bathrooms and put out fresh hand towels.

5. WELCOME YOUR GUESTS.

Make your guests feel welcomed even before they enter your house. Turn on the porch lights and open the front door. For one cocktail party that my husband and I threw, we borrowed tikki torches from my friend and neighbor Kimberley and set them along our front walkway to guide people to the door. It was a cold November evening and the party we were giving was not an "island" theme, but the blaze from the torches instantly lit up everyone's mood. (This same neighbor of mine also owns a giant inflatable green, gold, and purple court jester that she assembles in her front yard every February for her annual Mardi Gras party. She is a good neighbor to have.) If possible, be there to greet your guests when they arrive, or assign the task to a family member or a reliable friend who won't mind taking on the duty.

6. PROVIDE MUSIC.

Some people believe that life needs a soundtrack. I am not one of those people, but I do believe that music is an important part of entertaining. Play what you like; music is a personal choice, but decide what you are going to play beforehand so that you don't have to scramble at the last minute. Tone it down for a sedate dinner and turn it up for a big bash.

7. CHECK YOUR LIGHTING.

In my kitchen I have a large island that is topped with pure white Formica (thanks, previous owner!). Above the island is a giant fluorescent element that emits the most garish light you can imagine. I sometimes refer to the island as my autopsy table. Eventually I will get around to remodeling, but for now when I have people over I keep the overhead light off and line up several hurricane lamps with candles on the island. It makes a huge difference. Consider candlelight in other rooms as well— the living room and dining room, even a couple of votives in the bathroom. But please stay away from scented candles. They will interfere with all of the wonderful aromas emanating from your kitchen and give everyone a headache.

8. OFFER AN ASSORTMENT OF BEVERAGES.

For most casual gatherings I find that a selection of wine and beer, plus the makings for an occasional mixed drink, more than suffice. I also like to have some nonalcoholic choices for guests who prefer not to drink. At the table I set out a pitcher or two of ice water and, in keeping with Italian tradition, a couple of bottles of sparkling water, one each at either end. Keep fresh ice on hand for chilling beverages.

9. COOK WHAT YOU KNOW.

I was an English major in college, and more than one of my creative writing professors encouraged me to "write what you know" (which I guess is how I got into this business). I have heard the same advice applied to cooking—that is, cook what you know. Why try something you have never made before if you are going to be serving it to others? It is good advice, and yet, I have never been able to follow it. For me, part of the fun of being in the kitchen is trying new things and feeding the results to my friends. Has this backfired? You bet. Some years ago I cooked dinner for my husband's boss, a man who very much enjoyed eating and knew a thing or two about good food. I also happened to be a new parent of a particularly high-maintenance baby. So perhaps I was tired. Still, I opted to try to re-create an intricate pasta dish that my husband and I had eaten once in Italy, plus a labor-intensive veal roast. The pasta took forever to cook and was hideously chewy, and the veal roast fell apart. I don't remember what I served for dessert but I do remember that (mercifully) it turned out well, so at least that part of the meal was saved. I was terribly embarrassed about it then, but now the memory makes me laugh. Today, I would probably do things a little differently—I would cook something I know well for the boss and save the experiment for close friends.

10. KEEP A CASUAL ATTITUDE.

My point is this: not everything is going to be perfect every time. But so what? You do what you can, and the rest will take care of itself. A casual attitude, perhaps. But, happily, that's what casual entertaining is all about.

Buon Appetito!

Equipment

❧·✵·❧

Here is an alphabetical list of the equipment I have found useful when making and serving the recipes in this book.

❧·❧·❧

BAKING DISHES: I use ceramic and Pyrex oven-proof baking dishes, casseroles, shallow gratin pans, and deep lasagne pans for baking many of the recipes in this book. I seek out baking dishes that are attractive enough to go from oven to table.

BAKING SHEETS: I find rimmed baking sheets have many uses, from toasting bread for crostini and making focaccia to roasting whole beef tenderloin and large fillets of fish.

BLENDER OR IMMERSION BLENDER for pureeing Creamy Carrot Soup

CHAFING DISH for keeping eggs and ravioli warm on a buffet table

CHEESE KNIVES AND SPREADERS for cutting and spreading hard and soft cheeses

COLANDER for draining pasta and rinsing vegetables and other ingredients

COOKIE CUTTERS for butter cookies and decorative cut-outs for decorating the tops of tarts

COVERED DISHES: Oven-proof vessels with matching lids are useful for transporting hot dishes such as risotto or sautéed vegetables to the table.

CUSTARD CUPS: I find 6-ounce Pyrex custard cups are ideal for baking popovers.

CUTTING BOARDS: I use separate cutting boards for meat and poultry, fish, and vegetables.

DECORATIVE CERAMIC BOWLS of a variety of sizes to serve dips, salads, slaw, and various other dishes

DOUBLE BOILER: Not many recipes call for one these days, but I often use the enamel-coated double boiler that I bought at a tag sale years ago. In this book, only the recipe for Heavenly Eggs specifically calls for a double boiler. But if you are timid about making custard for gelato or a trifle without it curdling, I recommend you use a double boiler instead of setting your pot right on the stove.

DUTCH OVEN OR OTHER HEAVY-BOTTOMED LIDDED POTS in a couple of sizes for making soups and stews, risotto, polenta, and ragu

FINE-MESH SIEVE for straining liquid from shellfish and dried porcini soaking liquid and for straining custard

FOOD PROCESSOR for mixing pasta and pastry dough, grinding nuts, and finely chopping and pureeing ingredients

GARLIC PRESS for pureeing whole peeled garlic cloves

GRATERS: I use a Microplane grater-zester with fine rasps for grating Parmigiano and pecorino cheese, as well as for lemon and orange zest and nutmeg. I use the large holes on a box grater for shredding cheeses.

GRILL: I make use of both a charcoal and a gas grill for grilling meats, cheeses, vegetables, and breads.

ICE CREAM SCOOP for scooping ice cream, granita, and cheesecake sundaes

JUICER: For juicing lemons and limes I use a small gadget that presses half of the fruit at a time, capturing the seeds and sending the juice through a series of holes.

KNIVES: I use a paring knife for trimming and peeling vegetables and fruit and for cutting free-form cookie shapes, a 7-inch stainless-steel chef's knife for chopping and for crushing garlic, and a large serrated knife for slicing bread and tomatoes.

MANDOLINE for thinly slicing sweet potatoes for fried sweet potato chips

METAL BAKING PANS: I use a 9-by-13-inch pan for freezing granita and for baking pizza rustica. I use a metal loaf pan for freezing apricot semifreddo.

MIXING BOWLS of all sizes for mixing sauces and vinaigrettes and for holding ingredients, such as baking powder, flour, sugar, and salt, once they have been measured. Stock up on glass or stainless-steel bowls of varying sizes, as you will use them again and again.

PARFAIT GLASSES OR ICE CREAM BOWLS for serving granitas, gelato, and cheesecake sundaes

PASTA MACHINE for rolling pasta dough to make ravioli and lasagne sheets

PASTRY BRUSH for brushing glaze on grilled meats and roasted squash wedges

PEPPER MILL for seasoning many dishes with freshly ground pepper

POULTRY OR KITCHEN SHEARS for cutting up chicken

RING PANS, including a 10-inch tube pan and a Bundt pan, are used for making several of the desserts in this book, as well as a baked eggplant and rice timballo.

ROLLING PIN for rolling out pastry for sweet and savory tart crusts and cookies

SALAD SPINNER: If you are cleaning large quantities of lettuce for a party-size salad, this gadget is indispensable.

SAUCEPOTS: I use a 4-quart lidded pot with short handles that is made of stainless steel for making sauces and for simmering soups, and a 5-quart lidded pot for boiling water for pasta.

SERVING PLATTERS: I am partial to oval serving platters and own a number of them in a variety of sizes for serving everything from bite-size appetizers to roasts.

SKEWERS: I use 12-inch-long wooden skewers for shrimp, small cubes of meat for *arrosticini*, and vegetables.

SKILLETS AND SAUTÉ PANS: I use a 9-inch well-seasoned cast-iron skillet for making crepes for the Crepe Cannelloni (page 122). I use a heavy-bottomed stainless-steel skillet and a deep nonstick skillet for sautéing and pan-frying vegetables and for frying eggplant, zucchini blossoms, and meatballs.

SLOW-COOKER: I don't often use my slow-cooker for cooking, but I do use it to keep chowders and other substantial soups warm on the buffet table.

SPATTER SCREEN for preventing oil spatters during frying

SPOONS, SPATULAS, AND OTHER STIRRING UTENSILS: I use wooden spoons and silicon spatulas for stirring vegetables as they sauté and for stirring soups and sauces. For scraping out mixing bowls I use silicon and rubber spatulas. A large slotted spoon is useful for removing cooked ingredients from a pan or pot. I own several serving spoons that are useful for scooping out gratins and other baked foods at a buffet table.

SPRINGFORM PAN: I use a 9-inch aluminum springform pan for cakes and tortes and a 10-inch springform pan for the Pasta Timballo.

STAND MIXER: Until recently, I used my Kitchen Aid stand mixer primarily to mix cake batters. But when my small ice cream machine konked out on me, I purchased an ice cream attachment for my mixer rather than replace the ice cream machine. I find it does the job just as well.

STEAMING BASKET for steaming vegetables and shrimp

SUGAR SHAKER for dusting confectioners' sugar over cakes, tarts, and cookies

TART PANS: I use a 9-inch tart pan and an 11-inch tart pan with removable bottoms to bake sweet and savory tarts (*crostate*).

THERMOMETERS: I use an instant-read thermometer for checking the doneness of meat and fish, an oven thermometer to check the accuracy of the temperature in my oven, and a candy thermometer to check the temperature of custard.

TONGS for flipping meats on the grill, turning pieces of meat during browning, and removing vegetables from the steaming basket

TRIFLE BOWL: A straight-sided, footed glass bowl is ideal for serving trifle as it shows the various layers of cake, fruit, and custard.

WHISK for making custards, lightly whipping cream, and mixing vinaigrettes and dressings

WIRE RACK for cooling baked dishes, cookies, and tarts

Ingredients

❧·✦·❧

Following is an alphabetical list of special ingredients for the recipes in this book. Explanations for some ingredients can also be found in the recipes in which they appear.

❧·❧·❧

ANCHOVIES

For all of the recipes in this book that call for anchovies I use Rizzoli brand *alici in salsa piccante* (See Sources, page 218). The small, rectangular red-and-gold tins are packed with rolled anchovy fillets marinated in a mildly spicy olive oil sauce flavored with tuna. Although they are not widely available here, you can order them online. In their absence use the best-quality imported Italian or Spanish anchovy fillets in olive oil that you can find.

APPLES

If you are cooking or baking with apples in season there is no reason you should settle for bland supermarket apples. Seek out local varieties where you live. Some of my favorite apple varieties are Albemarle Pippin, Goldrush, Stayman, and Suncrisp.

ARUGULA

This spicy green adds color and zip to salads. I also use it as a garnish or a bed for grilled meats.

BACON

In Virginia, where I live, supermarkets have a good selection of high-quality thick-sliced hardwood-smoked bacon. If your supermarket does not carry good bacon, it is worth seeking out a butcher who supplies it.

BITTERSWEET CHOCOLATE

I am a lover of dark chocolate, so for the Bittersweet Mocha Grappa Torte with Walnuts (page 193) I use an extra bittersweet chocolate with at least 60 percent cacao. Be sure to use a high-quality chocolate, such as Callebaut, Valrhona, or Scharffen Berger. I have also found reasonably priced, good-quality 70-percent bittersweet Belgian chocolate slabs at Trader Joe's.

BLOOD ORANGES

These oranges have interiors ranging from deep crimson to bright orange with streaks of red. Their flavor ranges from sweet to tangy. As with any orange, seek out those that feel heavy for their size—they are the juiciest.

CAPERS

Capers packed in salt are more expensive than those preserved in brine, but I prefer them in most recipes. Those in brine tend to take on the flavor of the liquid, while the salt-packed capers have a more pure taste.

CHEESES

Many of the recipes in this book call for more than one type of cheese. With so many wonderful cheeses available to us nowadays, I feel compelled to take advantage of the selection. Here are brief descriptions of the cheeses used in this book:

ASIAGO: a cow's milk cheese produced in the Italian Alps. Fresh Asiago is a moist cheese suitable for slicing; aged Asiago has a more pronounced flavor and is a good grating cheese.

AURICCHIO: aged provolone that traditionally was produced in southern Italy. It has a sharp, buttery flavor and is much superior to the sliced provolone typically found in a supermarket deli.

BASKET CHEESE: a fresh, unsalted cow's milk cheese named for the way it is drained and formed inside a basket.

CACIO DI ROMA: a creamy, semi-firm sheep's milk cheese from Italy's Lazio region. It is available in the cheese section of well-stocked supermarkets, gourmet shops, and cheese shops. Substitute manchego if you are unable to find it.

DRY JACK: aged Monterey Jack cheese. It has the buttery quality of a good cheddar and is good for grating.

FONTINA VAL D'AOSTA: a dense, semi-firm cheese made in the Italian Alps near the French and Swiss borders. It has a somewhat sharp aroma and a nutty, slightly mushroomy flavor.

GORGONZOLA: a blue-veined cow's milk cheese made in Italy's Lombardy and Piedmont regions. Gorgonzola dolce is creamy and soft. Gorgonzola piccante or mountain gorgonzola is aged longer and has a sharper flavor and a more crumbly texture.

HALLOUMI: produced in Cyprus, traditionally from a combination of goat's and sheep's milk, but now often made with cow's milk. The cheese is sometimes flavored with mint. Its high melting point makes it ideal for grilling or frying.

MANCHEGO: a popular Spanish sheep's milk cheese aged for three months or longer. It has small holes and a rich golden color. Its flavor sharpens as it ages.

MASCARPONE: a triple-crème cheese originally produced in Lombardy. It is dense and buttery and is used in both baking and cooking, as well as for spreading.

MOZZARELLA: the name used for numerous fresh (that is, unripened) Italian cheeses that are shaped by spinning and then cutting the curd. The cheese can be made from the milk of cows or water buffalo. Fresh mozzarella is a good cheese for salads. Partially dried, aged mozzarella, such as the vacuum-packed variety commonly found in supermarkets, has a firmer texture and is good for shredding. *Ciliegine* are small whole mozzarellas about the size of a large olive. Smoked mozzarella typically contains less moisture than fresh mozzarella and is delicious in eggplant parmigiana and other baked dishes.

PARMIGIANO-REGGIANO: a hard, granular grating cheese essential to many of the recipes in this book. Its flavor is both sharp and rich. It is sold in chunks and keeps best tightly wrapped in plastic and refrigerated. Look for the words "Parmigiano Reggiano" stamped into the rind of the cheese to be sure you are getting the real thing. For the best flavor, grate it only as needed.

PECORINO ROMANO: an aged sheep's milk cheese that is paler in color than Parmigiano-Reggiano. It has a sharp, salty flavor and is an excellent grating cheese.

PECORINO TOSCANO: an aged sheep's milk cheese that is more mild and creamy than pecorino Romano. It is delicious as part of an Italian cheese platter, and also grilled and drizzled with honey.

QUESO BLANCO: a fresh and slightly salty cow's milk cheese from Mexico. It softens but does not melt when heated and is ideal for grilling.

RICOTTA: a fresh cheese made from whey, a by-product of cheese-making. Most ricotta available here is made from cow's milk rather than sheep's milk. Look for fresh ricotta at well-stocked grocery stores or cheese shops rather than the grainy mass-produced variety found in tubs at the supermarket.

ROBIOLA: a small square or round cheese made from a combination of cow's, goat's, and sheep's milk and produced in northern Italy's Piedmont region. It has a bloomy white rind (like brie), a creamy interior, and a high fat content.

SOTTOCENERE AL TARTUFO: a semi-soft cow's milk cheese produced in the Veneto region. It has an ash rind and is flecked with black truffle.

CHESTNUTS

Chestnuts appear in several forms in this book. Whole peeled and cooked chestnuts are available at well-stocked supermarkets and gourmet food shops. Chestnut jam, a sticky-sweet spread, is available at Italian delicatessens and gourmet food shops.

Chestnut honey has an assertive, slightly bitter flavor and a dark color. It is available in gourmet food shops and online. *Marrons glacés* are cooked chestnuts that have been poached in sugar syrup. They are available at gourmet food shops and are quite expensive. (For chestnut products see Sources, page 218.)

FLOUR

I use unbleached all-purpose flour for the desserts in this book and most other recipes. For pasta dough, I use "00" flour, a highly refined flour with the texture of talcum powder. If you are unable to find it substitute unbleached all-purpose flour.

GIARDINIERA

This is the Italian term for pickled vegetables, most often found as a mix of carrots, cauliflower, pearl onions, and red peppers. You can find jars of giardiniera at many supermarkets, as well as gourmet food shops and Italian delicatessens.

GREEK YOGURT

Thick, creamy Greek yogurt is made from either sheep's or cow's milk. To my mind, it has a much more pleasing texture and a richer, tangier taste than American yogurt, which seems grainy in comparison.

HERBS

I almost always prefer to cook with fresh herbs rather than dried ones. They usually have a brighter flavor and, when added at the end of a recipe, provide a splash of color as well. The herbs used most often in the recipes in this book are basil, flat-leaf parsley, rosemary, and sage. These herbs are available fresh year-round in small packages in the produce section of most supermarkets.

MARSALA

Named for its city of origin in Sicily, Marsala is a fortified blended wine that can be sweet, medium-dry, or dry. The recipes in this book call for dry Marsala.

MORTADELLA

This cured sausage, a specialty of Bologna, is nothing like its American imitator. It has a silky-smooth texture and is studded with pork fat and slivers of pistachio nuts.

OIL

Two kinds of olive oil are used throughout this book. Extra-virgin olive oil is used in most dishes for sautéing and flavoring. For frying I use either a good-quality olive oil that is not labeled extra-virgin or a vegetable oil such as canola or sunflower.

PANCETTA

This cut of Italian bacon is cured with salt, pepper, and other spices and comes from the belly of the pig. Pancetta is generally rolled up into a large sausage shape for curing and then sold sliced.

PORCINI

The recipes in this book call for dried porcini mushrooms to be reconstituted in water. Dried porcini have a strong, earthy mushroom aroma and lots of flavor. Look for dried porcini sold in well-sealed plastic packets. They should be in slices or large pieces; small bits indicate the mushrooms are old and therefore not as flavorful. Once the packet is opened, store the mushrooms in a zipper-lock plastic bag in the freezer. They will keep indefinitely.

PROSCIUTTO

Imported Prosciutto di Parma is cured with salt, air-dried, and aged for more than a year. Good Italian prosciutto is deliciously silky and rich and best appreciated raw as an antipasto or in a sandwich. I use a good-quality domestic prosciutto for the recipes in this book that call for cooking or grilling the ham. Prosciutto cotto is Italy's version of cooked ham. It is available at Italian delicatessens and at well-stocked supermarkets. It is sometimes flavored with rosemary. Use a good-quality American ham, sliced to order, if you are unable to find it.

PROSECCO

Prosecco is a straw-colored sparking Italian wine that tastes of fruit and has a refreshing dry finish. Since the recipe Seafood Risotto with Prosecco only calls for 1½ cups, I recommend you get out your champagne flutes and enjoy the rest by the glass.

RADICCHIO

This bitter green, a member of the chicory family, is actually a deep garnet red. The most common variety of radicchio available here is radicchio di Chioggia, a tight round head with red and white leaves. Radicchio di Verona, also red and white, is long and tapered and resembles a large Belgian endive.

RICE

I use two kinds of rice for recipes in this book. For risotto recipes and for rice salad I use Arborio, a pearly white, short-grain variety of rice with a high starch content. Carnaroli and Vialone Nano are two other types of rice suitable for risotto. For recipes that call for fragrant rice I use either long-grain basmati rice from India or jasmine rice.

SAFFRON

Red-gold saffron threads are the dried stigmas of a variety of crocus. As a spice, saffron is sold either as threads or as a powder. The powder dissolves more easily, but it is also more easily tampered with. To be sure you are getting pure saffron, buy the threads and gently pound them to a powder before using.

SOPRESSATA

This dry-cured salami is known for its distinctive flat shape, which comes from being pressed with a weight while drying. The seasoning varies from region to region but typically includes black pepper or hot pepper.

SOUR CHERRIES

Also known as pie cherries, sour cherries are primarily grown in Michigan, though I buy them at my local farmers' market in Virginia. They have a fleeting season that peaks in early July, but they freeze well. Pit a quart (or however many you want) of cherries and spread them out on a rimmed baking sheet or jellyroll pan. Put the pan in the freezer for 30 to 60 minutes, until the cherries are more or less frozen solid. Transfer the frozen cherries to a zipper-lock freezer bag, seal, and return to the freezer. They will last for up to a year. To use them in the Sour Cherry–Mascarpone Pound Cake recipe, just add the frozen cherries, without defrosting them first, to the cake batter as called for in the instructions.

Pitting sour cherries is easy. They are softer than their sweet cousins, and it is easy to push the pit out with your fingers by prying the cherries open at the stem end and gently squeezing. An even easier way is by using the paperclip trick. Unbend a clean paperclip so that you have a long S-shaped wire with two curved ends. Gently push the smaller curved end into the cherry through the stem end until you reach the pit; then just scoop it out.

TUNA

Imported Italian tuna preserved in olive oil is available in tins and jars. It is inconveniently expensive, so I use it sparingly. I buy Flott brand, imported from Sicily, which contains large pieces rather than small chunks. Ortiz, imported from Spain, is another good brand.

I consider appetizers and antipasti a sort of culinary welcome wagon. They are the first food that your guests will sample when they arrive at your home, and indeed they even help to set the tone for a social gathering: Are you serving little canapés piped with mousse and garnished with a tiny mound of caviar? Or beer nuts?

The appetizers here fall somewhere in between. They are more casual than a fancy hors d'oeuvre but definitely more special than a bowl of nuts. Some, such as Mini Rice Croquettes (page 25), Crostini with a Selection of Colorful Toppings (page 22), and Sea Salt and Rosemary Sweet Potato Chips (page 43), are finger foods. Others—Seaside Salad (page 37) and Shrimp alla Scapece (page 35), for example—are meant to be enjoyed as part of a buffet or sit-down dinner.

Remember that not all of your appetizers have to be homemade. I almost always set out bowls of green and purple olives (don't forget to put out a small vessel to collect the pits), an Italian Cheese Platter (page 39), and sliced cured meats such as dry salami and sopressata. And of course, don't forget about nuts such as marcona almonds and pistachios—or even beer nuts!

Over the years I have discovered that appetizers serve as more than just a palate teaser. You can use them to direct your guests to where you would like them to congregate. I know I am not the only one who finds that people seem to gravitate to the kitchen. Most of the time, this is just fine with me. But I also want my guests to feel comfortable, and to know that they are welcome to move around, to sit down in the living or family room or, on a nice afternoon or evening, gather outside. So that is where I set the food. I guarantee that if you put out a platter of Stuffed Olives (page 27) or Gorgonzola-Stuffed Dates (page 29) on your patio, your guests will follow.

BENVENUTI: APPETIZERS & ANTIPASTI

CH. **1**

Crostini with a Selection of Colorful Toppings

MAKES ABOUT 40 SLICES

Found in just about every restaurant throughout Umbria and Tuscany, crostini are simply thin slices of grilled or toasted baguette garnished with any number of savory toppings. Here is the basic recipe for making crostini, followed by a few classic topping combinations.

INGREDIENTS

For the crostini:

I THIN BAGUETTE OR FICELLE

EXTRA-VIRGIN OLIVE OIL FOR BRUSHING

Heat the oven to 375ºF. Cut the bread into ½-inch-thick slices and brush them on both sides with a little olive oil. Arrange half of the slices on a large rimmed baking sheet.

Place the baking sheet in the oven and toast the bread slices for 7 to 8 minutes, or until they are golden brown around the edge and pale golden in the center. Turn the slices over and continue to toast them for 5 minutes more, or until lightly browned on both sides. Remove the toasts from the oven and let them cool to room temperature. Brush the remaining slices of bread with olive oil and toast them in the oven in the same way.

Top the crostini with one or more of the following toppings, arrange them on platters, and serve.

DO AHEAD: The crostini may be made up to 3 days in advance and kept at room temperature in a tightly lidded container or zipper-lock bag. Garnish them with your topping of choice up to 30 minutes before serving.

INGREDIENTS

Anchovy Butter Topping

4 TABLESPOONS UNSALTED BUTTER, SOFTENED

3 TO 4 RIZZOLI BRAND *ALICI IN SALSA PICCANTE (page 16),* OR BEST-QUALITY ITALIAN ANCHOVY FILLETS IN OLIVE OIL, DRAINED AND FINELY CHOPPED

In a small bowl, combine the butter and anchovies and blend thoroughly with a fork or a spatula. Spread on crostini and serve.

DO AHEAD: The anchovy butter may be made up to 2 days in advance and kept in a tightly lidded container in the refrigerator. Remove the butter from the refrigerator and let it come to spreading consistency before using.

Gorgonzola Topping

4 OUNCES GORGONZOLA DOLCE

4 OUNCES MASCARPONE

I TABLESPOON COGNAC

FRESHLY GROUND BLACK PEPPER

Giardiniera Topping

2 TABLESPOONS EXTRA-VIRGIN OLIVE OIL

I CUP FINELY MINCED PARSLEY

½ CUP MINCED GIARDINIERA *(page 18)*

2 TABLESPOONS CAPERS, PREFERABLY IN SALT, RINSED, DRAINED, AND COARSELY CHOPPED

3 CLOVES GARLIC, FINELY MINCED

3 TEASPOONS WHITE WINE VINEGAR

I TEASPOON SUGAR

KOSHER OR SEA SALT

FRESHLY GROUND BLACK PEPPER

Combine the gorgonzola, mascarpone, and cognac in a small bowl and blend thoroughly with a fork or a spatula. Spread on crostini and sprinkle with a little pepper.

DO AHEAD: The gorgonzola topping can be made up to 2 days in advance and kept in a tightly lidded container in the refrigerator. Remove it from the refrigerator and let it come to spreading consistency before using.

Heat the oil in a medium skillet placed over medium heat. Add the parsley, giardiniera, capers, and garlic and sauté for 5 minutes, or until the garlic is soft and the vegetables have started to soften. Raise the heat to medium-high and stir in the vinegar and sugar. Sauté for a minute or two and then remove from the heat. Season with salt and pepper to taste and let cool to room temperature. Spoon the cooled topping onto crostini, arrange on a platter, and serve.

DO AHEAD: The topping can be made a day in advance and kept in a tightly lidded container in the refrigerator. Bring it to room temperature before using.

Mini Rice Croquettes

MAKES 24 TWO-INCH RISOTTO BALLS

೮ಽ·ಜ಼·೮ಽ

INGREDIENTS

For the risotto:

2 TABLESPOONS BUTTER

2 TABLESPOONS EXTRA-VIRGIN OLIVE OIL

1 SMALL YELLOW ONION, FINELY CHOPPED

¼ CUP DRY WHITE WINE

1 CUP ARBORIO RICE

1 CUP DICED CANNED TOMATOES

2 TO 3 CUPS HOMEMADE CHICKEN BROTH
(page 50) OR BEST-QUALITY FAT-FREE, LOW-
SODIUM CANNED CHICKEN BROTH

2 TABLESPOONS CHOPPED FRESH BASIL

½ TEASPOON KOSHER OR SEA SALT, OR TO TASTE

FRESHLY GROUND BLACK PEPPER

¾ CUP FRESHLY GRATED PARMIGIANO-REGGIANO

2 LARGE EGGS, LIGHTLY BEATEN

—

To make the croquettes:

1½ CUPS UNBLEACHED ALL-PURPOSE FLOUR

3 LARGE EGGS, LIGHTLY BEATEN WITH A PINCH OF SALT

1½ TO 2 CUPS UNSEASONED DRY BREAD CRUMBS

1 (8-OUNCE) BALL OF FRESH MOZZARELLA

VEGETABLE OR OLIVE OIL (NOT EXTRA-VIRGIN)
FOR FRYING

My mother's older sister Elsa was a professor of literature and a sports enthusiast. She much preferred teaching and skiing to cooking. There were, however, a few dishes she liked to prepare now and again, and an inviting platter of rice croquettes, with gooey mozzarella centers, was one of them. It is true that this recipe takes some work—making the rice, shaping the croquettes, and frying them. But all of the work can all be done in advance (see Do Ahead), which makes this savory treat great to serve at a buffet. The recipe here calls for a basic tomato-based risotto, but almost any kind of leftover risotto, including Vanishing Cheese Risotto (page 89), will do fine.

Make the risotto:

Heat the butter and oil in a heavy-bottomed saucepan placed over medium-low heat. When the butter has melted, add the onion and stir to coat thoroughly. Sauté the onion, stirring frequently, for 7 to 8 minutes, until it is soft and translucent. Increase the heat to medium-high and add the wine. Let it bubble for a minute or so, and then stir in the rice. When the liquid has nearly all been absorbed, add the diced tomatoes and stir to combine everything thoroughly.

Reduce the heat to medium and add 2 cups of broth, stirring to combine well. Cook the rice at a gentle simmer, reducing the heat to medium-low if necessary, and stirring often. Taste the rice for doneness after 20 minutes of cooking. It should be

CONTINUED ON NEXT PAGE . . .

tender but still a little firm at the center of each kernel. Add additional broth if necessary.

When the rice is cooked, remove it from the stove and stir in the basil, salt and pepper, and Parmigiano. Let the mixture cool for about 5 minutes before stirring in the lightly beaten eggs, taking care to add the eggs a bit at a time and to stir the mixture vigorously to prevent them from scrambling.

Turn the rice mixture onto a rimmed baking sheet or large glass baking dish and spread it out with a spatula to help it cool quickly. Cover with foil and refrigerate until thoroughly chilled.

To shape the croquettes:
Place the flour, lightly beaten eggs, and bread crumbs in three separate shallow bowls. Cut the mozzarella into ½-inch-thick slices and then cut the slices into ½-inch cubes (you may have leftover cheese depending on the individual size of the croquettes).

Remove the rice from the refrigerator and scoop up a rounded tablespoonful into the palm of your hand. Press a cube of mozzarella into the center of the rice and shape the mound into a ball or an oval, making sure that the cheese is completely encased in the center. Roll the rice ball in the flour, gently shaking off the excess. Transfer the rice ball to the bowl of beaten eggs and, using a fork, roll it around to coat it thoroughly. Transfer the croquette to the bowl of bread crumbs and roll it around several times (with your fingers or a fork) until it is thoroughly coated. Place the rice ball on a large rimmed baking sheet or platter.

Continue to make the croquettes in this way until you have used up all the rice; you should have about 24 balls that are slightly larger than golf balls. When you are finished, loosely cover the baking sheet or platter with aluminum foil and refrigerate the croquettes for at least 30 minutes and up to several hours.

To fry the croquettes:
Pour enough vegetable oil into a deep frying pan or straight-sided sauté pan to measure 1 inch. Heat the oil over medium-high heat until it registers 350°F on a candy thermometer. Carefully lower 6 rice balls into the pan and fry them for 3 to 4 minutes, turning them several times for even browning, until they are a deep golden brown. Using a slotted spoon, remove the rice balls to a platter lined with paper towels to drain. (Alternatively, you can place a brown paper shopping bag near the stove and remove the cooked rice balls to the bag to drain before placing them on a serving platter.) Continue until all of the croquettes have been fried.

Arrange the croquettes on a warmed ceramic platter or other decorative platter and serve immediately.

DO AHEAD: Croquettes may be made and fried ahead of time and frozen in containers or freezer bags for up to 3 months. To serve, place the frozen croquettes on a baking sheet and bake in a preheated 375°F oven for 15 to 20 minutes, or until completely heated through.

Stuffed Olives

MAKES 120 STUFFED OLIVES

INGREDIENTS

For the stuffing:

I TABLESPOON EXTRA-VIRGIN OLIVE OIL

I TABLESPOON UNSALTED BUTTER

5 OUNCES GROUND BEEF

5 OUNCES GROUND PORK

5 OUNCES GROUND VEAL

I SMALL YELLOW ONION, FINELY CHOPPED

I CLOVE GARLIC, SLICED PAPER-THIN

KOSHER OR SEA SALT

FRESHLY GROUND BLACK PEPPER

½ CUP DRY WHITE WINE

2 LARGE EGGS, LIGHTLY BEATEN

½ CUP FRESHLY GRATED PARMIGIANO-REGGIANO

2 OUNCES PROSCIUTTO DI PARMA,
FINELY JULIENNED

2 OUNCES MORTADELLA, FINELY CHOPPED

PINCH OF FRESHLY GRATED NUTMEG

For the olives:

120 PITTED LARGE GREEN OLIVES, SUCH AS
CERIGNOLA OR SICILIAN

2 CUPS UNBLEACHED ALL-PURPOSE FLOUR

PINCH OF KOSHER SEA SALT

FRESHLY GROUND BLACK PEPPER

5 LARGE EGGS

2 TO 3 CUPS DRY BREAD CRUMBS

VEGETABLE OR OLIVE OIL (NOT EXTRA-VIRGIN)
FOR FRYING

One-hundred-plus stuffed olives may sound like a lot, but I can tell you that if you put these out on your buffet table they will be gone within minutes. They are that good, and yes, they are worth the effort of stuffing and frying each and every one. The wonderful thing about these olives is that you can make them weeks in advance and freeze them (see Do Ahead). Just pop them, frozen, in the oven when it comes time to serve them. This recipe comes from my mother, Gabriella, who adapted it from one given to her years ago by a friend from Ascoli Piceno, the ancient town in Italy's Marche region from where the recipe is said to originate.

To make the stuffing:

In a skillet or sauté pan, heat the olive oil and butter over medium heat. When the butter has melted and begins to sizzle, add the beef, pork, veal, onion, and garlic. Use a wooden spoon to break up the large chunks of meat. Sauté, stirring, for 2 minutes, then cover and let the meat cook for 12 to 15 minutes, or until the onion is soft and the meat is cooked through but not browned. Season the mixture with the salt and pepper to taste. Raise the heat to medium-high and pour in the wine. Cook for 2 more minutes, or until most of the liquid has evaporated. Remove from the heat and let cool for 10 minutes.

Transfer the stuffing to a food processor and process for 10 to 15 seconds, or until it is finely ground but not a paste—you want it to have some body. Transfer the mixture to a bowl.

In a small bowl, stir together the eggs and cheese. Pour the egg mixture into the bowl with the meat. Add the prosciutto, mortadella, and nutmeg and mix everything together thoroughly. Cover tightly and refrigerate until chilled.

CONTINUED ON NEXT PAGE . . .

. . . CONTINUED

With a paring knife cut one side of an olive from top to bottom so that you can pry it open. Fill with about ½ teaspoon or a little more of stuffing and close the olive around the stuffing. It is okay if the two edges of the olive do not meet, as the olives will be better with a little more stuffing and the bread crumb coating will make them look uniform again.

Stuff all of the olives in the same way and set them aside while you prepare the ingredients for the coating. Place the flour in a shallow bowl and season it with a pinch of salt and a few grindings of pepper. Place the eggs in a second shallow bowl and beat them lightly with a fork. Place the bread crumbs in a third shallow bowl.

Roll an olive in flour and shake off any excess. Using a fork, transfer the olive to the egg and roll it around to coat it completely. Transfer the olive to the bread crumbs and coat it thoroughly. Set the dredged olive on a rimmed baking sheet. Continue to dredge the olives in the flour, egg, and bread crumbs until you have coated them all.

In a large skillet or sauté pan, heat ¾ inch of vegetable or olive oil over medium heat to 375°F. When the oil is hot, carefully set 10 to 12 olives in the skillet, taking care not to crowd the pan. Fry the olives in the hot oil for about 3 minutes, turning them once or twice, until they are golden brown all over. With a slotted spoon, transfer the olives to a rimmed baking sheet lined with paper towels or with a brown paper bag to allow them to drain.

When all the olives have been fried, arrange them on one or two decorative ceramic platters or shallow bowls and serve.

DO AHEAD: The olives may be prepared and fried in advance and frozen. Let them come to room temperature after you have fried them. Store them in tightly lidded containers or in zipper-lock freezer bags and freeze them for up to 3 months. When you want to serve them, simply take them from the freezer and place them on a rimmed baking sheet in a preheated 400°F oven for 15 minutes, or until they are completely warmed through.

Gorgonzola-Stuffed Dates

MAKES 24 STUFFED DATES

INGREDIENTS

24 MEDJOOL DATES

8 OUNCES GORGONZOLA DOLCE

Many supermarkets and gourmet markets carry Medjool dates, which are large, sweet, and succulent. They are easy to pit, making them a perfect vehicle for creamy, piquant, salty-sweet gorgonzola. While these dates make a fine appetizer, remember that you can also serve them as part of a cheese course or with seasonal fruit, such as pears or clementines, in place of dessert.

Using a sharp paring knife, slice the dates open lengthwise and pull out the pit. Stuff each pitted date with about a teaspoonful of gorgonzola. Arrange on a decorative platter and serve.

DO AHEAD: The dates may be stuffed several hours ahead and refrigerated. Remove them from the refrigerator an hour before serving.

Bruschetta with Roasted Cherry Tomatoes

MAKES 12 SERVINGS

Every bite of these tomato-topped bread slices is filled with the taste of summer. I like to serve them on a large white platter. It really makes the vibrant reds and greens stand out.

INGREDIENTS

I ROUND LOAF ITALIAN COUNTRY BREAD, CUT INTO ¾-INCH-THICK SLICES, LARGER SLICES CUT IN HALF CROSSWISE; 24 SLICES TOTAL

I CUP EXTRA-VIRGIN OLIVE OIL, PLUS ADDITIONAL FOR DRIZZLING

6 CUPS CHERRY TOMATOES, STEMS REMOVED

2 CLOVES GARLIC, FINELY MINCED

2 TABLESPOON CAPERS, PREFERABLY IN SALT, RINSED, DRAINED, AND COARSELY CHOPPED

2 TEASPOONS MINCED FRESH BASIL, PLUS 2 SPRIGS FRESH BASIL FOR GARNISH

2 TEASPOONS MINCED FRESH OREGANO

KOSHER OR SEA SALT

Heat the broiler and place the oven rack 4 inches from the heat source (see Cook's Note). Place the bread on a large rimmed baking sheet and brush the top of each slice with olive oil. Place the baking sheet in the oven and broil for 1 to 2 minutes, just until the edges of the slices are dark and the centers are golden. Remove the bread from the oven and transfer the slices to a large serving platter (use two if they don't all fit on one). Reduce the heat in the oven to 425ºF and, using oven mitts, move the oven rack to the center of the oven.

In a large bowl, toss the tomatoes with the garlic, capers, basil, and oregano, and ¼ cup olive oil. Wipe the baking sheet clean and spread the tomatoes on it in one layer. Roast the tomatoes in the oven for 15 to 20 minutes, until their skins are just starting to split.

Spoon the roasted tomatoes and all of their juices on top of the bread slices. Garnish the platter or platters with basil sprigs and sprinkle the bruschetta with a little salt and a little more olive oil. Serve warm.

COOK'S NOTE: For bruschetta on the grill, prepare a charcoal grill or heat a gas grill on high. Place the bruschetta on the grill grate and grill until the bottoms are slightly charred with grill marks; turn and grill the other side until lightly charred. Use tongs to remove the slices of bruschetta as they finish grilling.

DO AHEAD: You can brush the slices of bread with oil and have them ready to broil or grill up to 2 hours in advance. Cover the bread loosely with plastic wrap to prevent it from drying out. The tomatoes and other ingredients for roasting can be prepared up to 2 hours in advance and kept, covered with plastic wrap, at room temperature.

Basil-Stuffed Zucchini Blossoms

MAKES 24 STUFFED BLOSSOMS

❧·☙·❧

Delicate, perishable zucchini blossoms are one of summer's nicest treats. Here, they provide an attractive vessel for a classic trio of Italian flavors: milky mozzarella cheese, fresh basil, and piquant anchovies.

∼∼∼∼∼∼∼∼∼∼∼∼∼∼ INGREDIENTS ∼∼∼∼∼∼∼∼∼∼∼∼∼∼

I CUP UNBLEACHED ALL-PURPOSE FLOUR

I CUP SPARKLING SPRING WATER,
SUCH AS SAN PELLEGRINO

I LARGE EGG, LIGHTLY BEATEN *(see Cook's Note)*

½ TEASPOON KOSHER OR SEA SALT, PLUS AN
ADDITIONAL SPRINKLE AT SERVING TIME

24 ZUCCHINI BLOSSOMS, PREFERABLY WITH ABOUT
I INCH OF STEM ATTACHED

I (8-OUNCE) BALL FRESH MOZZARELLA, CUT INTO
24 (I INCH BY ½ INCH) PIECES

24 LARGE FRESH BASIL LEAVES, PLUS A
SPRIG FOR GARNISH

8 ANCHOVY FILLETS, PREFERABLY RIZZOLI BRAND
ALICI IN SALSA PICCANTE (page 16), CUT CROSSWISE
INTO THIRDS, TO MAKE 24 SMALL PIECES

VEGETABLE OR OLIVE OIL (NOT EXTRA-VIRGIN)
FOR FRYING

In a medium-size bowl, whisk together the flour, sparkling water, egg, and salt to make a smooth batter about the consistency of heavy cream. Add a little more sparkling water if the batter seems too thick. Set aside.

Gently rinse the zucchini blossoms and pat them dry with a paper towel. Gently pry them open and remove the pistil from the center of the blossom by pinching it with your fingertips (this step is optional). Carefully stuff each blossom with a piece of mozzarella cheese, a basil leaf, and a small piece of anchovy. Gently twist the tops of the blossoms to close them.

Pour enough oil into a medium-sized skillet or sauté pan to reach a depth of ½ to ¾ inch. Place the skillet over medium-high heat and heat it to 375ºF. To test, drop a small amount of batter into the hot oil. It should float to the surface, sizzle, and quickly turn golden.

Holding a zucchini blossom by the stem, gently dip it into the batter. Transfer the blossom to the hot oil, and then repeat with 3 more blossoms. Do not crowd the skillet or the blossoms will not fry properly. Fry the blossoms for about 2 minutes on one side, and then turn them using a fork or a slotted spoon. Fry them another 2 minutes, or just until they are golden. Remove the blossoms with a slotted spoon and drain them on a paper-towel-lined platter or on a large brown paper bag placed near the stove. Continue frying the blossoms until you have used them all.

To serve, arrange the warm zucchini blossoms on a decorative platter, sprinkle a little salt over them, and garnish with a sprig of basil.

❧·❧·❧

COOK'S NOTE: For a lighter batter you can omit the egg.

❧·❧·❧

DO AHEAD: You can fry the zucchini blossoms several hours ahead of time and serve them at room temperature. Or, to serve them warm, briefly reheat them in a low-temperature oven. Their batter coating will lose its crispiness but the blossoms will still taste delicious.

❧·❧·❧

SERVING SUGGESTION: These stuffed blossoms are beautiful fanned out on a round or oval platter and served as an appetizer. They also make a nice side dish to just about any grilled entrée. I have been known to pile the leftovers between two slices of good bread, along with some sliced tomatoes and a drizzle of olive oil and call it lunch.

Chef John Coletta's Calabrian Fennel Salad with Raisins and Red Finger Chiles

MAKES 6 TO 8 SERVINGS

John Coletta is chef-owner of a lovely restaurant in Chicago called Quartino that specializes in small plates. I fell head over heels for this salad when he served it at a party at his restaurant hosted by cookbook publicist and literary agent Lisa Ekus-Saffer. Chef John graciously agreed to share his recipe with me so that I could share it here.

About this recipe Chef John says: "This simple salad requires very little time and skill; however, the ingredients must be of high quality and flavor in order to achieve successful results. By roasting the fennel a layer of flavor is added, creating interest and comfort."

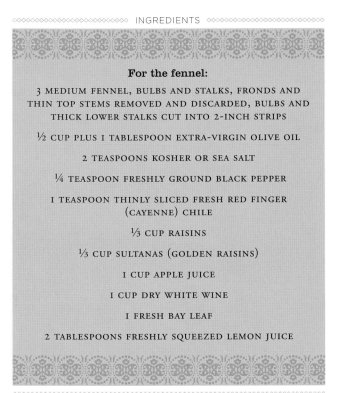

INGREDIENTS

For the fennel:

3 MEDIUM FENNEL, BULBS AND STALKS, FRONDS AND THIN TOP STEMS REMOVED AND DISCARDED, BULBS AND THICK LOWER STALKS CUT INTO 2-INCH STRIPS

½ CUP PLUS 1 TABLESPOON EXTRA-VIRGIN OLIVE OIL

2 TEASPOONS KOSHER OR SEA SALT

¼ TEASPOON FRESHLY GROUND BLACK PEPPER

1 TEASPOON THINLY SLICED FRESH RED FINGER (CAYENNE) CHILE

⅓ CUP RAISINS

⅓ CUP SULTANAS (GOLDEN RAISINS)

1 CUP APPLE JUICE

1 CUP DRY WHITE WINE

1 FRESH BAY LEAF

2 TABLESPOONS FRESHLY SQUEEZED LEMON JUICE

Heat the oven to 475°F.

In a medium-sized bowl combine the fennel, ½ cup olive oil, the salt and pepper and toss until the fennel is completely coated with the oil and seasoning. Spread the mixture onto a rimmed baking sheet and place in the oven. Roast the fennel, turning it once or twice, until it is golden and lightly caramelized, 20 to 25 minutes. Remove the pan from the oven and let the fennel cool to room temperature.

In a medium-sized heavy-bottomed pot, combine the remaining 1 tablespoon olive oil with the chile, raisins, apple juice, white wine, and bay leaf. Set the pot over medium heat and bring to a simmer. Cook at a gentle simmer until the raisins are soft, about 15 minutes. Using a slotted spoon, transfer the cooked raisins to a bowl and let cool. Discard the liquid and the bay leaf.

In a mixing bowl, fold together the roasted fennel and cooked raisins with the lemon juice. Adjust the seasoning with additional salt and pepper if necessary. Transfer the salad to a serving bowl or platter and serve.

Caponata

MAKES 8 APPETIZER OR 6 SIDE DISH SERVINGS

Caponata is a versatile dish. It can be served as a topping for Crostini (page 22) or Bruschetta (page 31), as a dip with baked pita chips, or as a side dish. It goes particularly well with grilled entrées such as Spatchcocked Herbed Chickens *alla Diavola* (page 117) or the Mixed Grill Platter (page 113).

INGREDIENTS

2 MEDIUM EGGPLANTS (1½ TO 2 POUNDS)

KOSHER OR SEA SALT

¼ CUP VEGETABLE OR OLIVE OIL
(NOT EXTRA-VIRGIN) FOR FRYING

⅓ CUP EXTRA-VIRGIN OLIVE OIL

1 LARGE YELLOW ONION, CUT INTO ¼-INCH DICE
(ABOUT 2 CUPS)

3 RIBS CELERY, TRIMMED AND CUT INTO ¼-INCH DICE

1 CUP PITTED AND COARSELY CHOPPED
GOOD-QUALITY MEATY GREEN OLIVES, SUCH AS
CERIGNOLA OR PICHOLINE

1 (14.5-OUNCE) CAN STEWED TOMATOES, CRUSHED
OR COARSELY CHOPPED

FRESHLY GROUND BLACK PEPPER

2 TABLESPOONS CAPERS (IN SALT OR IN BRINE),
RINSED, DRAINED, AND COARSELY CHOPPED

2 TABLESPOONS SUGAR

6 TO 7 TABLESPOONS GOOD-QUALITY
RED WINE VINEGAR

SPRIG OF FRESH BASIL OR FLAT-LEAF PARSLEY
FOR GARNISH

Trim the ends off the eggplants and cut them crosswise into ¾-inch-thick slices. Cut the slices into ¾-inch dice. Sprinkle the pieces of eggplant with salt and place them in a colander set in the sink. Put a plate over the eggplant and place a heavy object on top of it to weigh it down. This will help extract the bitter juices from the eggplant. Let the eggplant sit for 30 to 60 minutes. Pat the pieces dry with paper towels.

Heat ¼ cup vegetable oil in a large skillet or sauté pan placed over medium-high heat. When the oil is hot (375ºF), add enough eggplant cubes to fill the skillet without crowding it. Fry the eggplant cubes until they are golden brown, taking care to turn them once or twice so they brown on several sides. This should take about 5 minutes. Reduce the heat to medium if the eggplant seems to be browning too quickly. Use a large slotted spoon to remove the cooked eggplant to a platter lined with paper towels. Alternatively, you can drain the eggplant on a large brown paper shopping bag placed near the stove (but not next to the burner!). Continue to fry the eggplant, adding more oil as necessary, until you have cooked it all.

Wipe the skillet clean with a paper towel and pour in the ⅓ cup olive oil. Warm the oil over medium heat and add the onion and celery. Cook over medium to medium-low heat, stirring from time to time, until the onion is translucent and barely beginning to brown around the edges, about 10 minutes. Stir in the olives and chopped tomatoes and sprinkle with a little salt and pepper. Simmer for 5 minutes. Add the capers, sugar, vinegar, and the reserved eggplant and simmer for 10 minutes, until the celery is tender and the sauce has thickened. Remove from the heat, adjust the seasoning with additional salt and pepper if necessary, and leave to cool.

Refrigerate the caponata until ready to serve. Spoon it into a decorative ceramic bowl and garnish with a sprig of fresh basil or flat-leaf parsley.

DO AHEAD: Caponata may be served either cold or at room temperature, whichever you prefer, but its flavor improves over time, so be sure to make it a day or two in advance. Store the caponata in a tightly lidded container in the refrigerator.

Shrimp alla Scapece

MAKES 6 TO 8 SERVINGS

Alla Scapece is an Italian dialect term that means "marinated." Italians serve all manner of fresh seafood in this way; sometimes the fish is cooked and then marinated, and sometimes it is added to the marinade raw, leaving the acid in the marinade—usually lemon juice or vinegar—to "cook" the fish. This particular recipe calls for lightly steaming the shrimp just before marinating them, resulting in shellfish that are pink and tender, with just the right amount of firmness.

INGREDIENTS

1 GARLIC CLOVE, PRESSED

¼ CUP FRESHLY SQUEEZED LEMON JUICE

2 TABLESPOONS BALSAMIC VINEGAR

2 TEASPOONS SMOOTH DIJON MUSTARD

1 TEASPOON KOSHER OR SEA SALT

FRESHLY GROUND BLACK PEPPER

GENEROUS PINCH CRUSHED RED PEPPER

1 TEASPOON CHOPPED FRESH MINT

1 TEASPOON CHOPPED FRESH OREGANO

1 TEASPOON CHOPPED FRESH FLAT-LEAF PARSLEY

½ CUP EXTRA-VIRGIN OLIVE OIL

1½ POUNDS LARGE SHRIMP, PEELED AND DEVEINED

2 RIBS CELERY, THINLY SLICED ON THE DIAGONAL

¼ CUP VERY THINLY SLICED RED ONION

LARGE, UNBLEMISHED BUTTER LETTUCE
LEAVES FOR SERVING

Combine the garlic, lemon juice, vinegar, mustard, salt, pepper, red pepper, and herbs in a medium-sized bowl. Whisk everything together thoroughly. Gradually pour in the olive oil, whisking all the while, until the dressing has emulsified. Set aside to let the flavors mingle while you cook the shrimp.

Place a steaming basket in a sauce pot with a lid. Add just enough water to the pot so that the steaming basket is set right above the water but not immersed in it. Bring the water to a boil over medium-high heat. Reduce the heat to medium-low—it should be simmering gently—and add the shrimp. Cover the pot with the lid and steam the shrimp for 5 to 6 minutes, until they are just cooked through.

Drain the shrimp and place them in a bowl. Pour the dressing over the shrimp while they are still warm and toss them gently but thoroughly to combine. Mix in the celery and red onion. Cover with plastic wrap and refrigerate overnight. Serve the shrimp chilled in a decorative serving bowl or on a platter lined with pale green leaves of butter lettuce. To serve the salad individually, place one or two large cupped leaves of butter lettuce on each individual plate and spoon the shrimp salad on top, drizzling some of the dressing over the lettuce leaves.

DO AHEAD: These shrimp are best when made a day in advance. This gives the flavors a chance to mingle but allows the celery and onion to stay just crunchy enough to add some nice texture to the salad.

Seaside Salad

MAKES 8 SERVINGS

I call this Seaside Salad simply because it reminds me of all the wonderful little dishes of marinated antipasti I have enjoyed over the years in towns up and down the Adriatic and Mediterranean coasts. These appetizers always feature the freshest local catch—tender tiny cockles and succulent baby calamari. Use the freshest seafood you can find to make the most of this simple yet delectable salad.

INGREDIENTS

2 DOZEN MANILA OR LITTLENECK CLAMS, THOROUGHLY SCRUBBED AND RINSED

2 DOZEN MUSSELS, THOROUGHLY SCRUBBED, DEBEARDED IF NECESSARY, AND RINSED

I POUND CLEANED CALAMARI, BOTH SACS AND TENTACLES, SACS CUT INTO ½-INCH-WIDE RINGS AND TENTACLE CROWNS CUT IN HALF LENGTHWISE TO YIELD BITE-SIZED PIECES

I POUND MEDIUM OR LARGE SHRIMP, PEELED AND DEVEINED

JUICE OF I LEMON

I TEASPOON KOSHER OR SEA SALT

I CLOVE GARLIC, PRESSED

¼ CUP MINCED FLAT-LEAF PARSLEY

GENEROUS PINCH RED PEPPER FLAKES

¾ CUP EXTRA-VIRGIN OLIVE OIL

I LARGE OR 2 SMALL FRESH BAY LEAVES

Put the clams in a dry skillet or sauté pan, cover, and place the pan over medium-high heat. Cook until all of the clams have opened, 5 to 8 minutes. Discard any that have not opened within 10 minutes. Remove the clams from their shells and place them in a bowl large enough to fit all of the shellfish. Drain the liquid from the clams through a fine-mesh sieve lined with a damp paper towel into a bowl. Reserve the liquid.

Wipe the skillet clean and put the mussels in it. Cover and place the pan over medium-high heat and cook until all of the mussels have opened, about 5 to 8 minutes. Discard any that have not opened within 10 minutes. Remove the mussels from their shells and add them to the bowl with the clams. Drain the liquid through a fine-mesh sieve lined with a damp paper towel into the same bowl containing the clam juice. Reserve.

Bring a large pot of water to a boil. Add the calamari and cook for 5 minutes, or until they are opaque but still very tender. With a slotted spoon, remove the calamari to the bowl containing the clams and mussels but keep the pot on the heat.

Carefully set a steaming basket into the pot of water in which you boiled the calamari. The bottom of the steaming basket should be just above the water line, so carefully ladle out some water if necessary.

Place the shrimp in the steaming basket and cover the pot. Steam the shrimp for 5 minutes or until they are just cooked through. They should be pink and opaque but still tender and not at all stiff. Transfer the shrimp to the bowl with the other shellfish.

In a small bowl, stir together the lemon juice, reserved liquid from the clams and mussels, salt, garlic, parsley, and red pepper. Gradually whisk in the oil until the mixture is thoroughly combined. Pour the dressing over the shellfish and toss well to combine. Tuck the bay leaf or leaves in among the shellfish. Cover tightly with plastic wrap and refrigerate until thoroughly chilled. To serve, divide the salad among 8 small plates. Spoon the dressing from the bowl over the salad. Serve cold.

DO AHEAD: This salad is best after it has marinated for at least 4 hours. You can make it a day ahead or early on the day that you plan to serve it.

Italian Cheese Platter

I WHOLE ROBIOLA, A CREAMY TO RUNNY CHEESE
MADE IN PIEDMONT FROM A COMBINATION OF COW'S,
GOAT'S, AND SHEEP'S MILK, WITH A RICH, BUTTERY FLAVOR

I (4-OUNCE) WEDGE PECORINO TOSCANO, A SHEEP'S
MILK CHEESE THAT IS CREAMIER AND SOMEWHAT
MILDER THAN PECORINO ROMANO

I (4-OUNCE) WEDGE FONTINA VAL D'AOSTA, A DENSE,
SEMI-FIRM CHEESE WITH A SOMEWHAT SHARP AROMA
AND AN EARTHY, NUTTY FLAVOR

I (4-OUNCE) WEDGE GORGONZOLA DOLCE, A CREAMY,
IVORY-COLORED BLUE CHEESE WITH A SOFT, SPREADABLE
TEXTURE AND A SWEET-SALTY FINISH

I (4-OUNCE) PIECE BRESCIANELLA STAGIONATA,
A WASHED-RIND, SOFT COW'S MILK CHEESE FROM
LOMBARDY, WITH A STRONG AROMA AND A RICH,
OOZY INTERIOR

—

I RIPE PEAR OR APPLE, THINLY SLICED, OR I CLUSTER OF
GRAPES CUT INTO SMALLER CLUSTERS FOR EASY HANDLING

½ CUP SKINNED HAZELNUTS, TOASTED IN A 375°F OVEN
FOR 5 TO 10 MINUTES, OR UNTIL GOLDEN

PLAIN WATER CRACKERS

THIN SLICES OF BAGUETTE

This is a great time to be a cheese lover in the United States. Between well-stocked supermarkets, cheese shops, wine shops, and the Internet we have access to countless wonderful cheeses from all over the world. Here are some of my favorite Italian cheese selections to set out on a platter. Serve the cheeses with plain water crackers and thinly sliced baguette.

Let the cheeses sit out, still wrapped, at room temperature for at least 1 hour before serving, preferably longer.

Remove the cheeses from their wrappings. Arrange the cheeses on a platter with enough space between them to allow for cutting. If possible, set out enough knives and spreaders for each cheese. Garnish the platter with slices of fresh pear or apple, or small clusters of grapes. Scatter the hazelnuts in small clusters on the platter, or set them in a small bowl on the platter. Serve the cheese with the crackers and the baguette slices arranged in separate napkin-lined baskets.

COOK'S NOTE: I often serve a small platter of sliced dry salami to accompany the cheese.

Two Dips

Dips are among the easiest appetizers to prepare. They can usually be made well in advance, and they don't require any special cooking techniques or know-how. Plus, people love them; there is something convivial about a dish that is shared. It seems to promote socializing, and isn't that what you want at a party? Here are two of my favorites.

White Bean Dip with Rosemary and Sage

MAKES ABOUT 2 CUPS

Fresh cannellini beans are a staple in Tuscan cooking. The traditional method of preparing them was to place the fresh beans in a glass bottle or flask, along with salt, pepper, olive oil, and sage, and then place the flask among the ashes in the fireplace and allow the beans to cook slowly overnight. Here, I am availing myself of the modern convenience known as canned beans, which puree just as nicely. Fresh olive oil, sage, and rosemary contribute the classic flavors of Tuscany.

INGREDIENTS

2 (15-OUNCE) CANS CANNELLINI BEANS, DRAINED AND RINSED

¼ CUP EXTRA-VIRGIN OLIVE OIL, PLUS MORE FOR DRIZZLING

3 CLOVES GARLIC, CHOPPED

I TABLESPOON MINCED FRESH ROSEMARY LEAVES

I TABLESPOON MINCED FRESH SAGE LEAVES

¾ TEASPOON KOSHER OR SEA SALT, OR TO TASTE

FRESHLY GROUND PEPPER

2 TABLESPOONS WATER (OPTIONAL)

Combine the beans, oil, garlic, herbs, salt, and a liberal grinding of pepper in the bowl of a food processor. Process to a thick puree. If the mixture seems too dense, dribble a little water in through the feed tube while the processor is running, and process until smooth. Spoon the dip into a decorative bowl and drizzle with a little more olive oil.

DO AHEAD: The dip may be made up to 2 days in advance and refrigerated in a tightly lidded container. Bring it to room temperature and transfer it to a decorative bowl before serving.

SERVING SUGGESTION: Serve the dip with crostini, bread sticks, or thick slices of fresh country bread, and raw vegetables such as baby carrots and celery.

Spinach and Yogurt Dip

MAKES ABOUT 1½ CUPS

Cinnamon adds a sweet, exotic note to this Middle Eastern-style dip, which I like to serve with both fresh pita bread and crispy pita chips, for a contrast in texture.

INGREDIENTS

3 TABLESPOONS UNSALTED BUTTER

1 GARLIC CLOVE, MINCED

⅓ CUP FINELY CHOPPED YELLOW ONION

1 (9-OUNCE) BAG BABY SPINACH LEAVES, COOKED ACCORDING TO PACKAGE INSTRUCTIONS, SQUEEZED TO REMOVE EXCESS WATER, AND CHOPPED (ABOUT ⅔ CUP)

¾ TEASPOON KOSHER OR SEA SALT

1 CUP WHOLE MILK GREEK-STYLE YOGURT

¼ TEASPOON GROUND CINNAMON

FRESHLY GROUND PEPPER TO TASTE

Melt the butter in a large skillet placed over medium heat. Add the garlic and onion and cook, stirring frequently, until the onion is soft and translucent, about 7 minutes. Remove the pan from the heat and stir in the spinach and salt. Mix well to combine. Set the mixture aside to cool.

In a medium bowl, combine the yogurt, cinnamon, and a generous grinding of pepper. Fold in the cooled spinach mixture and mix until thoroughly combined. Let the dip sit for 30 minutes to allow the flavors to mingle. Refrigerate until thoroughly chilled.

DO AHEAD: This dip may be made up to 2 days in advance and refrigerated in a tightly lidded container. Transfer the dip to a decorative bowl before serving.

Sea Salt and Rosemary Sweet Potato Chips

MAKES 8 TO 10 SERVINGS

When my kids were quite young I used to make these chips in a (perhaps misguided) attempt to get them to try new vegetables. Of course they devoured them; what's not to love about fried sweet potatoes? The seasoned salt dresses them up just a bit.

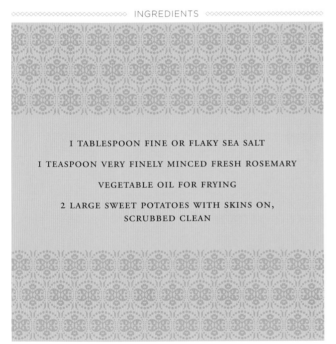

INGREDIENTS

1 TABLESPOON FINE OR FLAKY SEA SALT

1 TEASPOON VERY FINELY MINCED FRESH ROSEMARY

VEGETABLE OIL FOR FRYING

2 LARGE SWEET POTATOES WITH SKINS ON,
SCRUBBED CLEAN

In a small bowl, mix together the sea salt and rosemary. Set aside.

Pour enough oil into a large saucepan to reach a depth of 1 inch. Set the pan over medium heat and heat the oil to 350°F. Test the oil by dropping in a sliver of sweet potato. It should sizzle immediately.

Using a mandoline or a sharp chef's knife, slice the potatoes crosswise into very thin rounds, about 1/16 of an inch thick. Carefully drop a handful of potato slices into the hot oil. Use a skimmer or large slotted spoon to turn the potato slices frequently, and fry them for about 2 minutes, or just until they are golden brown. Carefully but quickly remove them from the oil to a large paper-towel-lined rimmed baking sheet or a large brown paper bag to drain. Continue to fry the sweet potatoes in batches until you have fried them all. Let the chips cool to room temperature.

Sprinkle some of the rosemary salt over the chips and place the chips in a decorative bowl or napkin-lined basket. Serve the chips at room temperature.

DO AHEAD: The chips may can be fried and salted several hours in advance and kept, uncovered, at room temperature.

Savory Cheese Biscotti

MAKES ABOUT 6 DOZEN BISCOTTI

Savory biscotti are every bit as delicious as their better-known sweet cousins, and they make a great addition to a buffet table or appetizer spread, placed near a bowl of mixed olives or a cheese platter. Once you get the hang of this recipe you can experiment with different nuts, such as walnuts to replace the almonds; different cheeses, such as cheddar or dry Jack; and a variety of herbs and spices, such as rosemary, cayenne, or crushed fennel.

INGREDIENTS

4 CUPS UNBLEACHED ALL-PURPOSE FLOUR

1 ½ TABLESPOONS FRESHLY GROUND BLACK PEPPER

2 TEASPOONS BAKING POWDER

2 TEASPOONS KOSHER OR SEA SALT

1 CUP GRATED AGED ASIAGO

1 CUP GRATED PECORINO ROMANO

1 CUP THINLY SLICED ALMONDS (WITH SKINS)

12 TABLESPOONS (1 ½ STICKS) COLD UNSALTED
BUTTER, CUT INTO ½-INCH PIECES

3 EGGS, LIGHTLY BEATEN, PLUS 1 ADDITIONAL EGG,
LIGHTLY BEATEN, FOR BRUSHING ON THE DOUGH

1 CUP WHOLE MILK

Put the flour, pepper, baking powder, salt, cheeses, and almonds in the work bowl of a food processor. Pulse briefly to combine. Add the butter and pulse briefly. Combine the 3 beaten eggs with the milk and pour the mixture into the food processor. Process just until the mixture begins to form a ball of dough.

Turn the dough out onto a large piece of waxed paper and pat it into a disk. Wrap the disk in the waxed paper and refrigerate it at least 2 hours and up to overnight.

Heat the oven to 350°F. Remove the dough from the refrigerator and let it sit at room temperature for about 15 minutes. Divide the dough into 4 equal pieces. Roll each piece into a log about 11 inches long, 2 inches wide, and ¾ to 1 inch thick. Place 2 logs each on 2 rimmed baking sheets. With a pastry brush, lightly brush the tops of the logs with the remaining beaten egg. Bake the logs for 30 minutes, rotating the baking sheets after 15 minutes. The logs should be golden on top and springy to the touch. Remove the logs from the oven and transfer them to a rack to cool for 20 minutes.

Reduce the oven temperature to 300°F. Place a log on a cutting board and, using a serrated knife, cut it on the diagonal into ⅓-inch-thick slices. Transfer the slices to a rimmed baking sheet.

Bake the biscotti for 35 to 40 minutes, turning them once halfway through the baking process, until they are golden and crisp. Remove the biscotti to a rack to cool completely. Repeat with the remaining logs.

DO AHEAD: The dough for the biscotti may be made in advance and refrigerated for up to 3 days or frozen in a zipper-lock freezer bag for up to 3 months. Baked biscotti will stay fresh at room temperature for up to 2 weeks in an airtight container.

Frank's Garlic Bread

MAKES 4 TO 6 SERVINGS

For many years when I was growing up, Saturday was steak night at our house: T-bones, which my dad broiled to perfectly rare doneness, tossed green salad, and Dad's crusty-on-the-outside-squishy-on-the-inside garlic bread. Set a basket or two of this bread on the table for your friends to make them feel right at home.

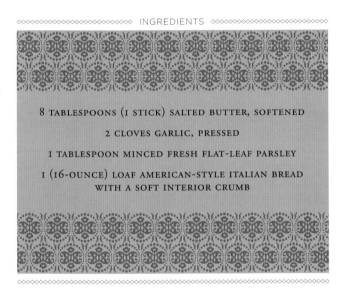

INGREDIENTS

8 TABLESPOONS (1 STICK) SALTED BUTTER, SOFTENED

2 CLOVES GARLIC, PRESSED

1 TABLESPOON MINCED FRESH FLAT-LEAF PARSLEY

1 (16-OUNCE) LOAF AMERICAN-STYLE ITALIAN BREAD
WITH A SOFT INTERIOR CRUMB

Heat the oven to 350°F.

Combine the butter, garlic, and parsley in a small bowl and mix thoroughly with a fork. With a serrated knife, cut 1-inch-thick slices into the bread, but do not cut through the bottom; the loaf should remain intact.

Gently pry open the bread where it is sliced and spread a little butter on each slice (you can butter one side of each slice or both sides; it's up to you). Wrap the bread in aluminum foil and bake for about 20 minutes, until the bread is hot, the butter is melted, and the crust is crispy. Transfer the loaf to a long cloth-lined bread basket and serve immediately.

DO AHEAD: You can spread the butter on the bread up to 2 hours in advance; wrap the bread in foil, and refrigerate it until you are ready to bake it. Bake it a few extra minutes to be sure that it gets nice and hot and the butter melts.

Walnut Focaccia

MAKES 6 TO 8 SERVINGS

INGREDIENTS

For the focaccia:

2 TEASPOONS ACTIVE DRY YEAST

I CUP WARM WATER (IIO°F)

I TABLESPOON HONEY

2 ½ CUPS UNBLEACHED ALL-PURPOSE FLOUR

¾ TEASPOON KOSHER OR SEA SALT

2 TABLESPOONS WALNUT OIL, PLUS ADDITIONAL
FOR GREASING BOWL AND PAN

CORNMEAL FOR SPRINKLING PAN

—

For the topping:

¼ CUP WALNUT OIL OR EXTRA-VIRGIN OLIVE OIL

2 TEASPOONS COARSELY CHOPPED
FRESH ROSEMARY

I TABLESPOON COARSE SEA SALT

¼ CUP CHOPPED WALNUTS

Nothing beats the warm, gentle aroma of bread dough rising—except the aroma of that same bread baking in the oven. I created this variation of classic focaccia after I found myself in possession of a bottle of walnut oil, which I had purchased for another use. Walnut oil is expensive, and although it will keep in the refrigerator for up to 6 months, I did not want it to go to waste, so I started trying new ways to use it before it lost its fresh taste. If you don't have walnut oil on hand, substitute extra-virgin olive oil; you can still add the walnut topping and end up with great, crispy-tender focaccia.

Stir together the yeast, water, honey, and 1 tablespoon of the flour until smooth. Let the mixture proof for about 15 minutes, until a creamy foam forms on top.

Put the remaining flour and the salt into the work bowl of a food processor and pulse briefly to combine. Add the 2 tablespoons of walnut oil and the yeast mixture to the bowl and process for about 30 seconds, until a ball of dough forms.

Turn the dough out onto a lightly floured work surface and knead for 5 minutes, adding additional flour if necessary to achieve a smooth, silky texture. Form the dough into a tight ball and place it into a glass or ceramic bowl greased with 1 tablespoon of walnut oil. Cover the bowl with plastic wrap and place it in a warm, draft-free spot for 2 hours to rise, until it is doubled in size.

Have ready an 8-by-11-inch rimmed baking sheet that has been lightly greased with walnut oil and sprinkled with cornmeal. Remove the dough from the bowl and knead it briefly to deflate it. Transfer the dough to the baking sheet and gently press it out with your fingertips until it covers the entire sheet to the rim. Cover with plastic and let the focaccia rise in a warm, draft-free spot for 30 minutes.

Uncover the dough and press your fingertips or knuckles into it to create depressions all over the surface. Cover the dough and let it rise again for another hour or so, until it is nicely puffed up.

Heat the oven to 400ºF while the dough is going through its final rise.

Uncover and drizzle or gently brush the ¼ cup walnut or olive oil all over the surface of the focaccia and sprinkle with the chopped rosemary and sea salt. Place the focaccia in the oven and bake for 10 minutes. Sprinkle the chopped walnuts over the top of the focaccia and bake an additional 10 to 15 minutes, until the top is golden and the bread sounds hollow when lightly tapped. Use an angled spatula to lift the focaccia out of the pan and transfer it to a rack to cool briefly. When ready to serve, slice the focaccia into rectangles and place in a bread basket. Serve warm or at room temperature.

✧·✧·✧·✧

DO AHEAD: Focaccia is best served on the day it is made, but it doesn't have to be piping hot when served. You can start the dough early in the day and attend to other tasks while it is rising and baking.

Many are the virtues of a good soup or salad. Soups are pleasing to just about anyone. Broth-based or creamy soups such as Egg Ribbons in Homemade Broth (page 50) and Creamy Carrot Soup with Rice and Caramelized Carrots (page 57) fit right in as a first course at an intimate dinner party. Farmers' Market Minestrone (page 55) can be a meal in itself when served in a generous quantity.

Every host appreciates the versatility of salads. They can be served at any point during dinner—as a starter, as a side dish to accompany the entrée, or as a refresher before dessert. The salads here provide a wide range of choices, from the lightly dressed Red, White, and Green Salad with Lemon-Balsamic Dressing (page 58) to the more substantial Mediterranean Composed Salad (page 66) to the heartiest salads featuring grains, such as Farro Salad (page 72) and Insalata di Riso (page 69), a beloved family recipe that comes from my mother's sister Gilda.

SOUPS & SALADS

Egg Ribbons in Homemade Broth

MAKES 6 FIRST-COURSE SERVINGS

❧·▦·❧

∞∞∞∞∞∞∞∞∞∞∞∞ INGREDIENTS ∞∞∞∞∞∞∞∞∞∞∞∞

For the Homemade Chicken Broth:

I (4-POUND) CHICKEN

3 CARROTS, TRIMMED, HALVED LENGTHWISE,
AND CUT INTO 2-INCH PIECES

2 RIBS CELERY, INCLUDING LEAFY TOPS,
TRIMMED AND CUT INTO 2-INCH PIECES

2 YELLOW ONIONS, QUARTERED, AND 2 QUARTERS
EACH STUCK WITH I WHOLE CLOVE

6 SPRIGS FLAT-LEAF PARSLEY

4 SPRIGS FRESH THYME

I CLOVE GARLIC, LIGHTLY CRUSHED WITH THE
SIDE OF A KNIFE BLADE

½ TEASPOON WHOLE BLACK PEPPERCORNS

4 TO 5 QUARTS WATER

KOSHER OR SEA SALT

—

For the egg ribbons:

4 LARGE EGGS

I CUP WHOLE MILK

2 TABLESPOONS MINCED FRESH FLAT-LEAF PARSLEY

½ TEASPOON KOSHER OR SEA SALT

PINCH OF FRESHLY GROUND NUTMEG

FRESHLY GROUND BLACK PEPPER

¾ CUP UNBLEACHED ALL-PURPOSE FLOUR, SIFTED

ABOUT 2 TABLESPOONS UNSALTED BUTTER

—

For serving the soup:

I CUP FRESHLY GRATED PARMIGIANO-REGGIANO

Broth-based soups are among my favorite foods. They are elegant and comforting and nourishing all at the same time. This recipe is especially appealing because everything can be made well in advance and then reheated just before serving.

To make the broth:

Put all of the ingredients except the water and salt into a large stockpot. Add the water, pouring in enough to cover the ingredients by about 2 inches. Bring the broth to a boil over medium-high heat, skimming any foam that forms on the surface with a skimmer. Reduce the heat to medium-low and simmer gently, uncovered, skimming any foam that forms on the surface during the first hour or so of cooking, for 3 to 4 hours, adding salt to taste during the last hour of cooking. The broth is ready when it is reduced by about one-half and has developed a rich, meaty flavor.

Strain the broth through a colander lined with damp cheese-cloth into a clean container. Discard the solids. (You can save the good, large chunks of chicken meat and large pieces of carrot and celery and refrigerate them. I enjoy them as a cold lunch, drizzled with olive oil and sprinkled with salt.)

Let the broth cool to room temperature, then cover and refrigerate until well chilled. Skim off and discard the congealed layer of fat on the surface before reheating.

To make the egg ribbons:

Combine the eggs, milk, parsley, salt, nutmeg, and a little pepper in a bowl and whisk together. Gradually whisk in the flour, taking care to avoid lumps. Cover the batter with plastic wrap and let stand at room temperature for 30 minutes.

Place a 9-inch nonstick skillet or sauté pan (I use a well-seasoned cast-iron skillet) over medium heat and coat the bottom with a film of butter. When the butter is hot, pour in a small ladleful of batter (less than ½ cup) and quickly swirl the pan so that the batter coats the entire bottom, forming a thin pancake. Cook for 30 to 45 seconds, or until just set. Using an offset spatula or pancake turner, flip the pancake and cook on the other side for 20 to 30 seconds, or until set. Transfer the pancake to a plate. Continue making the pancakes until you have used all the batter, taking care to add butter to the pan as needed. Stack the pancakes on the plate as you remove them from the skillet.

Roll the pancakes up, one or two at a time, and cut them crosswise into thin ribbons (⅛ to ¼ inch wide). Unravel the ribbons and place them on a plate or in a shallow bowl. Continue to roll and cut the pancakes until you have cut them all. Cover the ribbons with plastic wrap and set aside.

In a saucepan, bring the broth to a boil over medium heat. Add the egg ribbons to the boiling broth and cook for just a few minutes, until the ribbons are heated through. Ladle the soup into 6 shallow rimmed bowls and sprinkle each serving with cheese. Serve immediately.

෨·෨·෨

DO AHEAD: The broth may be made in advance and kept in a tightly lidded container in the refrigerator for up to 3 days or frozen for up to 3 months. The egg ribbons may be made up to 3 days in advance and kept in a tightly lidded container in the refrigerator.

Cold Curried Squash Soup

MAKES 4 TO 6 SERVINGS

◇◇◇◇◇◇◇◇◇◇◇◇◇◇◇◇◇ INGREDIENTS ◇◇◇◇◇◇◇◇◇◇◇◇◇◇◇◇◇

2 POUNDS YELLOW STRAIGHT OR
CROOK-NECKED SUMMER SQUASH, SHREDDED
ON THE LARGE HOLES OF A BOX GRATER
(ABOUT 8 TO 9 MEDIUM SQUASH OR
6 PACKED CUPS)

2 TABLESPOONS EXTRA-VIRGIN OLIVE OIL

1 TABLESPOON UNSALTED BUTTER

1 LARGE YELLOW ONION, CHOPPED (ABOUT 1 ½ CUPS)

1 TABLESPOON HOT CURRY POWDER

4 CUPS HOMEMADE CHICKEN BROTH *(page 50)*,
HOMEMADE VEGETABLE BROTH *(page 55)*, OR
BEST-QUALITY FAT-FREE, LOW-SODIUM CANNED
CHICKEN BROTH OR CANNED VEGETABLE BROTH

KOSHER OR SEA SALT

¼ CUP HEAVY CREAM OR LIGHT CREAM

—

Optional garnishes:

6 LARGE COOKED AND PEELED SHRIMP, CHILLED

1 LARGE, RIPE TOMATO, FINELY DICED

4 TO 6 TABLESPOONS CRÈME FRAÎCHE
OR SOUR CREAM

I don't often make cold soups; in summer I prefer soup—and most of my food, in fact—the Italian way, at room temperature or barely warm. However, summer days in Virginia can be awfully steamy, and every now and then a small serving of cold soup can really hit the spot.

Place the grated squash in a colander and let it drain for a few minutes. You can help it along by gently squeezing out the moisture with your hands.

Heat the oil and butter in a medium heavy-bottomed pot placed over medium heat. Add the onion and sauté over medium heat until the onion is soft and pale golden, about 8 minutes.

Sprinkle in the curry powder and stir to combine thoroughly. Add the drained squash and sauté, stirring frequently, until the squash is wilted, about 10 minutes. Pour in the broth and bring to a boil. Reduce the heat to medium-low and cook at a gentle simmer until the squash is completely tender, about 15 to 20 minutes. Taste and add salt if you like.

Remove the soup from the heat and let it cool for a few minutes. Purée the soup in a blender until it is completely smooth. Clean out the pot and return the soup to it. Stir in the cream. Transfer the soup to a tightly lidded container and refrigerate at least 2 hours, or until it is completely chilled.

Serve the soup cold, topped with one of the optional garnishes.

Farmers' Market Minestrone

MAKES 8 TO 10 FIRST-COURSE SERVINGS OR 6 MAIN-COURSE SERVINGS

This is one of those wonderful recipes that change each time I make it, depending on what's in the stalls at the farmers' market and what I have on hand in my pantry. Think of this version as a guideline and feel free to improvise. Adding the small meatballs featured in the Pasta Timballo (page 99) recipe was my daughter, Adriana's, inspired idea. They turn the soup into a one-dish meal, perfect for a casual gathering of family or friends.

INGREDIENTS

For the Homemade Vegetable Broth:

2 LARGE RIPE TOMATOES, CORED, SEEDED, AND CUT INTO LARGE CHUNKS, OR 1 (15-OUNCE) CAN DICED TOMATOES

3 CARROTS, TRIMMED AND CUT INTO 2-INCH PIECES

3 RIBS CELERY, TRIMMED AND CUT INTO 2-INCH PIECES

1 LARGE ONION, CUT INTO CHUNKS

3 SCALLIONS, BULBS AND STEMS CUT CROSSWISE INTO LARGE PIECES

STALKS AND FRONDS OF 1 FENNEL BULB, CUT INTO LARGE PIECES (RESERVE THE BULB FOR THE SOUP)

4 SPRIGS FRESH THYME

4 SPRIGS FRESH FLAT-LEAF PARSLEY

1 TEASPOON KOSHER OR SEA SALT

¼ CUP EXTRA-VIRGIN OLIVE OIL

8 CUPS (2 QUARTS) COLD WATER

¼ TEASPOON WHOLE BLACK PEPPERCORNS

INGREDIENTS

For the soup:

3 TABLESPOONS EXTRA-VIRGIN OLIVE OIL, PLUS ADDITIONAL FOR DRIZZLING

2 MEDIUM CARROTS, TRIMMED AND CUT INTO ½-INCH DICE

1 FENNEL BULB, CUT INTO ½-INCH DICE

3 PURPLE OR GREEN SCALLIONS OR SPRING ONIONS, BULBS AND TENDER STEMS CUT CROSSWISE INTO THIN SLICES

1 ZUCCHINI, CUT INTO ½-INCH DICE (ABOUT 1 CUP)

1 YELLOW SQUASH, CUT INTO ½-INCH DICE (ABOUT 1 CUP)

1 TEASPOON KOSHER OR SEA SALT

1 (15-OUNCE) CAN CHICKPEAS, DRAINED AND RINSED

1 CUP FRESH OR FROZEN CORN KERNELS (BRIEFLY THAWED IF FROZEN)

1 BATCH MEATBALLS FROM THE PASTA TIMBALLO (page 99)

2 CUPS SMALL SHELL-SHAPED PASTA

5 OUNCES FRESH SPINACH LEAVES

1 PACKED CUP SHREDDED FRESH BASIL LEAVES

1 CUP FRESHLY GRATED PARMIGIANO-REGGIANO

1 CUP FRESHLY GRATED PECORINO ROMANO

To make the broth:
Heat the oven to 450°F.

Combine all of the ingredients for the broth, except the water and peppercorns, in a large roasting pan and toss well to

CONTINUED ON NEXT PAGE...

... CONTINUED

combine. Place the pan in the oven and roast the vegetables for 30 to 40 minutes, turning every 15 minutes or so, until they are soft and browned in places.

Transfer the vegetables and their juices to a large pot and pour in the water. Add the peppercorns and bring the broth to a boil over medium-high heat. Reduce the heat to medium-low, cover partially, and cook for 45 minutes, until the broth is richly flavored.

Remove the broth from the heat and let sit for 5 minutes. Using a fine-mesh sieve lined with damp cheesecloth, strain the broth into a clean pot. Discard the solids. Return the broth to the burner, cover, and keep warm over low heat.

To make the soup:
In a large Dutch oven or other heavy-bottomed pot, warm the olive oil over medium heat. Add the carrots, fennel, and scallions and sauté, stirring frequently, for 10 minutes, until the carrots are bright and shiny and the scallions are softened. Add the zucchini and yellow squash and season with 1 teaspoon of salt. Cook for 3 minutes, just until the squashes start to soften.

Add the chickpeas and corn kernels and cook for a minute or two, then slowly pour in the warm broth. Add the meatballs. Bring the broth to a boil and stir in the shells. Cook for about 10 minutes or until the shells are al dente (cooking time will depend on the brand and type of pasta you use). Turn off the heat and add the spinach, stirring until it is wilted. Cover the pot and let the soup sit for just a minute or two. Stir in the basil and the cheeses.

Ladle the soup into individual shallow rimmed bowls and drizzle each serving with a little olive oil. Serve immediately.

DO AHEAD: The broth may be made in advance and kept in a tightly lidded container in the refrigerator for up to 3 days, or frozen for up to 3 months. The meatballs may be made up to 2 days in advance and refrigerated or up to 1 month ahead and frozen. If frozen, bring them to room temperature before using.

Creamy Carrot Soup with Rice and Caramelized Carrots

MAKES 6 FIRST-COURSE SERVINGS

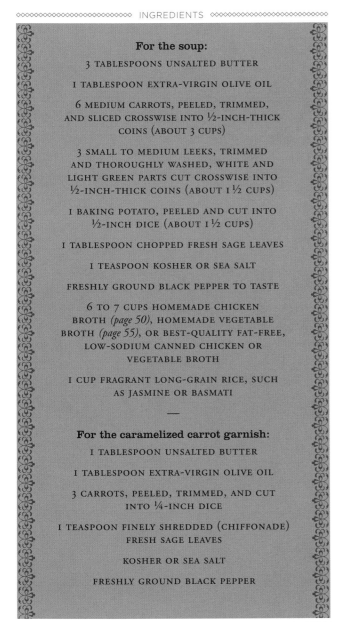

For the soup:

3 TABLESPOONS UNSALTED BUTTER

1 TABLESPOON EXTRA-VIRGIN OLIVE OIL

6 MEDIUM CARROTS, PEELED, TRIMMED, AND SLICED CROSSWISE INTO ½-INCH-THICK COINS (ABOUT 3 CUPS)

3 SMALL TO MEDIUM LEEKS, TRIMMED AND THOROUGHLY WASHED, WHITE AND LIGHT GREEN PARTS CUT CROSSWISE INTO ½-INCH-THICK COINS (ABOUT 1½ CUPS)

1 BAKING POTATO, PEELED AND CUT INTO ½-INCH DICE (ABOUT 1½ CUPS)

1 TABLESPOON CHOPPED FRESH SAGE LEAVES

1 TEASPOON KOSHER OR SEA SALT

FRESHLY GROUND BLACK PEPPER TO TASTE

6 TO 7 CUPS HOMEMADE CHICKEN BROTH (*page 50*), HOMEMADE VEGETABLE BROTH (*page 55*), OR BEST-QUALITY FAT-FREE, LOW-SODIUM CANNED CHICKEN OR VEGETABLE BROTH

1 CUP FRAGRANT LONG-GRAIN RICE, SUCH AS JASMINE OR BASMATI

—

For the caramelized carrot garnish:

1 TABLESPOON UNSALTED BUTTER

1 TABLESPOON EXTRA-VIRGIN OLIVE OIL

3 CARROTS, PEELED, TRIMMED, AND CUT INTO ¼-INCH DICE

1 TEASPOON FINELY SHREDDED (CHIFFONADE) FRESH SAGE LEAVES

KOSHER OR SEA SALT

FRESHLY GROUND BLACK PEPPER

Fragrant with fresh sage and long-grain rice, this soup makes a lovely first course for a spring dinner.

To make the soup:

In a large Dutch oven or other heavy-bottomed pot, warm the butter and oil over medium heat. When the butter is melted, add the carrots and leeks. Sauté the vegetables for about 10 minutes, or until they have begun to soften. Add the potato, sage, salt, and pepper and cook for 5 minutes. Stir in 6 cups of vegetable or chicken broth. Bring the soup to a boil, reduce the heat to medium-low, and simmer, partially covered, for 20 to 25 minutes, until all of the vegetables are tender. Remove from the heat and let the soup cool for 10 minutes. Purée the soup in a blender, in batches if necessary, or in the pot using an immersion blender. Set the soup aside while you cook the rice.

Bring 1½ cups of water to a rolling boil in a medium-size saucepan. Add a pinch of salt and stir in the rice. Return to a boil, reduce the heat to medium-low, cover, and cook the rice without stirring for 18 to 20 minutes, until water has been absorbed and the grains are tender but not mushy.

Stir the rice into the puréed soup. Reheat over medium heat just until the soup is completely heated through.

To make the caramelized carrot garnish:

Heat the butter and oil in a medium-size skillet or sauté pan placed over medium heat. When the butter is melted and begins to sizzle, stir in the diced carrots and shredded sage. Raise the heat to medium-high and sauté for 5 minutes, stirring frequently, until the carrots are tender and lightly browned. Season with a little salt and pepper and remove from the heat.

To serve, ladle equal portions of soup into six shallow rimmed bowls. Garnish each serving with a spoonful of the caramelized carrots and serve immediately.

Red, White, and Green Salad with Lemon-Balsamic Dressing

MAKES 8 SERVINGS

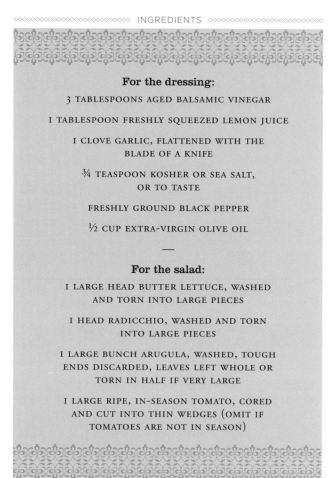

INGREDIENTS

For the dressing:

3 TABLESPOONS AGED BALSAMIC VINEGAR

1 TABLESPOON FRESHLY SQUEEZED LEMON JUICE

1 CLOVE GARLIC, FLATTENED WITH THE BLADE OF A KNIFE

¾ TEASPOON KOSHER OR SEA SALT, OR TO TASTE

FRESHLY GROUND BLACK PEPPER

½ CUP EXTRA-VIRGIN OLIVE OIL

—

For the salad:

1 LARGE HEAD BUTTER LETTUCE, WASHED AND TORN INTO LARGE PIECES

1 HEAD RADICCHIO, WASHED AND TORN INTO LARGE PIECES

1 LARGE BUNCH ARUGULA, WASHED, TOUGH ENDS DISCARDED, LEAVES LEFT WHOLE OR TORN IN HALF IF VERY LARGE

1 LARGE RIPE, IN-SEASON TOMATO, CORED AND CUT INTO THIN WEDGES (OMIT IF TOMATOES ARE NOT IN SEASON)

We have a tendency to dress up our salads when company's coming, with nuts, dried fruit, croutons, seeds, and sprouts. But there is something to be said for the appeal and practicality of a simple salad of greens—and tomatoes when in season—dressed with a light vinaigrette. It is easy to put together and goes well with just about any entrée. Here is my tried-and-true version.

To make the dressing:

In a small bowl, whisk together the vinegar, lemon juice, garlic, salt, and pepper. Slowly whisk in the oil to achieve an emulsified dressing. Cover and let sit for 15 to 30 minutes to let the garlic infuse the dressing. Discard the garlic just before pouring on the salad.

To assemble the salad:

Combine the lettuce, radicchio, and arugula in a salad bowl. Add the tomato slices, if using. Pour the dressing over the salad (you may not need all of it) and toss gently but thoroughly with salad tongs. Taste and adjust the seasoning with additional salt if necessary. Serve immediately.

DO AHEAD: The dressing may be prepared up to 2 hours in advance; remove the garlic after it has steeped for 30 minutes. Whisk the dressing before using. The salad greens may be washed several hours in advance; leave the leaves whole until you are ready to assemble the salad to prevent browning.

Spinach and Apple Salad

MAKES 4 TO 6 SERVINGS

INGREDIENTS

For the dressing:

3 TABLESPOONS FRESHLY SQUEEZED
ORANGE JUICE

3 TABLESPOONS FRESHLY SQUEEZED LIME JUICE

1 TABLESPOON DIJON MUSTARD

1 TABLESPOON HONEY

½ TEASPOON KOSHER OR SEA SALT, OR TO TASTE

FRESHLY GROUND PEPPER

⅓ TO ½ CUP EXTRA-VIRGIN OLIVE OIL

—

For the salad:

8 TO 10 CUPS FRESH BABY SPINACH LEAVES

1 LARGE FIRM, HIGHLY FLAVORED, SWEET-TART
APPLE, CORED AND THINLY SLICED
(LEAVE SKIN ON)

½ CUP RED ONION, PEELED AND THINLY SLICED

¼ CUP GORGONZOLA DOLCE OR GORGONZOLA
PICCANTE, CRUMBLED

In fall, I look for firm, dense apples with a good balance of sweetness and acidity, such as Goldrush, Albemarle pippin, Honeycrisp, and Suncrisp. This salad has a satisfying crunch and lots of good assertive flavor.

To make the dressing:
In a small bowl, combine the orange juice, lime juice, mustard, and honey. Season with a little salt and pepper. Slowly whisk in the oil to achieve an emulsified dressing.

To assemble the salad:
Put the spinach, apple, and red onion in a decorative salad bowl and toss with the dressing. Sprinkle blue cheese over the top and serve.

DO AHEAD: The dressing may be made up to 2 hours in advance and kept, covered, at room temperature. Whisk before dressing the salad.

Winter Endive and Orange Salad

MAKES 6 TO 8 SERVINGS

INGREDIENTS

For the dressing:

2 TABLESPOONS CIDER VINEGAR

2 TABLESPOONS HONEY

1 TABLESPOON SMOOTH DIJON MUSTARD

½ TEASPOON KOSHER OR SEA SALT

FRESHLY GROUND BLACK PEPPER

½ CUP EXTRA-VIRGIN OLIVE OIL

—

For the salad:

5 HEADS BELGIAN ENDIVE, CUT CROSSWISE INTO 2-INCH PIECES

1 LARGE HEAD RED LEAF LETTUCE, TORN INTO LARGE PIECES

1 LARGE OR 2 SMALL BUNCHES ARUGULA, TOUGH END STEMS REMOVED

2 JUICY CHILLED ORANGES, PEELED WITH ALL WHITE PITH REMOVED FROM THE EXTERIOR, SLICED INTO THIN ROUNDS

My family has been making this salad for years. It is easy to prepare, and I have never served it to anyone who didn't immediately love it.

To make the dressing:
In a bowl, whisk together the vinegar, honey, mustard, salt, and pepper. Gradually incorporate the oil, pouring it in a thin stream and whisking all the while to achieve an emulsified dressing. Taste and adjust the seasoning with additional salt if necessary.

To assemble the salad:
Mix all of the greens together and arrange them in a large, deep serving platter. Arrange the orange slices on top of the greens. Drizzle the dressing over the salad. Serve immediately.

DO AHEAD: The greens may be washed several hours in advance and stored in zipper-lock bags in the crisper compartment of the refrigerator. Leave the leaves whole until you are ready to assemble the salad to prevent browning. The oranges may be prepared several hours in advance and stored in a tightly lidded container in the refrigerator. The dressing may be prepared several hours in advance and kept, covered, at room temperature. Whisk before using.

Caesar Salad

MAKES 6 TO 8 SERVINGS

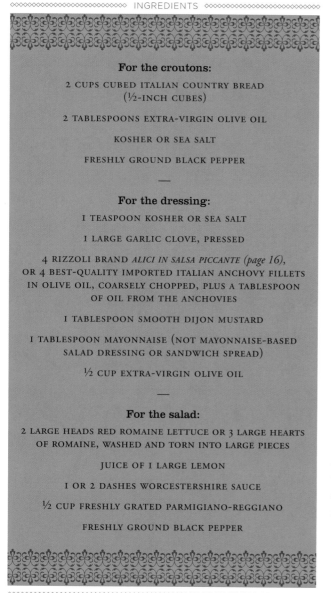

INGREDIENTS

For the croutons:

2 CUPS CUBED ITALIAN COUNTRY BREAD
(½-INCH CUBES)

2 TABLESPOONS EXTRA-VIRGIN OLIVE OIL

KOSHER OR SEA SALT

FRESHLY GROUND BLACK PEPPER

—

For the dressing:

1 TEASPOON KOSHER OR SEA SALT

1 LARGE GARLIC CLOVE, PRESSED

4 RIZZOLI BRAND *ALICI IN SALSA PICCANTE (page 16)*,
OR 4 BEST-QUALITY IMPORTED ITALIAN ANCHOVY FILLETS
IN OLIVE OIL, COARSELY CHOPPED, PLUS A TABLESPOON
OF OIL FROM THE ANCHOVIES

1 TABLESPOON SMOOTH DIJON MUSTARD

1 TABLESPOON MAYONNAISE (NOT MAYONNAISE-BASED
SALAD DRESSING OR SANDWICH SPREAD)

½ CUP EXTRA-VIRGIN OLIVE OIL

—

For the salad:

2 LARGE HEADS RED ROMAINE LETTUCE OR 3 LARGE HEARTS
OF ROMAINE, WASHED AND TORN INTO LARGE PIECES

JUICE OF 1 LARGE LEMON

1 OR 2 DASHES WORCESTERSHIRE SAUCE

½ CUP FRESHLY GRATED PARMIGIANO-REGGIANO

FRESHLY GROUND BLACK PEPPER

Although the original recipe for Caesar Salad apparently did not include anchovies, I wouldn't dream of making it without them as their salty sharpness really enhances the dressing. The other change I made is to omit the coddled (briefly boiled) egg because I am just not fond of its slick texture. Instead, I use a bit of Dijon mustard and mayonnaise to bind the dressing. This is one of my all-time favorite salads, and when I am not serving it to company I often make it as a main course for family dinner, topped with shredded roast chicken. Even my ultra-picky son, Nick, loves it.

To make the croutons:
Heat the oven to 400ºF.

Spread the bread cubes on a large rimmed baking sheet and drizzle the olive oil over them. Toss well with a wooden spoon or a spatula. Sprinkle on a little salt and a few grindings of pepper, toss again, and spread into a single layer.

Place the baking sheet in the oven and toast the croutons, stirring them once at the midpoint, for 15 minutes, or until they are evenly browned and crisp. Remove from the oven and let cool to room temperature.

To make the dressing:
In a medium bowl, stir together the salt and garlic clove to form a paste. Add the anchovies and their oil, the mustard, and the mayonnaise, and whisk to combine. Slowly add the olive oil, whisking all the while, until you have added it all and the mixture is thick and emulsified.

To assemble the salad:

Place the lettuce leaves in a large bowl. Pour the olive-oil dressing over the lettuce leaves and toss well to combine. Pour the lemon juice over the leaves and toss again. Add the Worcestershire sauce, the cheese, and a generous grinding of pepper and toss again. Transfer the salad to a large salad bowl or decorative serving bowl and top with the croutons. Serve immediately.

℘·℘·℘

DO AHEAD: The croutons may be made up to 3 days in advance and kept at room temperature in a tightly lidded container or a zipper-lock storage bag. The lettuce may be cleaned and kept in a large zipper-lock bag in the refrigerator until you are ready to assemble the salad. Don't tear the leaves until just before assembling, to prevent any browning of the edges. The ingredients for the dressing may be mixed together up to 2 hours in advance and kept, tightly covered, at room temperature. Whisk before pouring over the salad.

Tomato and Cheese Salad over Bruschetta

MAKES 6 SERVINGS

INGREDIENTS

3 POUNDS RIPE HIGH-SUMMER HEIRLOOM
TOMATOES OF VARYING SHAPES, SIZES,
AND COLORS

3 MIDDLE EASTERN CUCUMBERS OR
1 ENGLISH CUCUMBER, SEEDED, HALVED
LENGTHWISE, AND CUT CROSSWISE INTO
½-INCH-THICK STRIPS

¼ CUP SHREDDED OR COARSELY CHOPPED
FRESH BASIL, PLUS A COUPLE OF SPRIGS
FOR GARNISH

¼ CUP COARSELY SHREDDED FRESH MINT, PLUS
A COUPLE OF SPRIGS FOR GARNISH

1½ TABLESPOONS BEST-QUALITY
BALSAMIC VINEGAR

1 TABLESPOON BEST-QUALITY
RED WINE VINEGAR

¼ CUP EXTRA-VIRGIN OLIVE OIL

FINE SEA SALT

FRESHLY GROUND BLACK PEPPER

6 SLICES BRUSCHETTA *(page 31)*

½ CUP CRUMBLED RICOTTA SALATA
OR IMPORTED GREEK FETA

This salad is so simple to make it can hardly be called a recipe. It is practically a fixture at my table in mid- to late summer when tomatoes are at their finest. There is only one thing to remember with a salad like this: it is only as good as the ingredients that comprise it. So please don't skimp.

Cut the tomatoes in half, core them, and slice them into thin wedges. Place the tomatoes in a bowl. Add the cucumbers, basil, and mint and gently combine. Sprinkle in the balsamic and red wine vinegars and mix again. Drizzle the olive oil over the salad and season with salt and pepper to taste. Mix everything together gently but thoroughly. Cover with plastic wrap and let sit for 30 minutes. Stir well just before serving and adjust the seasoning with additional salt if necessary.

Place the bruschetta slices on a large serving platter and spoon the salad over the bread. Scatter the crumbled ricotta salata on top and garnish with a few sprigs of basil and mint. Serve immediately.

To serve individually, place a slice of bread on each of 6 salad plates and divide the salad evenly among them. Garnish with the crumbled cheese. Tear up a few leaves of basil and mint and sprinkle on top of each plate.

Red Slaw with Tart Cherries

MAKES 10 SERVINGS

INGREDIENTS

10 CUPS FINELY SLICED RED CABBAGE
(ABOUT 1 HEAD)

1 CUP THINLY SLICED RED ONION

1¼ CUPS SHREDDED CARROTS (ABOUT 2 MEDIUM)

¾ CUP DRIED TART CHERRIES

¾ CUP MAYONNAISE (NOT MAYONNAISE-BASED
SALAD DRESSING OR SANDWICH SPREAD)

½ CUP RED WINE VINEGAR

3 TEASPOONS SUGAR

1 TEASPOON KOSHER OR SEA SALT

FRESHLY GROUND BLACK PEPPER

Over the years I have brought this salad to countless picnics and cookouts and have received compliments even from those who profess to despise mayonnaise. Allowing the salad to sit overnight in the refrigerator tenderizes the cabbage and plumps up the cherries.

Place the cabbage, red onions, carrots, and cherries in a large bowl and toss to combine. In a bowl, whisk together the mayonnaise, vinegar, sugar, salt, and pepper. Pour the dressing over the salad and mix thoroughly. Taste and adjust the seasoning with additional salt if necessary. Spoon the salad into a large container that has a tight-fitting lid. Cover and refrigerate overnight. To serve, transfer the salad into a decorative serving bowl. Serve cold.

Mediterranean Composed Salad

MAKES 6 SERVINGS

For the dressing:

⅓ CUP FRESHLY SQUEEZED LEMON JUICE

2 CLOVES GARLIC, PRESSED

1 TABLESPOON SMOOTH DIJON MUSTARD

1 TEASPOON MINCED FRESH OREGANO

1 TEASPOON MINCED FRESH FLAT-LEAF PARSLEY

1 TEASPOON MINCED FRESH THYME

¾ TEASPOON KOSHER OR SEA SALT, OR TO TASTE

FRESHLY GROUND BLACK PEPPER

½ TO ¾ CUP EXTRA-VIRGIN OLIVE OIL

—

For the salad:

2 POUNDS RED-SKINNED OR
YELLOW-FLESHED POTATOES

KOSHER OR SEA SALT

1 POUND TENDER GREEN BEANS, TRIMMED

3 (5.5-OUNCE) CANS BEST-QUALITY ITALIAN OR
SPANISH TUNA IN OLIVE OIL, DRAINED

4 HARD-BOILED EGGS, PEELED AND SLICED
OR QUARTERED LENGTHWISE

1½ CUPS PURPLE OLIVES, SUCH AS
GAETA OR KALAMATA

2 (8-OUNCE) BALLS FRESH MOZZARELLA,
CUT INTO THICK SLICES

2 LARGE PERFECTLY RIPE SUMMER TOMATOES,
CUT CROSSWISE INTO THICK SLICES

A composed salad is nothing more than a salad in which the ingredients are artfully arranged on a platter rather than tossed together in a bowl. Deciding how to arrange the various components is part of the fun of making this dish. Resembling a niçoise salad, it makes a nice centerpiece for a summer luncheon. Serve the salad with a loaf of fresh country bread cut into thick slices. For dessert? Orange or coffee granitas (pages 183 and 184).

To make the dressing:

In a small bowl, whisk together the lemon juice, garlic, mustard, herbs, salt, and several grindings of pepper. Slowly whisk in the oil to achieve an emulsified dressing. Cover with plastic wrap and let stand.

To prepare the vegetables:

Put the potatoes in a large pot and cover with cold water by 1 inch. Salt the water generously. Set the pot over medium-high heat and bring to a boil. Cook the potatoes for about 20 minutes, until they are just tender. Drain and let sit until the potatoes are cool enough to handle but still quite warm. Peel the potatoes, cut them into 2-inch chunks, and place them in a bowl. Drizzle some of the dressing over the potatoes and mix to combine thoroughly. Set aside.

Pour 1 or 2 cups water into a pot with a lid and fit a steaming basket inside the pot. The water should reach just below the basket. Add or remove water as needed. Set the pot on medium-high heat and bring to a boil. Add the green beans to the steaming basket and let them steam, uncovered, for about a minute. Cover the beans and steam 3 to 4 minutes longer, until they are bright green and crisp-tender. Using tongs, quickly transfer the beans to a bowl and drizzle a little dressing over them, taking care to reserve some of the dressing. Toss to coat thoroughly.

To assemble the salad:
Choose a decorative platter large enough to hold all of the salad components. It can be round, oval, or rectangular. Mound the tuna into the center of the platter. Arrange the potatoes, green beans, eggs, olives, cheese, and tomatoes on the platter around the tuna. Here is where creative license comes in; you can arrange everything as you see fit. For example, you can alternate slices of tomato with slices of mozzarella. You can form a ring around the tuna with the dressed potatoes or the slices of egg. Or you can divide each component in half and arrange them symmetrically on the platter. Be as artful as you like.

Drizzle the remaining dressing over the salad (do not toss!). Serve immediately.

છ·છ·છ

DO AHEAD: The dressing may be made several hours in advance and refrigerated. Bring it to room temperature and whisk well before using. I don't recommend dressing the green beans in advance as the acid in the lemon will dull their bright green color.

Pear Salad with Walnuts, Pecorino, and Chestnut Honey

MAKES 6 SERVINGS

I enjoyed a similar version of this salad at a small restaurant in Umbria a few years ago. What I liked about it, in addition to the drizzle of chestnut honey on top, was the way that the pears and the cheese, which were the same creamy hue, were also cut to the same size, making it hard to tell which was which until you took a bite. Be sure to choose pears that are just starting to soften at the stem but are still fairly firm to the touch at their widest point; these can be cut cleanly without turning mushy. Anjou, Bartlett, Bosc, and Comice are all good choices for this salad.

INGREDIENTS

4 RIPE BUT STILL-FIRM PEARS

1 TO 2 TABLESPOONS FRESHLY SQUEEZED LEMON JUICE

6 OUNCES PECORINO TOSCANO

FRESHLY GROUND BLACK PEPPER

1 CUP COARSELY CHOPPED TOASTED WALNUTS
(see Cook's Note)

½ CUP CHESTNUT HONEY (page 17)

Peel and core the pears and cut them into ½-inch dice. Put the pieces of pear in a bowl and squeeze 1 to 2 tablespoons of lemon juice over them so that they are very lightly coated. Be careful not to overdo it with the lemon juice or it will make the salad too tart.

Cut the pecorino cheese into ½-inch dice and add to the bowl with the pears. Season with a few grindings of pepper and gently fold everything together. Transfer the pears and pecorino to an oval serving platter. Scatter the walnuts on top of the pears and cheese and drizzle the honey over everything. Serve immediately.

To serve individually, divide pears and cheese among 6 small salad plates. Sprinkle each plate with some of the walnuts and drizzle honey over each serving.

COOK'S NOTE: To toast walnuts, spread one rounded cupful of walnut halves on a rimmed baking sheet. Toast in a 350°F oven for 7 to 10 minutes, until they are fragrant. Be careful not to overcook.

Remove from the oven and let cool. Chop walnuts coarsely before sprinkling them on salad.

Insalata di Riso

SERVES 5 TO 6 AS A MAIN COURSE AND 10 TO 12 AS A SIDE DISH

INGREDIENTS

1 ½ CUPS ARBORIO, CARNAROLI, OR OTHER
SHORT-GRAIN RISOTTO RICE

¼ CUP EXTRA-VIRGIN OLIVE OIL

8 OUNCES BEST-QUALITY CANNED OR JARRED TUNA
IN OLIVE OIL, DRAINED

3 HARD-BOILED EGGS, QUARTERED LENGTHWISE
OR SLICED CROSSWISE

2 RIZZOLI BRAND *ALICI IN SALSA PICCANTE* (page 16)
OR BEST-QUALITY ITALIAN ANCHOVY FILLETS IN
OLIVE OIL, DRAINED AND CHOPPED

1 CUP DICED JARRED GIARDINIERA (page 18)

½ CUP FROZEN PEAS, THAWED

½ CUP DICED CELERY

½ CUP PICKLED COCKTAIL (PEARL) ONIONS,
DRAINED, AND HALVED IF THEY ARE ANY LARGER
THAN A MARBLE

⅓ CUP DICED JARRED ROASTED RED BELL PEPPERS,
OR A COMBINATION OF ROASTED RED AND YELLOW
BELL PEPPERS IF YOU CAN FIND THEM AT YOUR
SUPERMARKET OR GOURMET FOOD STORE

¼ CUP GREEN OLIVES, SUCH AS PICHOLINE

¼ CUP PURPLE OLIVES, SUCH AS
GAETA OR KALAMATA

2 TABLESPOONS MINCED FLAT-LEAF PARSLEY

1 TABLESPOON CAPERS, PREFERABLY IN SALT,
RINSED, DRAINED, AND COARSELY CHOPPED

JUICE OF 1 LARGE LEMON

¼ CUP MAYONNAISE (NOT MAYONNAISE-BASED
SALAD DRESSING OR SANDWICH SPREAD)

KOSHER OR SEA SALT TO TASTE

FRESHLY GROUND BLACK PEPPER TO TASTE

Of the many recipes in this book, this appetizing salad may be my favorite. It is based on a dish that my Zia Gilda, my mother's eldest sister, used to make every summer for my sister and me. If we were lucky, she might have a bowl of it waiting for us when we arrived from the airport to the apartment in Rome that she shared with my mother's other two sisters, Adriana and Elsa. Gilda was a person who loved fine things, like Bruno Magli shoes and Luisa Spagnoli dresses. But she was also modest, and the styles she chose were simple. It was the same with her cooking: the food she prepared was always simple, unadorned home fare. But she went to the open-air market in the piazza near her house every day to find the freshest ingredients, and whatever she made was always delicious. Gilda passed away some years ago, never having written down her recipes, but with my sister's help I have recreated her rice salad here to the best of my memory. I think she would have approved. I like to serve this as a refreshing alternative to potato salad at a backyard cookout, or as the main course at a casual summer luncheon.

Bring a large pot of salted water to a boil over medium-high heat. Pour in the rice. When the water returns to a boil, reduce the heat to medium-low, cover, and cook the rice at a gentle simmer for 20 minutes, or until it is al dente (tender but still a little firm and not at all mushy). Drain the rice in a colander in the sink and rinse it under cold water to stop the cooking process and to cool it. Drain thoroughly and transfer the rice to a large bowl. Toss the rice with the olive oil. Add the remaining ingredients except for the lemon juice, mayonnaise, and salt and pepper, and gently fold everything together. Stir in the lemon juice and mayonnaise and season to taste with salt and pepper. Spoon the rice salad into a decorative serving bowl, cover, and let it sit at room temperature for 30 to 60 minutes to allow the

CONTINUED ON NEXT PAGE . . .

. . . CONTINUED

flavors to mingle. Just before serving, toss the salad again and bring it to the table with a large serving spoon to allow your guests to serve themselves.

∾·∾·∾·∾

DO AHEAD: My sister and I agree that this salad is at its absolute best when made up to 1 hour in advance so that the rice has time to absorb the flavors but is still just the slightest bit warm. However, the ingredients may be chopped and prepared ahead of time and set aside or refrigerated until you are ready to use them. Bring them to room temperature before mixing them into the rice.

Farro Salad

MAKES 8 TO 10 SERVINGS

Farro is a wonderfully versatile grain that is said to have nourished the soldiers of ancient Rome. It has enjoyed a renaissance in popularity in recent years and is now found in many supermarkets and gourmet food shops. The grain, a cousin to the wheat berry, is equally at home in soups, stews, and salads such as this one. This is a great recipe for a casual buffet or to take on a picnic; it is festive in appearance and hearty in flavor, feeds a good number of people, and is always a crowd pleaser.

INGREDIENTS

For the dressing:

I TABLESPOON FRESHLY SQUEEZED LEMON JUICE

I TABLESPOON RED WINE VINEGAR

I TEASPOON GOOD-QUALITY BALSAMIC VINEGAR

I TABLESPOON DIJON MUSTARD

I TEASPOON KOSHER OR SEA SALT

FRESHLY GROUND BLACK PEPPER

I WHOLE GARLIC CLOVE, FLATTENED WITH THE BLADE OF A KNIFE

½ CUP EXTRA-VIRGIN OLIVE OIL

INGREDIENTS

For the salad:

1 ½ CUPS FARRO, RINSED AND DRAINED

3 CUPS HOMEMADE VEGETABLE BROTH *(page 55)* OR BEST-QUALITY FAT-FREE, LOW-SODIUM CANNED VEGETABLE BROTH

I TEASPOON KOSHER OR SEA SALT

4 OUNCES GREEN BEANS, TRIMMED AND CUT INTO I-INCH PIECES (I CUP)

3 CARROTS, PEELED, TRIMMED, AND CUT INTO ½-INCH COINS OR HALF-COINS (¾ CUP)

I SMALL FENNEL BULB, STALKS REMOVED, CHOPPED (⅔ CUP)

½ CUP CHOPPED SCALLIONS (BOTH WHITE AND GREEN PARTS)

½ CUP FROZEN PEAS, THAWED

½ CUP FROZEN ROASTED CORN KERNELS, THAWED (IF YOU CAN'T FIND FROZEN ROASTED CORN, USE REGULAR FROZEN CORN KERNELS)

¼ CUP CHOPPED GREEN OLIVES, SUCH AS PICHOLINE

¼ CUP CHOPPED PURPLE OLIVES, SUCH AS KALAMATA

½ CUP BOTTLED ROASTED OR MARINATED ARTICHOKE HEARTS, DRAINED AND CUT INTO PIECES

½ CUP BOTTLED ROASTED RED OR YELLOW PEPPERS, OR A COMBINATION OF BOTH, DRAINED AND DICED

½ CUP DICED PECORINO ROMANO OR PECORINO TOSCANO

2 TABLESPOONS CHOPPED FLAT-LEAF PARSLEY

To make the dressing:

Combine the lemon juice, wine and balsamic vinegars, Dijon mustard, salt, pepper, and garlic clove in a medium bowl. Slowly whisk in the olive oil to achieve an emulsified dressing. Set the dressing aside while you prepare the salad.

To make the salad:

Combine the farro and vegetable broth in a medium pot and place over medium-high heat. Bring to a boil; reduce the heat to medium-low and cook, partially covered, for 20 to 25 minutes, or until the farro is tender but still a little firm and chewy (al dente). It should not be at all mushy. Turn off the heat, cover completely, and let the farro sit for 10 minutes. Fluff with a fork.

While the farro is cooling, bring a quart of water to a boil in another pot. Add the salt. Place a bowl of ice water near the stove. When the water is boiling, add the green beans and cook for about 3 minutes, then sample a bean. It should taste cooked but still be bright green and somewhat crunchy. When the beans reach this state, use a slotted spoon to remove them to the bowl of ice water. Use the same boiling water to cook the carrots in the same way, blanching them for 3 minutes. With the slotted spoon transfer the carrots to the ice bath, adding additional ice cubes if necessary. Drain the green beans and carrots in a colander as soon as they are cool.

Put the cooked farro in a large mixing bowl. Add the blanched green beans and carrots, as well as the remaining vegetables, the pecorino, and the parsley. Remove the garlic clove from the dressing and discard. Pour the dressing over the salad and fold everything together gently but thoroughly with a large wooden spoon or silicon spatula. Taste, and adjust the seasoning with additional salt and pepper if necessary. Spoon the salad into a decorative serving bowl, cover with plastic wrap, and let it sit at room temperature for 30 minutes before serving (see Do Ahead). Toss again just before bringing it to the table.

COOK'S NOTE: This is a good salad with which to improvise. Try adding some good-quality tuna in olive oil, diced boiled potatoes, chopped hearts of palm, marinated mushrooms, or additional chopped herbs. Or keep it simple and toss the cooked farro with olive oil, lemon juice, garlic, diced tomatoes, mozzarella, and basil.

DO AHEAD: This salad may be made several hours or up to a day in advance and refrigerated. Remove it from the refrigerator 30 to 60 minutes before serving.

Potato Salad

MAKES 8 SERVINGS

Here is the potato salad that I grew up with. No mayo, no diced pickles or chopped egg; just a simple yet somehow divine mix of potatoes, olive oil, salt and pepper, and a little chopped scallion.

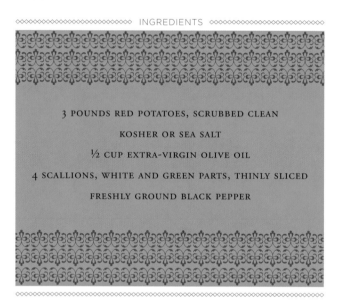

INGREDIENTS

3 POUNDS RED POTATOES, SCRUBBED CLEAN

KOSHER OR SEA SALT

½ CUP EXTRA-VIRGIN OLIVE OIL

4 SCALLIONS, WHITE AND GREEN PARTS, THINLY SLICED

FRESHLY GROUND BLACK PEPPER

Place the potatoes in a large pot and cover with cold water by 1 inch. Salt the water generously. Set the pot over medium-high heat and bring to a boil. Cook the potatoes for 20 to 25 minutes, until they are just tender. Drain and let sit until the potatoes are cool enough to handle but still quite warm.

Peel the potatoes and cut them into large dice or into ¼-inch-thick slices and place them in a bowl. Drizzle the olive oil over the potatoes while they are still warm and mix well. Add the scallions and salt and pepper to taste. Fold everything together. Serve the salad warm or at room temperature.

COOK'S NOTE: This is a great recipe to play around with. Try chives or red onion in place of the scallion, or dress it up with some chopped parsley, white wine vinegar, chopped anchovies, and capers.

Grilled Vegetable Salad

MAKES 8 TO 10 SERVINGS

◈◦▩◦◈

◇◇◇◇◇◇◇◇◇◇◇◇◇◇ INGREDIENTS ◇◇◇◇◇◇◇◇◇◇◇◇◇◇

For the dressing:

3 TABLESPOONS AGED BALSAMIC VINEGAR

1 TABLESPOON RED WINE VINEGAR

2 CLOVES GARLIC, PRESSED

¾ TEASPOON KOSHER OR SEA SALT, OR TO TASTE

FRESHLY GROUND BLACK PEPPER

½ CUP EXTRA-VIRGIN OLIVE OIL

—

For the grilled vegetables:

1 (1-POUND) EGGPLANT, CUT CROSSWISE
INTO ¾-INCH-THICK SLICES

KOSHER OR SEA SALT

VEGETABLE OIL OR HIGH-HEAT COOKING SPRAY
FOR GREASING THE GRILL GRATE

2 MEDIUM ZUCCHINI, HALVED LENGTHWISE

2 YELLOW CROOKNECK SQUASH, HALVED LENGTHWISE

EXTRA-VIRGIN OLIVE OIL

FRESHLY GROUND BLACK PEPPER

1 RED BELL PEPPER, TRIMMED AND CUT
INTO 2-INCH PIECES

1 YELLOW BELL PEPPER, TRIMMED AND CUT
INTO 2-INCH PIECES

1 GREEN BELL PEPPER, TRIMMED AND CUT
INTO 2-INCH PIECES

2 MEDIUM-TO-LARGE RED ONIONS, QUARTERED

2 DOZEN LARGE BUTTON MUSHROOMS, ENDS TRIMMED

1 PINT CHERRY TOMATOES

—

WOODEN SKEWERS, SOAKED FOR 30 MINUTES
IN COLD WATER AND DRAINED

—

¼ CUP COARSELY CHOPPED FRESH BASIL LEAVES

Spectacular colors—warm reds, cool purples, and bright greens and yellows—and the smoky flavor that comes from grilling make this a stand-out salad. Don't take the vegetables off the grill too soon; they should be tender enough so that they can absorb the dressing.

To make the dressing:
Combine the vinegars, garlic, salt, and pepper in a bowl and whisk to combine. Slowly whisk in the oil to achieve an emulsified dressing. Cover with plastic wrap and let the flavors blend while you prepare the vegetables.

To prepare the vegetables:
Layer the eggplant slices in a colander in the sink and sprinkle salt over each layer. Place a plate over the slices and weigh them down with a heavy object. Let the eggplant drain for 30 to 60 minutes. Wipe the slices dry with paper towels.

Prepare a charcoal grill or heat a gas grill to medium-high. Brush the grate with vegetable oil or spray with high-heat cooking spray.

Brush both sides of the eggplant, zucchini, and yellow squash with olive oil and sprinkle with a little salt and pepper. Skewer the peppers, onions, mushrooms, and tomatoes separately to insure that they will cook properly. Brush the skewered vegetables liberally with olive oil and season them with salt and pepper.

Place the eggplant, zucchini, and yellow squash on the grill grate and grill, turning frequently, about 12 minutes for the yellow squash, 15 minutes for the zucchini, and 17 minutes for the eggplant, or until they are charred here and there on the outside and softened somewhat but still a little firm. Transfer the eggplant and squashes to a platter or baking dish.

CONTINUED ON NEXT PAGE...

. . . CONTINUED

Place the skewered vegetables on the grill grate and grill, turning frequently, about 5 minutes for the tomatoes, 10 minutes for the mushrooms, and 14 to 15 minutes for the onions and peppers. The vegetables should be charred in places on the outside and softened somewhat, but still a little firm. Remove the vegetables from the grill as they finish cooking and place them on a large platter. Set the platters of vegetables near a cutting board.

Cut the eggplant disks into quarters, and cut the zucchini and yellow squashes crosswise into 1-inch pieces. Place them in a bowl large enough to hold all of the grilled vegetables. Remove the skewered vegetables from the skewers. Cut the peppers into bite-size pieces, and cut the mushrooms into quarters. Put them in the bowl, along with the onions and tomatoes. Scatter the chopped basil over the vegetables.

Pour the dressing over the vegetables and fold gently to combine. Taste and adjust the seasoning with additional salt and pepper if necessary. Cover with plastic wrap and let sit for 30 to 60 minutes. Or, refrigerate the salad until thoroughly chilled and serve cold.

DO AHEAD: This salad is best prepared several hours or up to a day in advance so that the vegetables take on the flavor of the dressing.

Most of us know how to toss a dish of pasta with some sauce, or butter and Parmigiano cheese, and call it dinner. I do it all the time for my family.

The pasta and other savory dishes in this chapter, however, are in a different realm. Spaghettini with Shrimp and Squash Blossoms (page 87) and Vanishing Cheese Risotto (page 89) are easy to make but stand out because of their special ingredients.

Others dishes are true labors of love. My mother's Lasagne Verde alla Bolognese (page 91) falls into this latter category. It requires several steps, including preparing a long-simmered sauce and making and rolling out homemade spinach pasta sheets. And yet, as involved as it sounds, this is a perfect dish to make for a dinner party. All of the work can be done ahead: the sauce can be made and frozen; the pasta sheets can be cut and dried until ready to use. The lasagne can even be assembled and refrigerated or frozen, so that all you have to do is pop it in the oven.

This chapter also includes three spectacular savory tortes: Eggplant and Rice Timballo (page 102), Pasta Timballo (page 99), and Pizza Rustica (page 97), a cheese- and cured meat–stuffed torte that Italians favor at Easter and I favor anytime.

I urge you to try some of these more involved recipes. Such kitchen projects give the recreational cook a wonderful sense of accomplishment. And if you want to bring on extra hands to help you fill and shape the *O Sole Mio* Ravioli (page 81) or roll out the dough for the Pizza Rustica, all the better.

CH. 3 PASTA, RICE & SAVORY TORTES

O Sole Mio Ravioli in Saffron-Butter Sauce

MAKES ABOUT 50 RAVIOLI, TO FEED 8 TO 10 AS A FIRST COURSE

INGREDIENTS

For the filling:

I POUND FRESH RICOTTA

I ½ CUPS SHREDDED CACIO DI ROMA

I LARGE EGG, PLUS I LARGE EGG YOLK,
LIGHTLY BEATEN TOGETHER

½ TEASPOON KOSHER OR SEA SALT, OR TO TASTE

FRESHLY GROUND BLACK PEPPER

—

For the pasta dough:

3 ½ TO 4 CUPS "OO" PASTA FLOUR *(see page 18)*, OR
3 TO 4 CUPS UNBLEACHED ALL-PURPOSE FLOUR

½ TEASPOON FINE KOSHER OR SEA SALT

4 EXTRA-LARGE EGGS

¼ TEASPOON SAFFRON THREADS, LIGHTLY
POUNDED TO A POWDER

I TABLESPOON EXTRA-VIRGIN OLIVE OIL

SEMOLINA FLOUR, FOR SPRINKLING ON
THE WORK SURFACE

—

For the Saffron-Butter Sauce:

12 TABLESPOONS (I ½ STICKS) UNSALTED BUTTER

¾ TEASPOON SAFFRON THREADS, LIGHTLY
POUNDED TO A POWDER

KOSHER OR SEA SALT

3 TABLESPOONS SNIPPED CHIVES
(ABOUT ¾-INCH-LONG PIECES)

—

I ½ CUPS FRESHLY GRATED
PARMIGIANO-REGGIANO

With their golden hue and round shape, these cheese-filled ravioli look like little suns, and they are even prettier bathed in their radiant orange-gold sauce. The warm, earthy aroma and unique flavor of saffron (not to mention its price) make this a fitting dish to celebrate a special occasion.

To make the filling:
If the ricotta cheese is very moist, put it in a cheesecloth-lined sieve or colander and let it drain for 30 minutes. If it is not too moist, drain it briefly, gently squeezing out any excess moisture. Put the ricotta in a large bowl and mash it with a fork to break it up. Stir in the cacio, egg, and egg yolk, and season with salt and pepper. Cover the bowl tightly with plastic wrap and refrigerate until ready to use.

To make the dough:
Put the flour and salt in the work bowl of a food processor fitted with the metal blade. Pulse briefly to combine. In a bowl, lightly beat together the eggs with the saffron until the saffron begins to dissolve. With the motor running on the food processor, pour the eggs and then the oil into the work bowl through the feed tube and process just until the mixture starts to form crumbs that look like small curds. This should take 20 seconds or less. Pinch together some of the mixture and roll it around. It should form a soft ball. If it seems dry, add a few drops of water or oil—no more than a tablespoon—and process briefly.

Turn the mixture out onto a clean work surface and press it together with your hands to form a rough ball. If the mixture seems sticky, sprinkle a little bit of semolina flour on the work surface. Knead the dough, using the palm of your hand to push it gently but firmly away from you and then fold it over toward you.

CONTINUED ON NEXT PAGE . . .

. . . CONTINUED

Give the dough a quarter-turn and continue to knead and turn for several minutes until the dough is smooth. Form it into a ball, wrap it tightly in plastic wrap, and let it rest at room temperature for 20 to 30 minutes.

To make the ravioli:

Set up your pasta machine with the rollers on the widest setting (number 1 on my machine). Scatter a little pasta flour and a little semolina flour on the work surface around the machine and have more on hand for sprinkling on the dough. Spread a clean cotton tablecloth on a table or large flat space and sprinkle it with semolina flour. This is where you will put the finished ravioli.

Cut the dough into 4 equal portions and rewrap 3 portions. Knead the fourth portion briefly on the work surface. Then, using a rolling pin or the flat of your hand, form it into an oval 5 to 6 inches long and 3 to 4 inches wide. Feed the dough through the rollers of the pasta machine and lay the strip on your work surface. Fold the dough into thirds, like folding a business letter, sprinkle it with a little flour if necessary, and pass it through the rollers again. Repeat the folding and rolling process 3 or 4 more times, or until the strip of dough is smooth. Move the roller setting to the next notch and feed the strip of dough through the setting twice, sprinkling it with a little flour if necessary to keep it from sticking. Continue to pass the dough through the rollers of the pasta machine twice on each setting until you get to the second-narrowest setting (6 on my machine). Roll the dough through the machine once. If you are

able to see the shadow of your hand through the strip of dough, it is thin enough to form into ravioli. If your hand is not visible through the dough, move the notch to the narrowest setting and pass the strip through the machine one more time.

At this point you will have a long, thin ribbon of dough. Lay the ribbon flat on a work surface dusted with semolina flour. For ravioli, it is best to fill and shape the first ribbon of dough before stretching the next.

Remove the filling from the refrigerator and set it nearby. Have on hand a 3-inch round cookie cutter for cutting the ravioli, a cake tester or toothpick for poking tiny holes in the ravioli, and a fork for sealing them.

Place teaspoons of filling at 3-inch intervals along the center of the strip. Stop when you get halfway across the strip of dough. Lift the empty half of the strip and fold it over the other half, to cover the mounds of filling. Gently press all around the mounds of filling with your fingers to separate and seal them. With the cookie cutter, cut out rounds of ravioli, making sure the filling is in the center of each of the ravioli. Gather up the leftover scraps of dough, press them into a ball, and wrap them tightly in plastic wrap. You will be able to roll these one more time to make more ravioli. Press the tines of the fork around the edges of the ravioli to seal them. Poke 6 little holes into the center mounds to release air. Transfer the shaped ravioli to the semolina-dusted tablecloth. Continue to roll out, fill, and shape the remaining pasta dough. Reroll the scraps once to form additional ravioli. Do not reroll the scraps after the second time. You should end up with about 50 ravioli.

If you plan to serve the ravioli on the day you make them, leave them out to dry until it is time to cook them. If you are making them in advance, freeze them until you wish to serve them. To freeze, sprinkle some semolina flour on a rimmed baking sheet that will fit in your freezer. Place a single layer of ravioli on the sheet, taking care that they do not touch each other. Freeze the ravioli for 45 minutes, or until completely firm. Transfer the ravioli to a zipper-lock freezer bag and return to the freezer until you use them. (To cook frozen ravioli, do not defrost them; just transfer them right from the freezer to the pot of boiling water.)

To make the sauce and cook the ravioli:
Place the butter and crushed saffron in a large skillet or sauté pan and set the skillet over medium-low heat. As the butter melts, stir it gently to help dissolve the saffron. When the butter is completely melted and starts to sizzle, turn off the heat and sprinkle in some salt and the chives. Stir to combine and then cover to keep the sauce warm while the ravioli cook.

Bring a large pot of generously salted water to a rolling boil. Gently drop in some of the ravioli, taking care not to crowd the pot or they will stick together. Cook the ravioli for about 5 minutes, until they are just al dente. Use a large slotted spoon or skimmer to remove the cooked ravioli to a large warmed serving bowl. Drizzle a little of the saffron butter sauce over

them and sprinkle a little Parmigiano on top. Continue until you have cooked all of the ravioli and transferred them to the serving bowl. Drizzle the top with any remaining sauce and sprinkle with any remaining cheese. Bring to the table and serve immediately. To serve the ravioli individually, divide the cooked ravioli among 8 to 10 individual shallow rimmed bowls. Drizzle a little of the sauce over each serving and sprinkle each serving with cheese.

DO AHEAD: The ravioli may be made up to a month in advance and frozen.

Double Carbonara

MAKES 4 TO 6 SERVINGS

What can I say? I love pancetta *and* bacon, so I put both into this deluxe version of Spaghetti alla Carbonara. After that was settled I figured I shouldn't have to choose between Parmigiano-Reggiano and pecorino, either. Although this dish involves some quick last-minute tossing of pasta with eggs and cream to create a smooth sauce, I am not averse to a little drama in the kitchen, especially when I am making a casual dinner for a small group of family or friends.

INGREDIENTS

3 TABLESPOONS EXTRA-VIRGIN OLIVE OIL

4 CLOVES GARLIC, FLATTENED WITH THE BLADE
OF A KNIFE

4 THICK SLICES SMOKY BACON, SLICED CROSSWISE
INTO ½-INCH-WIDE STRIPS

4 (¼-INCH-THICK) SLICES PANCETTA (ABOUT ½ POUND),
CUT INTO ¾-INCH-LONG STRIPS

⅓ CUP DRY WHITE WINE

1 TABLESPOON COGNAC

4 LARGE EGGS

4 TABLESPOONS HEAVY CREAM

½ CUP FRESHLY GRATED PARMIGIANO-REGGIANO

½ CUP FRESHLY GRATED PECORINO ROMANO

¼ CUP MINCED FLAT-LEAF PARSLEY

FRESHLY GROUND BLACK PEPPER

KOSHER OR SEA SALT

1 POUND SPAGHETTI

Put the oil and garlic in a medium-sized skillet or sauté pan placed over medium heat. Sauté the garlic over medium heat until it just starts to turn golden, 3 to 5 minutes. Add the bacon and pancetta and sauté until they are lightly browned and just beginning to crisp, about 10 minutes. Raise the heat to medium-high and pour in the wine, letting it bubble off for about 2 minutes, until it is almost but not entirely evaporated. Sprinkle in the cognac and let it bubble for just a minute. Turn off the heat.

Break the eggs into a large serving bowl and beat lightly with a whisk. Add the cream, the cheeses, the parsley, and a few grindings of pepper. Whisk everything together.

Bring a large pot of salted water to a rolling boil. Cook the spaghetti until it is al dente (cooking time will depend on the brand of pasta). While the pasta is cooking, reheat the bacon and pancetta until they are sizzling. Remove from the heat. Drain the pasta in a colander, reserving about 1 cup of the cooking water in a heat-proof cup.

Transfer the pasta to the serving bowl and very vigorously toss it with the egg-cheese mixture until the strands are well-coated. You will need to work quickly to prevent the eggs from scrambling. Add a splash or two of reserved pasta water to loosen the consistency a bit if the spaghetti is clumping together. Pour the bacon and pancetta and any drippings from the pan over the spaghetti and toss everything again thoroughly. Finish with several more grindings of black pepper. Bring the bowl to the table and serve immediately.

DO AHEAD: The bacon and pancetta may be sautéed up to 2 hours in advance, covered, and kept at room temperature.

Fettuccine al Forno with Porcini, Shiitakes, and a Hint of Truffle

MAKES 8 TO 10 SERVINGS

✧·✧·✧

INGREDIENTS

For the mushrooms:

1 OUNCE (1 CUP) DRIED PORCINI

1 CUP BOILING WATER

3 TABLESPOONS UNSALTED BUTTER, PLUS
ADDITIONAL FOR GREASING A BAKING DISH

3 TABLESPOONS EXTRA-VIRGIN OLIVE OIL

3 CLOVES GARLIC, MINCED

2 POUNDS MIXED FRESH MUSHROOMS, INCLUDING
SHIITAKES, PORTOBELLAS, AND ANY OTHERS
THAT CATCH YOUR EYE, THINLY SLICED

1 TABLESPOON MINCED FRESH OREGANO

1 TABLESPOON MINCED FRESH THYME

½ CUP DRY MARSALA

1 TEASPOON KOSHER OR SEA SALT

FRESHLY GROUND BLACK PEPPER

¼ CUP MINCED FLAT-LEAF PARSLEY

—

For the béchamel sauce:

6 TABLESPOONS UNSALTED BUTTER, PLUS MORE
TO BUTTER THE BAKING DISH

6 TABLESPOONS FLOUR

4 CUPS WHOLE MILK OR 2 CUPS WHOLE MILK
AND 2 CUPS LIGHT CREAM, HEATED TO A SIMMER

KOSHER OR SEA SALT

FRESHLY GROUND BLACK PEPPER

PINCH OF FRESHLY GRATED NUTMEG

—

2 POUNDS FETTUCCINE

1½ CUPS FRESHLY GRATED PARMIGIANO-REGGIANO

1½ CUPS SHREDDED *SOTTOCENERE AL TARTUFO*
(*see Cook's Note, page 86*)

Fall is the time for this ultra-rich baked pasta dish. The whisper of truffle comes from *sottocenere al tartufo,* a creamy textured cow's milk cheese from the Veneto region that is laced with bits of black and white truffle and has a fine coating of ash and spices (see Cook's Note).

To prepare the mushrooms:

Put the dried porcini in a small heatproof bowl and pour the boiling water over them. Let them stand for 20 to 30 minutes, or until softened. Drain the porcini in a fine-mesh sieve lined with damp paper towels or cheesecloth, reserving the liquid. Chop the mushrooms coarsely and set the mushrooms and liquid aside separately.

In a large skillet or sauté pan, heat 3 tablespoons of butter and the oil over medium heat. Add the garlic and sauté for 3 to 4 minutes, until the garlic is softened but not browned. Add the fresh mushrooms, oregano, and thyme and sauté for 10 minutes, or until the liquid the mushrooms release has evaporated and they are tender. Stir in the reserved porcini mushrooms. Raise the heat to medium-high and pour in the Marsala. Cook for 2 minutes, or until the wine has evaporated. Season the mushrooms with salt and pepper, stir once more, and remove from the heat. Stir in the parsley.

To make the béchamel sauce:

Melt the 6 tablespoons of butter in a heavy-bottomed saucepan placed over medium-low heat. Sprinkle in the flour, stirring vigorously with a whisk until the mixture is smooth. Cook for 2 minutes, and then gradually pour in the heated milk, whisking all the while to prevent scorching. Cook the béchamel sauce for 10 minutes, stirring constantly, until it is nicely thickened. Stir in the reserved porcini liquid, taking care to incorporate it well. Turn off the heat and season the sauce with a few pinches

CONTINUED ON NEXT PAGE ...

of salt, a few grindings of pepper (some cooks prefer to use white pepper here, but I don't mind the little black specks from black pepper), and the fresh nutmeg.

To prepare the fettuccine:
Heat the oven to 400°F. Lightly butter a large oven-proof baking dish.

Bring a large pot of salted water to a rolling boil. Cook the pasta until it is slightly undercooked (cooking time will depend on the brand of pasta). Drain the pasta in a colander placed in the sink, reserving about 1 cup of the pasta water in a heatproof cup.

Return the fettuccine to the pot in which you cooked it. Add the reserved béchamel sauce, the mushrooms, 1 cup of the Parmigiano-Reggiano, and all of the *sottocenere* cheese. If the pasta is clumping together, add a little of the reserved pasta water to loosen it a bit.

Pile the pasta into the baking dish, spreading it out evenly. Sprinkle with the reserved ½ cup of Parmigiano. Cover the dish with foil and bake for 20 minutes. Uncover and bake for 15 minutes more, until the top is golden. Serve immediately.

❧·❧·❧·❧

DO AHEAD: The mushrooms may be sautéed a day in advance and refrigerated in a tightly lidded container. Reheat them on the stove top before tossing them with the cooked fettuccine and sauce. The béchamel sauce may be made in advance and refrigerated for up to 3 days in a tightly lidded container. Bring it to a simmer on the stove top before mixing it with the cooked fettuccine.

❧·❧·❧·❧

COOK'S NOTE: If you are unable to find *sottocenere al tartufo,* substitute imported fontina Val d'Aosta.

Spaghettini with Shrimp and Squash Blossoms

MAKES 4 TO 6 SERVINGS

Shrimp and zucchini flowers complement each other in many ways: their vivid hues, their tender yet satisfying, slightly crunchy textures, their delicate yet distinct flavors. Together, they really dress up a simple dish of pasta. I like to serve this as a summer entrée, or sometimes as a first course followed by Escarole and Swiss Chard Torte (page 163).

INGREDIENTS

KOSHER OR SEA SALT

1 POUND SPAGHETTINI

3 TABLESPOONS UNSALTED BUTTER

3 TABLESPOONS EXTRA-VIRGIN OLIVE OIL

4 CLOVES GARLIC, MINCED

1½ POUNDS LARGE SHRIMP, PEELED AND DEVEINED

A GENEROUS PINCH OF CRUSHED RED PEPPER

JUICE AND ZEST OF 1 LEMON

2 TABLESPOONS MINCED FLAT-LEAF PARSLEY

⅓ CUP COARSELY CHOPPED FRESH BASIL

24 ZUCCHINI BLOSSOMS, SLICED CROSSWISE
INTO ½-INCH-THICK STRANDS

Have all your ingredients for the sauce prepped and ready to go, as you will be making this quick sauce while the pasta cooks.

Bring a large pot of salted water to a boil. Add the spaghettini and cook until it is slightly undercooked (cooking time will depend on the brand of pasta).

While the pasta is cooking, heat the butter, olive oil, and garlic in a large skillet or sauté pan placed over medium heat. When the butter is melted and begins to sizzle, add the shrimp to the pan and cook them for about 3 minutes, until they have changed color. Season with salt and red pepper and then add the lemon juice, zest, and parsley. Let the juice bubble for about a minute and then stir in the basil and the zucchini blossoms, and gently toss to combine everything thoroughly. Reduce the heat to low.

Drain the pasta in a colander, reserving some of the pasta water in a heat-proof cup. Return the skillet with the sauce to medium heat and toss the drained pasta with the sauce, using tongs or a serving fork to combine. Add a splash or two of the reserved pasta water to prevent the strands of pasta from sticking. When the pasta is al dente (this will take just a minute or so), remove the skillet from the heat.

Divide the spaghettini between four individual shallow rimmed bowls, arranging a few shrimp on top of each. Spoon any sauce left in the pan over the pasta and serve immediately.

Pork Ragù for a Crowd

MAKES ABOUT 3 QUARTS, ENOUGH TO SAUCE AT LEAST 3 POUNDS OF PASTA

If you are looking for a simple recipe to feed the multitudes, look no further. This robust sauce of stewed pork and sausages is easy to prepare and can be made well in advance. In fact, it is one of those magical recipes whose flavor improves if it is made ahead and then reheated. I like to serve this sauce over short sturdy pasta, such as rigatoni.

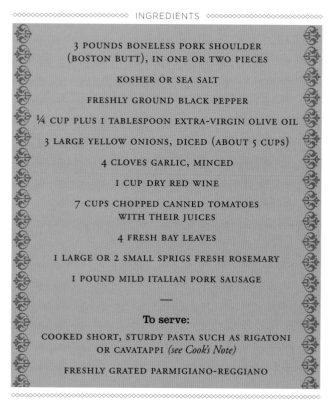

INGREDIENTS

3 POUNDS BONELESS PORK SHOULDER
(BOSTON BUTT), IN ONE OR TWO PIECES

KOSHER OR SEA SALT

FRESHLY GROUND BLACK PEPPER

¼ CUP PLUS 1 TABLESPOON EXTRA-VIRGIN OLIVE OIL

3 LARGE YELLOW ONIONS, DICED (ABOUT 5 CUPS)

4 CLOVES GARLIC, MINCED

1 CUP DRY RED WINE

7 CUPS CHOPPED CANNED TOMATOES
WITH THEIR JUICES

4 FRESH BAY LEAVES

1 LARGE OR 2 SMALL SPRIGS FRESH ROSEMARY

1 POUND MILD ITALIAN PORK SAUSAGE

—

To serve:

COOKED SHORT, STURDY PASTA SUCH AS RIGATONI
OR CAVATAPPI (*see Cook's Note*)

FRESHLY GRATED PARMIGIANO-REGGIANO

Generously season the pork all over with salt and pepper. Heat the oil in a large heavy-bottomed Dutch oven or other heavy-bottomed pot placed over medium-high heat. Set the pork in the pot and let it brown on one side for 3 to 4 minutes, then turn. Continue to brown the pork in this way until it is nicely seared all over. Remove the pork to a large bowl or plate.

Reduce the heat to medium and add the onions to the pot. Stir to coat them well, adding the 1 tablespoon of additional oil if necessary. Add the garlic. Sauté the onions and garlic until the onions are softened and translucent, about 10 minutes. Return the pork to the pot, raise the heat to medium-high, and pour in the wine. Let it bubble for a minute or so, and then add tomatoes, the bay leaves, and the rosemary. Reduce the heat to medium-low.

Remove the sausages from their casings and crumble the meat into the sauce. Cover the pot and simmer the sauce gently (reduce the heat further if necessary) for 2 to 2½ hours, or until the meat is fork-tender and shreds easily. Remove the meat to a cutting board and shred it. Return it to the pot and cook over low heat until the meat and sauce are completely heated through. Taste, and adjust the seasoning with additional salt if necessary.

To serve, toss the sauce with cooked pasta—the amount of pasta and sauce you use will, of course, depend on the number of people you are serving and how hungry they are. Count on at least ¼ pound per person if you are serving this dish as a main course. You can serve the pasta in a large, warmed serving bowl and let your guests help themselves at the table. Or you can dish it out into individual shallow rimmed bowls. Either way, sprinkle lots of freshly grated Parmigiano-Reggiano on top of the dressed pasta.

COOK'S NOTE: This recipe makes a lot of sauce, enough to serve up to 12 people as a main course with a salad on the side. Use as much as you need, depending on the number of people you are feeding (I generously estimate about a cup of sauce per serving) and freeze what is left in quart-sized containers.

Vanishing Cheese Risotto

MAKES 6 FIRST-COURSE OR 8 TO 10 SIDE-DISH SERVINGS

When we were kids, my sister decided to make risotto for dinner. This was while our parents were away and we were being supervised by a cousin who had come to visit from Italy. Without our mother's watchful eye in the kitchen, my sister saw an opportunity to make risotto the way she liked it best: with lots of cheese and lots of butter. The more she cooked and stirred the rice, the more she added chunks of butter and mozzarella and handfuls of Parmigiano, and the more she added them, the more quickly they disappeared into the pot. I am sure our cholesterol levels have never been the same. The version I present here is somewhat more restrained (though by no means light) and more refined. It is not something to eat every day, and of course you can serve it in judicious portions. But it is definitely worth the occasional splurge.

INGREDIENTS

2 TABLESPOONS EXTRA-VIRGIN OLIVE OIL

2 TABLESPOONS UNSALTED BUTTER

½ CUP DICED SHALLOTS

3 CUPS ARBORIO, CARNAROLI, OR OTHER
SHORT-GRAIN RISOTTO RICE

½ CUP DRY WHITE WINE

8 TO 10 CUPS HOMEMADE VEGETABLE BROTH *(page 55)*,
HOMEMADE CHICKEN BROTH *(page 50)*, OR BEST-QUALITY
FAT-FREE, LOW-SODIUM CANNED CHICKEN BROTH,
HEATED TO A SIMMER BUT NOT BOILING

1 WHOLE 8-OUNCE BLOCK IMPORTED ROBIOLA, CUT INTO
MEDIUM-SIZE PIECES, RIND INCLUDED *(page 17)*

1 CUP FRESHLY GRATED PARMIGIANO-REGGIANO, PLUS
A HANDFUL OF SHAVINGS FOR GARNISH

KOSHER OR SEA SALT

FRESHLY GROUND PEPPER

Heat the oil and the butter in a large Dutch oven or other heavy-bottomed pot placed over medium heat. When the butter has melted and begins to sizzle, add the shallots and sauté, stirring, until they are softened, about 7 minutes. Add the rice and stir to coat it thoroughly. Cook the rice for about 5 minutes, stirring constantly to prevent it from sticking, until the grains are shiny and translucent. Raise the heat to high and pour in the wine, stirring and letting it bubble for a minute or so. When most of the wine has been absorbed, reduce the heat to medium and add a ladleful of hot broth. Cook, stirring frequently, until almost all of the broth is absorbed. You do not need to stir the risotto continuously, but be sure to stir it often, and take care that the grains do not stick to the bottom of the pot. Continue to cook the risotto in this way for about 20 minutes or a little bit longer, adding broth by the ladleful, until the rice is almost but not completely cooked. It should be creamy but still al dente—a little bit firm in the center.

Turn off the heat and stir in the robiola and Parmigiano cheeses, stirring vigorously to incorporate them. Taste and season the risotto with salt and lots of freshly ground pepper. Spoon the risotto into a warmed serving bowl and garnish with an additional grinding of black pepper and a scattering of Parmigiano shavings. You may also serve the risotto in individual shallow-rimmed bowls. Garnish each bowl with some pepper and a few Parmigiano shavings.

Gabriella's Lasagne Verde alla Bolognese

MAKES 8 GENEROUS SERVINGS

I couldn't possibly write this book without including my mother's spectacular recipe for spinach lasagne with Bolognese sauce. The tender green pasta has a lovely earthy note and just a hint of nutmeg. The rich sauce is enhanced with cream and finely julienned strips of mortadella ham. In between the sheets of pasta are layers of fresh, oozy mozzarella and creamy béchamel sauce. Not even in the city of Bologna itself will you find lasagne that surpasses this one. This recipe is divided into four parts: the Bolognese sauce, the béchamel sauce, the pasta dough, and the assembling and baking of the lasagne. Most of the work can be done in advance, leaving only the baking for the last minute.

In a large Dutch oven or other heavy-bottomed pot, warm the oil and the butter over medium heat. When the butter has melted and begins to sizzle, add the garlic, carrots, celery, onion, and parsley and stir well to combine. Reduce the heat to medium-low and sauté the vegetables for about 10 minutes, or until they are softened and golden. Add the beef, veal, and pork and mix well, using a wooden spoon to break up the meats. Cook the meat over medium-low to low heat until it is deeply brown. Stir the meat frequently as it cooks. This will take about an hour or slightly longer.

When the meat is dark brown and crumbly, raise the heat to medium and stir in the wine, mixing for about a minute or so until the wine is evaporated. Season with a little salt, pepper, and nutmeg, and stir in the milk. Cook, stirring, until the milk has been absorbed. In a small bowl, dilute the tomato paste with a splash or two of beef broth and add it to the sauce. Mix well, and then add the remaining broth. Cover the pot partially with a lid, reduce the heat to low, and let the sauce simmer slowly for 2 hours, until it is very thick and all of the vegetables have more or less melted into the sauce. Stir in the cream and mortadella and heat through.

INGREDIENTS

For the Bolognese sauce:

3 TABLESPOONS EXTRA-VIRGIN OLIVE OIL

3 TABLESPOONS UNSALTED BUTTER

2 CLOVES GARLIC, MINCED

2 LARGE CARROTS, FINELY CHOPPED

2 LARGE RIBS CELERY, FINELY CHOPPED

I LARGE ONION, FINELY CHOPPED

I TABLESPOON MINCED FRESH FLAT-LEAF PARSLEY

I POUND GROUND BEEF

I POUND GROUND VEAL

I POUND GROUND PORK

I CUP DRY WHITE WINE OR DRY SHERRY

KOSHER OR SEA SALT

FRESHLY GROUND BLACK PEPPER

PINCH OF FRESHLY GRATED NUTMEG

I CUP WHOLE MILK

I (7-OUNCE) CAN TOMATO PASTE

2 CUPS BEST-QUALITY FAT-FREE, LOW-SODIUM CANNED BEEF BROTH

I CUP HEAVY CREAM OR LIGHT CREAM

¼ POUND THINLY SLICED MORTADELLA, CUT INTO JULIENNED STRIPS

DO AHEAD: The sauce may be made in advance and kept in a tightly lidded container in the refrigerator for up to 3 days or in the freezer for up to 3 months.

CONTINUED ON NEXT PAGE . . .

. . . CONTINUED

For the béchamel sauce:

3 CUPS WHOLE MILK

4 TABLESPOONS UNSALTED BUTTER

4 TABLESPOONS UNBLEACHED ALL-PURPOSE FLOUR

1 TEASPOON KOSHER OR SEA SALT

FRESHLY GROUND BLACK PEPPER

PINCH OF FRESHLY GRATED NUTMEG

In a large saucepan, bring the milk just to the boiling point over medium heat. Do not let it boil over. Remove from the heat.

In a heavy-bottomed saucepan, melt the butter over medium heat. Whisk in the flour and cook, stirring constantly, for 2 minutes. Add the milk in driblets, whisking constantly and taking care to avoid lumps and scorching. Cook the béchamel for 10 to 13 minutes, stirring it frequently with a wooden spoon, until it is thick enough to coat the back of the spoon. Season the béchamel with salt, pepper, and nutmeg, and remove from the heat.

DO AHEAD: The béchamel sauce may be made in advance and kept in a tightly lidded container in the refrigerator for up to 3 days. Reheat it in a saucepan over low heat, adding a splash or two of milk if necessary to loosen it.

INGREDIENTS

For the *pasta verde* (spinach pasta):

9 OUNCES FRESH SPINACH, OR 5 OUNCES THAWED FROZEN CHOPPED OR WHOLE-LEAF SPINACH

2 EXTRA-LARGE EGGS

2 CUPS "00" PASTA FLOUR (*see page 18*), PLUS ADDITIONAL FOR KNEADING AND DUSTING THE WORK SURFACE

2 TABLESPOONS SEMOLINA FLOUR, PLUS MORE FOR DUSTING THE WORK SURFACE

¾ TEASPOON KOSHER OR SEA SALT

PINCH OF FRESHLY GRATED NUTMEG

Pour a small amount of water into a pot and bring it to a boil over medium-high heat. Add the spinach, cover, and cook until the spinach is wilted and tender, 3 to 5 minutes. Drain the spinach in a colander and rinse under cold water. Drain thoroughly, using your hands to squeeze out as much excess liquid as possible. Put the spinach and one of the eggs in the work bowl of a food processor fitted with the metal blade. Process to a puree. Scoop the puree into a bowl. Wash and dry the work bowl and blade of the food processor.

Put the pasta flour, semolina flour, salt, and nutmeg in the work bowl and pulse briefly to combine. Add the spinach and the remaining egg to the bowl and process until the dough starts to form crumbs that look like small curds.

Turn the mixture out onto a lightly floured work surface and press it together with your hands to form a rough ball. Knead the dough, using the palm of your hand to push it gently but firmly away from you and then fold it over toward you. Give the dough a quarter-turn and continue to knead and turn for several more minutes, until the dough is smooth. Form it into a ball, wrap it tightly in plastic wrap, and let it rest at room temperature for 20 to 30 minutes.

To make the lasagne sheets:
Set up your pasta machine with the rollers on the widest setting (number 1 on my machine). Scatter a little pasta flour and a little semolina flour on the work surface around the machine and have more on hand for sprinkling on the dough. Spread a clean cotton tablecloth on a table or large flat space and sprinkle it with semolina flour. This is where you will put the lasagne sheets.

Cut the dough into 3 equal portions and rewrap 2 portions. Knead the third portion briefly on the work surface. Then, using a rolling pin or the flat of your hand, form it into an oval 5 to 6 inches long and 3 to 4 inches wide. Feed the dough through the rollers of the pasta machine and lay the strip on your work surface. Fold the dough into thirds, like folding a business letter, sprinkle it with a little flour if necessary, and pass it through the rollers again. Repeat the folding and rolling process 3 or 4 more times, or until the strip of dough is smooth. Move the roller setting to the next notch and feed the strip of dough through the setting twice, sprinkling it with a little flour if necessary to keep it from sticking. Continue to pass the dough through the rollers of the pasta machine twice on each setting until you get to the second-narrowest setting (6 on my machine). Roll the dough through the machine once. If you are able to see the shadow of your hand through the strip of dough, it is thin enough. If your hand is not visible through the dough, move the notch to the narrowest setting and pass the strip through the machine one more time. (Becoming adept at stretching the dough through the narrowest setting takes time and practice but will eventually become easier the more you do it. If you are having difficulty with the last setting, stop after stretching the dough through the second-narrowest setting.)

At this point you will have a long, thin ribbon of dough. Lay the ribbon flat on a work surface dusted with semolina flour. Cut the ribbon into 4-inch-by-5-inch rectangles and set the rectangles on the tablecloth. Continue stretching and cutting the remaining portions of dough. You should end up with about 24 rectangles. Leave the rectangles of pasta on the tablecloth until you are ready to cook them and assemble the lasagne.

DO AHEAD: The pasta sheets may be rolled and cut a day in advance. Leave them on the tablecloth to dry overnight. Their edges may curl as they dry but will flatten out once the pasta sheets are boiled.

INGREDIENTS

To assemble and bake the lasagne:

2 TO 3 (8-OUNCE) BALLS OF FRESH MOZZARELLA, THINLY SLICED

2½ CUPS FRESHLY GRATED PARMIGIANO-REGGIANO

UNSALTED BUTTER FOR GREASING THE DISH

KOSHER OR SEA SALT

Lay several clean dishcloths out on a clean, flat surface near the stove. Have ready the Bolognese sauce, heated to a simmer; the béchamel sauce, heated to a simmer; the pasta sheets; and the mozzarella and Parmigiano cheeses.

Heat the oven to 375°F.

Lightly coat the interior of a 9- by-13-inch oven-proof lasagne dish with butter.

Bring a large pot of salted water to a boil. Carefully drop in 4 to 6 sheets of lasagne, taking care not to crowd the pot. Boil the pasta for just a couple of minutes; fresh pasta cooks quickly and the lasagne sheets should be slightly underdone. Use a large skimmer to remove the lasagne sheets from the pot and spread them out on the clean dish towels. Continue to cook and spread out the lasagne sheets until you have used them all.

Spread a ladleful of Bolognese sauce and a little of the béchamel sauce in the bottom of the lasagne pan. Arrange a single layer of pasta sheets over the sauce. Spread just enough Bolognese sauce over the pasta to cover it, and spread a little of the béchamel on top of the sauce. Lay several slices of mozzarella over the top and sprinkle with a little Parmigiano. Continue to layer the pasta, sauces, and cheeses until you have at least 5 layers, ending with a layer of lasagne sheets and reserving a little sauce and Parmigiano cheese for the top. Spread a thin layer of sauce over the pasta and sprinkle the Parmigiano on top.

Cover the lasagne with foil and bake for 15 to 20 minutes. Uncover and bake for an additional 10 to 15 minutes, or until it is bubbling and the top is golden. Remove the lasagne from the oven and let it sit for 10 minutes before cutting. To serve, cut the lasagne into individual portions and with a spatula transfer the slices to shallow rimmed bowls. Serve immediately.

DO AHEAD: The lasagne may be assembled in advance and refrigerated, tightly covered, for up to 2 days or frozen for up to 1 month. Bring the lasagne to room temperature before baking it.

Seafood Risotto with Prosecco

MAKES 8 TO 10 FIRST-COURSE SERVINGS OR 5 TO 6 MAIN-COURSE SERVINGS

INGREDIENTS

I POUND MEDIUM OR LARGE SHRIMP,
PEELED AND DEVEINED, SHELLS WASHED
AND RESERVED

2 LOBSTER TAILS (½ POUND TOTAL),
REMOVED FROM THEIR SHELLS,
CUT CROSSWISE INTO I-INCH PIECES,
WITH SHELLS WASHED AND RESERVED

8 CUPS HOMEMADE VEGETABLE BROTH
(*page 55*) OR BEST-QUALITY LOW-SODIUM
CANNED VEGETABLE BROTH

I ½ CUPS PROSECCO

2 TABLESPOONS PLUS ¼ CUP
EXTRA-VIRGIN OLIVE OIL

2 DOZEN LITTLENECK OR OTHER SMALL CLAMS,
THOROUGHLY SCRUBBED AND RINSED

2 DOZEN MUSSELS, THOROUGHLY SCRUBBED,
DEBEARDED, IF NECESSARY, AND RINSED

½ POUND CALAMARI, BOTH SACS AND
TENTACLES, WASHED AND PATTED DRY
WITH PAPER TOWELS

2 TABLESPOONS MINCED FLAT-LEAF PARSLEY

I TABLESPOON FINELY MINCED GARLIC

GENEROUS PINCH OF RED PEPPER FLAKES

3 CUPS ARBORIO, CARNAROLI, OR OTHER
SHORT-GRAIN RISOTTO RICE

KOSHER OR SEA SALT

I spent a good portion of my summers traveling around Italy with my parents and my older sister when I was growing up. I remember one summer in particular, when we were in Venice, my sister, who was already a risotto lover (see Vanishing Cheese Risotto, page 89), became obsessed with *risotto ai frutti di mare* ("fruit of the sea risotto"), ordering it for every meal we ate out. I can't claim that my version here is perfectly authentic, as the shellfish in the United States differs from varieties harvested in the Mediterranean and Adriatic seas. But I can tell you that my sister loves it and makes it often for guests.

This is a dish to make for friends who like hanging out with you in the kitchen. While much of the work can be done ahead, the actual cooking and stirring of the risotto must be done just prior to serving. Recruit a couple of friends to help with the stirring: you can bribe them with the remainder of the prosecco not used to cook the rice.

Put the shrimp shells, lobster shells, vegetable broth, and ½ cup prosecco in a large pot. Bring the liquid to a boil over medium-high heat. Reduce the heat to medium-low and let the broth simmer, uncovered, for 25 to 30 minutes, until it is fragrant and somewhat reduced in volume. Strain the broth through a fine-mesh sieve lined with a layer of damp paper towel placed over a bowl. Discard the solids and return the strained broth to the pot. You should have 6 to 7 cups of strained liquid. Cover the pot and keep the broth warm on a very low flame.

Coat the bottom of a large, lidded skillet or sauté pan with 2 tablespoons of olive oil. Set the pan over medium-high heat and tip in the clams and mussels. Cover and cook, shaking the pan every so often, until the shellfish open, about 5 minutes. Give any that lag behind a couple more minutes to open, then discard any that remain closed. Remove the meat from the clams and mussels and reserve it in a bowl; discard the shells. (If you like, leave some of the clams and mussels in their shells to garnish the finished risotto.) Strain the liquid through a fine-mesh sieve lined with a layer of damp paper towel placed over a bowl. Reserve the liquid.

Using kitchen scissors, cut the calamari sacs into ½-inch-wide rings. Cut each crown of tentacles in half lengthwise to yield bite-sized pieces. Set aside in a bowl.

Put the remaining ¼ cup olive oil, together with the minced parsley, garlic, and red pepper flakes, in a large Dutch oven or other heavy-bottomed pot placed over medium heat. Cook, stirring frequently, until the garlic is slightly softened and fragrant, but not browned, about 3 minutes. Pour in the rice and stir to coat all of the grains well. Cook, continuing to stir, for 2 to 3 minutes, until the grains of rice are translucent. Raise the heat to medium-high and pour in the remaining 1 cup of prosecco. Stir and let the mixture bubble for about a minute. Reduce the heat to medium-low and pour in the reserved liquid from the clams and mussels. Cook, stirring constantly, until almost all of the liquid is absorbed. Begin to add the reserved shrimp and lobster broth, one ladleful at a time, to the risotto, stirring frequently, until the liquid is nearly all absorbed. You do not need to stir the risotto constantly, but be sure that you do stir it often, and take care that the grains do not stick to the bottom of the pot. Continue to cook the risotto in this way for about 18 to 20 minutes, adding broth by the ladleful, until the rice is almost but not completely cooked. It should still be very al dente—still rather firm and chalky at the center.

Add the reserved shrimp, lobster, and calamari to the risotto and cook, stirring, for 6 to 8 minutes, continuing to add broth as necessary, until the shellfish is just cooked through. Gently mix in the reserved clams and mussels, along with a splash of broth. Taste for doneness and season the risotto with salt—the amount you need to add will depend on the saltiness of the broth and the reserved liquid from the clams and mussels. The risotto is done when the grains of rice are tender yet just a bit firm at their very center. The consistency should be neither too soupy nor too dry.

Ladle the risotto into shallow rimmed bowls. Garnish with reserved clams and mussels in their shells, if using. Serve immediately.

❦·❦·❦·❦

DO AHEAD: The shellfish-infused broth may be made up to a day in advance and stored in the refrigerator. Store the shelled shrimp and lobster in a tightly covered container in the refrigerator. Bring the shellfish to room temperature before adding it to the risotto. The seafood may be cleaned and prepared several hours in advance. The clams and mussels can be steamed several hours in advance. Refrigerate the reserved liquid and the meat from the clams and mussels in tightly covered containers. Bring the shellfish and liquid to room temperature before adding them to the risotto.

Three Savory Tortes

Savory Pastry Dough with Lemon

MAKES DOUGH FOR A TWO-CRUST 9- TO 10-INCH ROUND TORTE
OR A 9-BY-13-INCH RECTANGULAR TORTE

INGREDIENTS

2½ CUPS UNBLEACHED ALL-PURPOSE FLOUR,
PLUS MORE FOR THE WORK SURFACE

½ CUP (1 STICK) UNSALTED BUTTER, CHILLED
AND CUT INTO PIECES

¼ TEASPOON KOSHER OR SEA SALT

2 LARGE EGGS

4 TO 5 TABLESPOONS FRESHLY SQUEEZED
LEMON JUICE

This pastry dough is pliant and easy to work with. Even pastry phobes should not have any problems rolling it out.

If making by hand: Using 2 table knives or a pastry cutter, combine the flour, butter, and salt in a large bowl, cutting the mixture together until it resembles small peas. Work in the eggs until the pieces of dough begin to adhere. Sprinkle the lemon juice over the dough and work only until the dough comes together.

If using a food processor: Combine the flour, butter, and salt in the work bowl of the food processor and pulse briefly until combined. Add the eggs and the lemon juice and pulse just until a ball of dough begins to form, less than 10 seconds.

Turn the dough onto a lightly floured work surface. Gently pat the dough into a disk. Do not knead or overmix. Wrap the disk tightly in plastic wrap and refrigerate until needed.

VARIATION: To make Savory Pastry Dough with White Wine, substitute 4 to 5 tablespoons dry white wine for the lemon juice.

Pizza Rustica

MAKES 10 OR MORE SERVINGS

INGREDIENTS

For the filling:

I POUND FRESH, UNSALTED CHEESE SUCH AS BASKET CHEESE
(see Cook's Note, page 98) OR IMPORTED GREEK FETA

I (8-OUNCE) BALL FRESH MOZZARELLA, DICED

I POUND FRESH RICOTTA

I CUP (4 OUNCES) SHREDDED SHARP, AGED PROVOLONE,
SUCH AS AURICCHIO

1½ CUPS (6 OUNCES) FRESHLY GRATED
PARMIGIANO-REGGIANO

½ CUP (2 OUNCES) GRATED PECORINO ROMANO

4 OUNCES MORTADELLA, CUT INTO SMALL DICE
(ABOUT ⅔ CUP)

4 OUNCES PROSCIUTTO, CUT INTO SMALL DICE
(ABOUT ⅔ CUP)

4 OUNCES SOPRESSATA, CUT INTO SMALL DICE
(ABOUT ⅔ CUP)

KOSHER OR SEA SALT

FRESHLY GROUND PEPPER

3 LARGE EGGS, LIGHTLY BEATEN

¼ CUP HALF-AND-HALF OR WHOLE MILK

—

To assemble the pizza:

BUTTER FOR THE PAN

I BATCH SAVORY PASTRY DOUGH *(facing page)*,
SLIGHTLY COOLER THAN ROOM TEMPERATURE

UNBLEACHED ALL-PURPOSE FLOUR FOR THE WORK SURFACE

I EGG, LIGHTLY BEATEN WTH 2 TABLESPOONS WATER

This is not pizza in the way that most of us have come to think of pizza—that is, a thin saucer of dough topped with tomato sauce, cheese, and other goodies and baked in the oven. Pizza rustica is something entirely different; a pastry crust filled with half a dozen cheeses and diced cured meats. It is what many Italians have traditionally brought to the table to break the Lenten fast at Easter. This version, created by my mother, is exceedingly rich and delicious. A sliver is all you need, especially if you are serving it as an appetizer. But also consider serving it as an entrée for a spring luncheon, accompanied by a salad and a light dessert. That is, if you can bring yourself to share it.

To make the filling:
Using a wooden spoon, a fork, or your fingers, crumble the basket cheese or feta into a large bowl. Add the mozzarella, ricotta, provolone, Parmigiano-Reggiano, and pecorino Romano cheeses. Fold everything together with a wooden spoon or a sturdy spatula. Add the mortadella, prosciutto, and sopressata and mix again. Taste and adjust the seasoning with salt and pepper if necessary.

Pour the beaten eggs over the mixture and stir until thoroughly combined. The filling should be dense and thick enough to stand a spatula or wooden spoon in, but it should not be so thick that you can't incorporate the ingredients. Add the half-and-half or milk and mix well. Cover the filling with plastic wrap and set aside.

To assemble the pizza:
Heat the oven to 350ºF.

Generously butter a 9-by-13-inch pan or a 10-inch round springform pan with sides at least 2½ inches deep.

CONTINUED ON NEXT PAGE . . .

Cut the dough into 2 portions, one slightly larger than the other. Rewrap the portion you are not using and set it aside. On a lightly floured work surface, roll out the larger portion of dough into a rectangle or circle, depending on the shape of your pan, so that it is large enough to cover the bottom and sides of the pan with some overhang. The dough should be about ⅛ inch thick. Place your rolling pin on the edge of the dough closest to you and gently wrap the dough around the rolling pin. Lift the dough over the pan, then carefully unroll it. Gently press the dough into the pan. Spoon the filling into the pan and smooth out the top.

Roll out the remaining portion of dough and drape it over the filling. Gently press it directly against the surface of the filling. Trim the top and bottom crusts so that only 1 inch of overhang remains, then press them together to seal. Roll the overhang in toward the center of the dough to form an edge. Continue to roll the edge until you have gone all the way around the pan. Press down on the rolled edge with the tines of a fork to seal and form a decorative crust. If desired, use leftover dough to cut out shapes (I use cookie cutters to make baby chicks and eggs at Easter) and arrange them on top of the pie, using a little of the egg mixed with water to help them adhere. Using a sharp knife, cut 4 slits in the top of the pizza. Lightly brush the top crust surface with the egg wash.

Set the pizza rustica in the oven and bake it for about an hour, until the top is deeply golden. Transfer the pan to a wire rack to cool for 20 to 30 minutes. If using a rectangular pan, carefully invert the pizza onto a platter or cutting board, and then re-invert it onto the rack. Let cool completely. If using a springform pan, remove the sides and carefully transfer the pie to a large plate or platter. Alternatively, cut the pizza into bite-sized pieces and arrange on a platter.

Serve warm, at room temperature, or cooled and chilled.

ↄↄ·ↄↄ·ↄↄ

COOK'S NOTE: Basket cheese is usually sold in 2-pound plastic baskets. It can be hard to find but is usually available at Easter time at Italian markets and can be special-ordered at many well-stocked cheese counters. If you can't find it, use imported Greek feta instead. In this case you will most likely not need to add additional salt.

ↄↄ·ↄↄ·ↄↄ

DO AHEAD: The pastry dough may be made and stored, tightly wrapped in plastic, in the refrigerator, a day in advance, or frozen for up to 1 month. Bring the dough to slightly cooler than room temperature before rolling it out. The filling may be made up to a day in advance and kept, in a tightly lidded container, in the refrigerator. The pizza rustica may be baked a day in advance, wrapped tightly in plastic, and stored in the refrigerator, or frozen for up to 1 month. Reheat it, uncovered, in a moderate oven (350°F) until completely warmed through.

Pasta Timballo

MAKES 8 TO 10 SERVINGS

I became obsessed with making a timballo after I saw the movie *Big Night,* in which the pasta-, meat-, and cheese-stuffed baked "drum" is featured practically as a leading character. Two days after seeing the film I gave birth to my first child, so I was a little busy. Still, I was determined to make this amazing concoction, so I set about doing it in stages—making and freezing the dough for the crust, making and freezing the ragù sauce, frantically rolling and frying tiny meatballs while my poor infant son wailed in his carriage not five feet away. Naturally I have no memory of what that first endeavor looked or tasted like, and it was some years before I decided to tackle a timballo again. Now that my once-colicky baby is a good-natured 12-year-old boy, it's a lot easier. I still make it in stages, but now I have fun doing it, and even more fun serving it. This is a show stopper.

To make the meatballs:

Line a large baking sheet or platter with waxed paper. In a small bowl, combine the bread crumbs and milk and let sit for 5 minutes. Squeeze out any excess milk and discard. Put all of the meats in a medium bowl and add the moistened bread crumbs, egg, garlic, cheeses, parsley, salt, and several grindings of pepper. Mix everything together with your hands or a wooden spoon. Dampen your hands with cold water, pinch off a small piece (about 2 teaspoons) of the meatball mixture, and roll it into a ball. Place it on the prepared baking sheet. Continue to form the meatballs until you have used all the mixture. Keep your hands moistened with cold water to prevent the mixture from sticking to them. You should end up with about 45 meatballs.

Pour enough vegetable oil into a large skillet or sauté pan to reach a ¼-inch depth. Place the skillet over medium-high heat

CONTINUED ON NEXT PAGE . . .

INGREDIENTS

For the meatballs:

I CUP FRESH BREAD CRUMBS

¼ CUP WHOLE MILK, HEATED TO A SIMMER

¼ POUND GROUND BEEF

¼ POUND GROUND PORK

¼ POUND GROUND VEAL

I LARGE EGG, LIGHTLY BEATEN

I GARLIC CLOVE, PRESSED

2 TABLESPOONS FRESHLY GRATED PARMIGIANO-REGGIANO

2 TABLESPOONS FRESHLY GRATED PECORINO ROMANO

I ½ TABLESPOONS MINCED FLAT-LEAF PARSLEY

½ TEASPOON KOSHER OR SEA SALT

FRESHLY GROUND PEPPER

VEGETABLE OR OLIVE OIL (NOT EXTRA-VIRGIN) FOR FRYING

—

For the timballo:

¾ POUND (12 OUNCES) DRY RIGATONI OR PENNE RIGATE PASTA

I ½ QUARTS PORK RAGÙ FOR A CROWD *(page 88)*, HEATED TO A GENTLE SIMMER

3 HARD-BOILED EGGS, PEELED AND COARSELY CHOPPED

I CUP DICED CACIO DI ROMA

I CUP DICED FRESH MOZZARELLA OR SMOKED MOZZARELLA

½ CUP FRESHLY GRATED PARMIGIANO-REGGIANO

½ CUP FRESHLY GRATED PECORINO ROMANO

KOSHER OR SEA SALT

FRESHLY GROUND PEPPER

I BATCH SAVORY PASTRY DOUGH WITH WHITE WINE *(page 96)*, AT ROOM TEMPERATURE

I EGG, LIGHTLY BEATEN WITH 2 TABLESPOONS WATER

. . . CONTINUED

and heat it to 375°F. To test, pinch off a tiny piece of meatball mixture and drop it into the hot oil. It should sizzle upon hitting the oil. Carefully lower 8 to 10 meatballs into the oil, taking care not to crowd the skillet. Fry them for about 2 minutes, until golden brown on the bottom. Gently roll them over with a fork and fry for another 2 minutes. Use a large slotted spoon or a skimmer to remove the meatballs to a paper-towel-lined platter or a large brown paper bag placed near the stove. Continue to fry the meatballs until you have fried them all.

To assemble and bake the timballo:
Heat the oven to 375°F.

Bring a large pot of generously salted water to a boil. Cook the pasta until it is very al dente; that is, slightly underdone. Drain the pasta in a colander placed in the sink and transfer the pasta to a large bowl. Toss the pasta with 1 quart (4 cups) of the ragù. This may seem like a lot of sauce, but the pasta and other ingredients will absorb it while the timballo bakes. Add the reserved meatballs, the hard-boiled eggs, and the cheeses. Fold everything together. Season to taste with salt and pepper.

Divide the pastry dough into two pieces, one slightly larger than the other. Rewrap the smaller piece and set aside. On a lightly floured work surface, roll the larger piece into a disk large enough to cover the bottom and sides of a 10-by-3-inch round springform pan with some overhang. Trim the overhang to about ¾ inch. The dough should be about ⅛ inch thick. Place your rolling pin on the edge of the dough closest to you and gently wrap the dough around the rolling pin. Lift the dough over the pan and carefully unroll it, gently pressing it into the pan. Spoon half of the pasta filling into the pastry-lined pan. Spread 1 cup of the remaining ragù over the filling. Spoon the remaining filling on top of the sauce, pressing down gently to pack in the filling. Top with the remaining cup of sauce.

Roll the smaller portion of the pastry dough into a disk large enough to cover the top of the timballo with a little overhang. Place your rolling pin on the edge of the dough closest to you and gently wrap the dough around the rolling pin. Lift the dough over the pan and carefully unroll it to cover the filling. Gently press the overhanging edges of the top and bottom crusts together. Use a little water to moisten the dough to help seal it if necessary. Using your fingers, roll the crust in toward the pan to create a rolled seam. Continue to roll along the circumference of the pan until you have fully sealed the crust.

Brush the top of the torte with the egg wash. With a sharp paring knife, cut three 2-inch slits across the top of the timballo.

Bake the timballo for 45 to 50 minutes, or until the crust is golden brown. Remove the timballo from the oven and let it cool on a rack for 10 minutes. Remove the springform ring from around the timballo. Slide an angled metal spatula between the bottom of the timballo and the bottom of the cake pan to loosen it. Gently slide the timballo onto a large serving platter and bring it to the table. Use a large serrated knife to cut the timballo into wedges.

ტ3·ტ3·ტ3

DO AHEAD: The pastry dough may be made 1 day ahead and refrigerated or up to 1 month ahead and frozen. Bring it to room temperature before rolling it out. The ragù may be made up to 3 days ahead and refrigerated or up to 3 months ahead and frozen. The meatballs may be made up to 2 days ahead and refrigerated or up to 1 month ahead and frozen. If frozen, bring them to room temperature before using.

Eggplant and Rice Timballo

MAKES 8 TO 10 SERVINGS

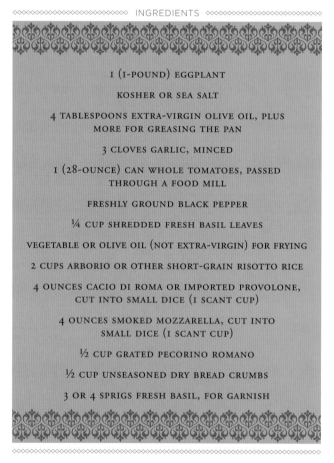

INGREDIENTS

1 (1-POUND) EGGPLANT

KOSHER OR SEA SALT

4 TABLESPOONS EXTRA-VIRGIN OLIVE OIL, PLUS
MORE FOR GREASING THE PAN

3 CLOVES GARLIC, MINCED

1 (28-OUNCE) CAN WHOLE TOMATOES, PASSED
THROUGH A FOOD MILL

FRESHLY GROUND BLACK PEPPER

¼ CUP SHREDDED FRESH BASIL LEAVES

VEGETABLE OR OLIVE OIL (NOT EXTRA-VIRGIN) FOR FRYING

2 CUPS ARBORIO OR OTHER SHORT-GRAIN RISOTTO RICE

4 OUNCES CACIO DI ROMA OR IMPORTED PROVOLONE,
CUT INTO SMALL DICE (1 SCANT CUP)

4 OUNCES SMOKED MOZZARELLA, CUT INTO
SMALL DICE (1 SCANT CUP)

½ CUP GRATED PECORINO ROMANO

½ CUP UNSEASONED DRY BREAD CRUMBS

3 OR 4 SPRIGS FRESH BASIL, FOR GARNISH

This beautiful, molded rice is almost always on my summer buffet table. It is adapted from a recipe in one of my favorite cookbooks, *Verdura: Vegetables Italian Style,* by Viana La Place. I bake the timballo in a basic ring pan, and when it is unmolded it is as pretty to look at as it is good to eat, which makes it a great addition to a summer buffet table. I have served it both warm and at room temperature. The leftovers are delicious cold.

Trim the ends off the eggplant and cut crosswise into ¼-inch-thick slices. Salt the slices lightly and layer them in a colander. Set a plate over the eggplant slices and weight it down with a heavy object. Let drain for 30 minutes.

Place the 4 tablespoons of extra-virgin olive oil and the garlic in a medium sauté pan or skillet. Turn the heat to medium-low and cook 2 to 3 minutes, stirring with a wooden spoon from time to time, until the garlic is fragrant and slightly softened but not brown. Stir in the tomatoes, and season with a little salt and pepper. Bring to a simmer and cook the sauce for 15 minutes, or until slightly thickened. Remove from the heat and stir in the basil.

Dry the eggplant slices with paper towels. Heat about ¼ inch of oil in a large sauté pan or skillet over medium-high heat. Fry the eggplant slices, a few at a time, turning once, until golden brown on both sides, about 5 minutes total per batch. Drain the slices on a paper towel–lined plate or a large brown paper bag. Set aside.

Place 7 cups of water in a medium to large pot and add a tablespoon of salt. Bring the water to a boil over medium-high heat and add the rice. Boil the rice, uncovered, for 13 to 15 minutes, reducing the heat to medium if necessary to prevent it from boiling over, just until the rice is al dente (tender but still a bit firm in the center). Drain the rice in a colander and put it in a large mixing bowl.

Stir the tomato sauce into the rice and add the cheeses. Gently mix together until the ingredients are thoroughly combined.

Grease a ring pan with a little extra-virgin olive oil and coat with half the bread crumbs. Spoon one-third of the rice and cheese mixture into the pan, smoothing it out with a wooden spoon or spatula to make an even layer. Using half the eggplant slices, arrange a layer of eggplant over the rice. Spoon a second layer of rice over the eggplant, and then arrange the remaining eggplant slices over that. Top with the remaining rice. Sprinkle the remaining bread crumbs over the top. The timballo may be refrigerated at this point for several hours or overnight if you don't plan to bake it immediately. Remove it from the refrigerator and let it return to room temperature before baking.

Heat the oven to 450ºF. Bake the timballo for 20 minutes, or until the cheese melts and the bread crumbs are golden brown. Remove from the oven and let cool for 10 minutes. Unmold the timballo onto a large platter and garnish with fresh basil leaves. Serve warm or at room temperature. To serve, cut into wedges.

DO AHEAD: The timballo may be made several hours in advance and served at room temperature.

The recipes in this chapter are organized by cooking technique, or rather, appliance—grill, oven, and stove top. I find it is easier to plan a menu if I know whether my oven will be free to bake a gratin or busy cooking the Roast Pork Loin with Carrots, Fennel, and Onions (page 131).

I naturally look to the grill when I am planning a warm-weather gathering or a casual party. My husband, Scott, and I have become avid grillers, and we get lots of use out of our charcoal kettle grill and our gas grill (plus a smoker that we share with two of our neighbors). I have to confess that Scott is usually the one who stands in the heat, flipping the steaks and chops for the Mixed Grilled Platter found on page 113 (hey, I made the marinade!) and poking the thermometer into the thigh of the Spatchcocked Herbed Chickens alla Diavola (page 117).

To me, a roast cooked in the oven implies a slightly more elegant affair, whether it's Poached and Roasted Capon with Porcini Butter (page 129) or Slow-Roasted Arctic Char with Sautéed Fennel and Pernod (page 127). Even so, plenty of comfort food emerges from my oven as well, including Eggplant Parmigiana Deluxe (page 138) and Crepe Cannelloni with Zucchini and Cheese Stuffing (page 122).

From the stove top come two chowders—Smoky Ham and Corn Chowder (page 149) and Spicy Seafood Chowder with Sweet Fennel (page 146)—plus a sublime slow-simmered Fresh Tuna Stew with Olives and Herbs (page 145), my sister Maria's Beef and Chestnut Stew with Marsala (page 154), and a red-hot Beef Brisket Chili served over Polenta (page 151), among other choices.

Here you will also find, under the heading Goes With, recommendations for what to serve with the recipes in this chapter. I use the term Goes With rather than Serve With because it better represents my intentions. Three-Cheese-Stuffed Red and Yellow Peppers (page 141) make a great vegetarian entrée for a casual gathering, but they are also a wonderful side dish for Beef Tenderloin alla Bandiera Italiana (page 133) or Rosemary-Rubbed Butterflied Leg of Lamb (page 112). Use these recommendations as a guideline, but I also encourage you to take advantage of the versatility of many of the recipes in this chapter and in others to come up with your own pairings.

CH. 4 MAIN COURSES

Arrosticini

MAKES 4 TO 6 SERVINGS

These appetizing little lamb skewers are from Italy's Abruzzo region, where my mother was raised and where I spent my summers when I was growing up. As teenagers, my sister and I would drive with our friends up into the hills searching for the telltale aroma of meat grilling on a wood-burning fire, which meant that an open-air restaurant was serving the regional specialty. We would devour dozens of these skewers, and with them, platefuls of grilled bread and piles of roasted potatoes.

INGREDIENTS

2 POUNDS BONELESS LEG OF LAMB WITH SOME MARBLING OF FAT *(see Cook's Note)*, CUT INTO ¾-INCH CUBES

3 CLOVES GARLIC, PRESSED

¼ CUP EXTRA-VIRGIN OLIVE OIL

I SPRIG FRESH ROSEMARY, CUT INTO 2-INCH PIECES, PLUS SEVERAL ADDITIONAL SPRIGS FOR GARNISHING THE SERVING PLATTER

KOSHER OR SEA SALT

FRESHLY GROUND PEPPER (OPTIONAL)

I LEMON, SLICED INTO ROUNDS FOR GARNISH

—

12-INCH WOODEN SKEWERS, SOAKED IN COLD WATER FOR 30 MINUTES AND DRAINED

Place the cubes of lamb, garlic, oil, and the cut-up rosemary sprig in a bowl and toss everything together until well combined. Cover with plastic wrap and marinate at room temperature for 1 hour or in the refrigerator for several hours or up to overnight. Remove the meat from the refrigerator and let it come to room temperature before grilling.

Prepare a hot charcoal grill or heat a gas grill to high. Thread the lamb cubes on the skewers, leaving no room between the pieces of meat. Sprinkle a little salt and pepper, if using, over the skewers. Place the skewers on the grill and sear for 3 minutes, until browned. Turn and sear for 2 more minutes. The interior of the meat should still be slightly pink. Using tongs, pile the skewers onto an oval serving platter or arrange them like spokes on a round serving platter. Garnish the platter with a few rosemary sprigs and some lemon slices. Serve immediately.

COOK'S NOTE: The traditional meat for arrosticini is *castrato*, a young ram that has been neutered shortly after birth to produce meat with a good marbling of fat. Lamb from the leg or the loin makes a good substitute as long as it has a little fat in it.

DO AHEAD: The meat may be marinated a day ahead and refrigerated. The cubes may be threaded onto the soaked skewers several hours ahead of time. Cover the threaded skewers with plastic wrap and refrigerate them. Bring them to room temperature before proceeding with grilling.

GOES WITH:

Bruschetta, page 31

Olive Oil–Roasted Potatoes, page 158

September Gratin, page 175

Artichokes alla Romana, page 160

Grilled Caesar Flank Steaks with Lemon-Anchovy Butter

MAKES 12 SERVINGS

All the bright, assertive flavors that make up a great Caesar salad come together in this delicious entrée: fresh lemon, Worcestershire sauce, garlic, and anchovies. It has the added appeal of being quick and easy to make; the little prep work involved is done a day in advance. Marinating the flank steak overnight not only gives you a jump start, it enhances the meat's flavor and tenderizes it.

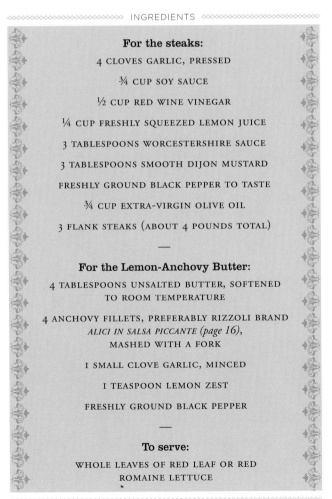

◇◇◇◇◇◇◇◇◇◇◇◇◇◇◇◇◇◇◇ INGREDIENTS ◇◇◇◇◇◇◇◇◇◇◇◇◇◇◇◇◇◇◇

For the steaks:

4 CLOVES GARLIC, PRESSED

¾ CUP SOY SAUCE

½ CUP RED WINE VINEGAR

¼ CUP FRESHLY SQUEEZED LEMON JUICE

3 TABLESPOONS WORCESTERSHIRE SAUCE

3 TABLESPOONS SMOOTH DIJON MUSTARD

FRESHLY GROUND BLACK PEPPER TO TASTE

¾ CUP EXTRA-VIRGIN OLIVE OIL

3 FLANK STEAKS (ABOUT 4 POUNDS TOTAL)

—

For the Lemon-Anchovy Butter:

4 TABLESPOONS UNSALTED BUTTER, SOFTENED
TO ROOM TEMPERATURE

4 ANCHOVY FILLETS, PREFERABLY RIZZOLI BRAND
ALICI IN SALSA PICCANTE (page 16),
MASHED WITH A FORK

I SMALL CLOVE GARLIC, MINCED

I TEASPOON LEMON ZEST

FRESHLY GROUND BLACK PEPPER

—

To serve:

WHOLE LEAVES OF RED LEAF OR RED
ROMAINE LETTUCE

To marinate the steaks:

In a medium bowl, whisk together the garlic, soy sauce, vinegar, lemon juice, Worcestershire sauce, mustard, and black pepper. Slowly whisk in the olive oil. Place two of the flank steaks in a gallon-size zipper-lock freezer storage bag and the third in another gallon-size freezer bag. Hold the bags upright and divide the marinade among them, adding a little more to the bag that contains two steaks. Carefully seal the bags shut, pressing out as much air as you can without letting any of the marinade escape. Flatten the bags out and place them on a small rimmed baking sheet or in a baking dish (in case of leakage) and refrigerate overnight.

To make the Lemon-Anchovy Butter:

In a small bowl, combine the softened butter, anchovies, garlic, lemon zest, and black pepper to taste. Spoon the butter onto a sheet of waxed paper and roll the paper around the butter, forming the butter into a 2-inch-thick cylinder as you roll. Tightly twist the ends of the paper shut. Place the cylinder of butter in the refrigerator to harden overnight. (I usually set the cylinder in a concave dish that is meant to hold a corn cob; this allows the butter to keep its cylinder shape as it hardens.)

To grill the steaks:

Remove the steaks from the refrigerator up to 1 hour before you plan to grill them. Remove the lemon-anchovy butter from the refrigerator 15 to 20 minutes before you plan to serve the steaks.

Prepare a charcoal grill (see Cook's Note, page 110) or preheat a gas grill to medium-high and lightly oil the grate. Set the steaks on the grill over direct heat and grill them for 5 to 8 minutes per side, or until an instant-read thermometer registers 120°F for rare and 130°F for medium-rare. Remove the steaks

CONTINUED ON NEXT PAGE . . .

... CONTINUED

to a carving board and loosely tent them with foil. Let them sit for about 10 minutes before slicing.

To serve, cut the steaks across the grain into ½-inch-thick slices, or thinner if you like. Arrange the slices on a large serving platter lined with the lettuce leaves. Cut the cylinder of lemon-anchovy butter into thin disks and place the disks here and there over the slices of steak (you may not use all the butter; return the unused portion to the refrigerator for another use, or freeze it).

DO AHEAD: Both the flank steak and the lemon-anchovy butter should be made a day in advance but may be made up to 2 days in advance.

GOES WITH:

Caesar Salad, page 62

Grilled Vegetable Salad, page 75

Bruschetta, page 31

Frank's Garlic Bread, page 45

Chestnut Honey–Glazed Country Pork Ribs

SERVES 4 TO 6

If you are looking to give your guests a rib fix but don't have the time to slow-smoke a rack of baby backs, country ribs are a great alternative. They are not really ribs at all; they are part of the bone-in loin closest to the shoulder of the pig. Like the loin, country ribs are lean, so treat them like pork chops rather than ribs and take care not to overcook them or they will be tough instead of succulent. An instant-read thermometer will help determine when they are done. This recipe is easily doubled to serve a small crowd.

INGREDIENTS

For the ribs:

4 POUNDS BONE-IN PORK LOIN RIBS (ALSO CALLED COUNTRY-STYLE LOIN RIBS), ABOUT 8 OUNCES EACH

EXTRA-VIRGIN OLIVE OIL

KOSHER OR SEA SALT

FRESHLY GROUND BLACK PEPPER

2 CLOVES GARLIC, CUT INTO PAPER-THIN SLIVERS

—

For the glaze:

¾ CUP FRESHLY SQUEEZED ORANGE JUICE, PLUS SEVERAL SLICES OF FRESH ORANGE FOR GARNISHING THE SERVING PLATTER

¾ CUP SOY SAUCE

¾ CUP CHESTNUT HONEY *(see page 18)* OR OTHER ROBUST FLAVORED HONEY

2 CLOVES GARLIC, FLATTENED WITH THE BLADE OF A KNIFE

I SPRIG ROSEMARY, PLUS ADDITIONAL SPRIGS FOR GARNISHING THE SERVING PLATTER

To season the ribs:

Drizzle a little oil on the ribs and rub it in with your fingers to coat the meat evenly. Sprinkle the ribs on all sides with salt and pepper and put them in a baking dish. Tuck the garlic slivers among the ribs. Cover with plastic wrap and set aside while you prepare the glaze.

To make the glaze:

Combine the orange juice, soy sauce, honey, flattened garlic cloves, and rosemary in a medium sauce pan. Bring to a boil over medium-high heat, reduce the heat to medium-low, and simmer the sauce until it is thickened and somewhat reduced, 15 to 20 minutes. Remove from the heat and discard the rosemary sprig and garlic cloves.

To grill the ribs:

Prepare a medium-hot charcoal grill (see Cook's Note, page 110) or heat a gas grill to medium-high. If you are using a charcoal grill, spread the hot coals across ⅔ of the charcoal grate and leave the remaining portion clear. If you are using gas, turn one of the burners to low to create a cooler zone. Brush the ribs on all sides with a little of the glaze. Using tongs, lay the ribs on the grate and grill for 5 to 6 minutes per side, 20 to 25 minutes total. Brush the ribs with additional glaze each time you turn them. If you find that the meat is searing too quickly on the charcoal grill, move the ribs to the cooler side and continue to cook them over indirect heat. Reduce the heat on the gas grill to medium if necessary to prevent excessive charring (a little is good, though!). Remove the ribs from the grill when their internal temperature at the meaty end registers 160°F on an instant-read thermometer.

Arrange the ribs on a large serving platter and garnish with sprigs of rosemary and slices of orange. Serve immediately.

CONTINUED ON NEXT PAGE ...

... CONTINUED

COOK'S NOTE: I like to use natural hardwood lump charcoal rather than pressed carbon charcoal briquettes as the hardwood imparts an alluring smokiness to the meat. For some reason I am also (oddly) drawn to the delicate glass tinkling sound of the wood as it burns.

DO AHEAD: The ribs may be seasoned a day ahead and refrigerated. Bring them to room temperature before grilling. The glaze may be made a day ahead and refrigerated. Bring it to a simmer in a saucepan before grilling the ribs.

GOES WITH:

Red Slaw with Tart Cherries, page 65

Potato Salad, page 74

Squash Gratin, page 177

Grilled Pork Tenderloins with Red Wine and an Orange Marmalade Glaze

MAKES 6 TO 8 SERVINGS

Here is one of several recipes that I "borrowed" and adapted from my sister, Maria. She is a talented improvisational cook and has come up with lots of great marinades, especially for pork. Lean pork tenderloin is sometimes derided as tasteless, but it is quick-cooking, easy to slice and serve, and with a flavorful marinade such as this, can definitely hold its own at a backyard party.

INGREDIENTS

For the marinade:

I CUP DRY RED WINE

½ CUP AGED BALSAMIC VINEGAR

2 GARLIC CLOVES, PRESSED

KOSHER OR SEA SALT

FRESHLY GROUND BLACK PEPPER

—

3 (I-POUND) PORK TENDERLOINS, TRIMMED OF EXCESS FAT AND SILVERSKIN

2 TABLESPOONS EXTRA-VIRGIN OLIVE OIL

—

For the glaze:

¼ CUP ORANGE MARMALADE

2 TEASPOONS AGED BALSAMIC VINEGAR

—

FRESH ORANGE SLICES FOR GARNISH

To marinate the meat:

In a bowl, mix together the wine, balsamic vinegar, garlic, and a little salt and pepper. Place the tenderloins in one or two large plastic zipper-lock freezer bags and pour the marinade over them. Seal the bag or bags tightly, pressing out as much air as possible without letting any marinade escape. Refrigerate for 4 hours or up to overnight. Remove the tenderloins from the refrigerator 30 to 45 minutes before grilling.

Prepare a medium-hot charcoal grill (see Cook's Note, facing page) or heat a gas grill to medium-high.

Remove the pork tenderloins from the marinade and pat dry. Set them on a baking dish or platter and rub them with the olive oil.

In a small bowl, whisk together the orange marmalade and vinegar. Set aside.

Place the tenderloins on the grill and grill for 3 to 4 minutes per side, giving the meat a quarter-turn each time until it is nicely seared all over. Brush the meat with the orange marmalade glaze, turning and coating all of the sides, and continue to grill for 10 minutes longer, or until an instant-read thermometer inserted into the center registers 155° to 160°F. Remove the pork from the grill and set it on a cutting board. Tent loosely with foil and let it rest for 5 to 10 minutes. Slice the meat thickly and arrange on a serving platter. Garnish the platter with orange slices, if desired.

DO AHEAD: The tenderloins may be marinated up to 2 days in advance and kept, tightly sealed in zipper-lock bags, in the refrigerator.

GOES WITH:

Farm Stand Sauté, page 159

Farro Salad, page 72

Potato Salad, page 74

Spinach and Apple Salad, page 59

Red Slaw with Tart Cherries, page 65

Rosemary-Rubbed Butterflied Leg of Lamb

MAKES 8 SERVINGS

This recipe was a last-minute entry. My friend Michelle Andonian and I created it on the fly one summer evening when my family and I were visiting her at her lake house in Michigan's Irish Hills area. It was so good, and so simple, that I couldn't leave it out. Michelle studded the meat with thin slivers of garlic while I made up a quick, aromatic paste using fresh rosemary from her garden. My daughter, Adriana, seized the opportunity to get her hands messy and rubbed the paste into the lamb. But I have to give most of the credit to my husband, Scott, who grilled the meat perfectly, so that it was deeply seared and crusty on the outside, and rosy and juicy on the inside.

INGREDIENTS

6 LARGE CLOVES GARLIC

2 TABLESPOONS MINCED FRESH ROSEMARY, PLUS SEVERAL SPRIGS FOR GARNISHING THE SERVING PLATTER

1 TEASPOON KOSHER OR SEA SALT

FRESHLY GROUND BLACK PEPPER

ABOUT 2 TABLESPOONS EXTRA-VIRGIN OLIVE OIL

1 (5-POUND) BONELESS LEG OF LAMB, TRIMMED OF EXCESS FAT

With a sharp paring knife, cut 2 of the cloves of garlic into paper-thin slices and set aside.

Pass the remaining 4 cloves of garlic through a garlic press. In a small bowl, mix together the puréed garlic, rosemary, salt, a generous quantity of pepper, and enough olive oil to make a thick paste.

Place the lamb on a clean work surface. Use the paring knife to cut several deep slits into the meat and with your fingers stuff the slits with the garlic slices. Rub the paste all over the lamb, taking care to coat the surface of the meat thoroughly. Place the meat in a large zipper-lock storage bag and set the bag on a plate or in a baking dish. Refrigerate for at least 1 hour and up to overnight. Remove the meat from the refrigerator 45 to 60 minutes before you plan to grill.

Prepare a medium-hot charcoal grill (see Cook's Note, page 110) or heat a gas grill to medium-high and lightly oil the grate. Set the lamb on the grill over direct heat and grill for 6 to 7 minutes, until seared. Turn and grill the other side for 6 to 7 minutes, until well seared. Continue to grill the meat, turning it from time to time, until an instant-read thermometer registers 130°F for medium-rare, about 40 to 45 minutes. Remove the lamb to a carving board and loosely tent it with foil. Let the meat rest for 10 minutes.

Cut the lamb on the diagonal into thin slices and arrange on a serving platter. Garnish with the rosemary sprigs and serve.

GOES WITH:

Grilled Vegetable Salad, page 75

September Gratin, page 175

Farm Stand Sauté, page 159

Tomato and Cheese Tart, page 170

Olive Oil-Roasted Potatoes, page 158

Mixed Grilled Platter of Steaks, Chops, Thighs, and Sausages

MAKES 8 TO 10 SERVINGS

INGREDIENTS

For the marinade:

I CUP EXTRA-VIRGIN OLIVE OIL

I CUP DRY RED WINE

8 GARLIC CLOVES, PRESSED

½ CUP CHOPPED FRESH OREGANO

2 TEASPOONS KOSHER OR SEA SALT

FRESHLY GROUND BLACK PEPPER

—

For the mixed grill:

2 POUNDS CHICKEN THIGHS (ABOUT 6)

2 POUNDS RIB-EYE OR NEW YORK STRIP STEAKS (ABOUT 2)

I POUND VEAL CHOPS (ABOUT 2)

I ½ POUNDS LAMB LOIN CHOPS (ABOUT 6)

I ½ POUNDS ITALIAN PORK SAUSAGE, HOT OR SWEET OR A MIX (ABOUT 6 LINKS)

—

KOSHER OR SEA SALT

—

For garnish:

FRESH OREGANO SPRIGS AND LEMON SLICES

Italian restaurants often serve what is known as a *grigliata mista,* or mixed grill, featuring a variety of fish or, as in this case, meat. Although the idea of grilling different meats may sound complicated, you will see that it is really quite simple once you've got the cooking times down. This recipe further simplifies things by using one basic marinade rather than separate seasonings for each kind of meat. I promise you that this gorgeous platter of glistening, char-grilled meat will satisfy even the most ravenous carnivore in your midst. Lest you think I have forgotten the vegetarians among us, let me direct your attention to Vegetarian Mixed Grill (page 119). There, now everyone's happy.

Whisk together all of the ingredients for the marinade.

Place each of the meats except the sausages in large zipper-lock freezer bags. Divide the marinade among the bags and seal tightly, pressing out as much air as possible without letting any marinade escape. Refrigerate for several hours or up to overnight.

Remove all of the meat from the refrigerator about 30 minutes before grilling.

Prepare a medium-hot charcoal grill (see Cook's Note, page 110) or heat a gas grill to medium-high. If you are using a charcoal

CONTINUED ON NEXT PAGE . . .

. . . CONTINUED

grill, spread the hot coals across ⅔ of the charcoal grate and leave the remaining portion clear. If you are using a gas grill, turn one of the burners to medium-low to create a cooler zone.

Remove the chicken thighs, steaks, veal chops, and lamb chops from the marinade and season them on both sides with salt.

Set the chicken on the grill first, placing the thighs skin-side-down on the direct-heat portion of the grill. Cover and grill for 5 minutes, turn, and grill another 5 minutes. Transfer the chicken thighs to the cooler side of the grill, cover the grill, and continue to cook for another 10 minutes or so, turning them occasionally and checking them for doneness (their juices will run clear). Remember to keep the grill covered unless you are checking or turning the pieces.

While the chicken is cooking on the cooler side of the grill, place the steaks, veal chops, lamb chops, and sausages on the direct-heat side of the grill, placing the sausages closest to the indirect-heat portion to prevent their skins from drying out and turning tough. Cover and grill for 4 to 5 minutes. Turn, and continue to grill for another 5 minutes or so for medium-rare, checking the pieces often to prevent excessive charring.

Transfer all of the meats to a large roasting pan and tent loosely with foil. Let everything rest for 5 to 10 minutes. Cut the sausages in half and the larger chops and steaks into serving-size pieces. Arrange the meat on one very large or two medium serving platters. Garnish the platter or platters with sprigs of oregano and slices of lemon.

DO AHEAD: The meat may be marinated a day in advance. Remove it from the refrigerator 30 to 45 minutes before grilling.

GOES WITH:

Tomato and Cheese Tart, page 170

Potato Salad, page 74

Insalata di Riso, page 69

Frank's Garlic Bread, page 45

Spatchcocked Herbed Chickens alla Diavola

MAKES 6 TO 8 SERVINGS

Spicy-hot char-grilled chickens are a classic Italian preparation. When my parents were engaged and living in New York City in the 1950s, they used to dine at a wonderful Old World Italian restaurant called Gino. It is still operating and is as famous for its red-white-and-black jumping zebra wallpaper as it is for its southern Italian specialties. One of my parents' favorite dishes was the char-grilled half chicken *alla diavola*, made with an abundance of garlic and pepper. Here is my version. Instead of using half chickens, I "spatchcock" or butterfly the birds by removing their backbones and flattening them. This makes for quick, even cooking and a dramatic grilling presentation.

INGREDIENTS

1 CUP PLUS 1 TABLESPOON MINCED FRESH HERBS
(I USE A MIX OF BASIL, OREGANO, AND THYME)

8 CLOVES GARLIC, PRESSED

1½ TEASPOONS KOSHER OR SEA SALT

A GENEROUS QUANTITY OF FRESHLY
GROUND BLACK PEPPER

1½ TEASPOONS CRUSHED RED PEPPER OR TO TASTE

ZEST OF 2 LEMONS, PLUS THINLY SLICED
LEMON ROUNDS FOR GARNISH

4 TO 6 TABLESPOONS EXTRA-VIRGIN OLIVE OIL

2 WHOLE CHICKENS, 3½ TO 4 POUNDS EACH

VEGETABLE OIL OR HIGH-HEAT GRILL SPRAY
FOR OILING THE GRILL GRATE

In a small bowl, combine 1 cup of the herbs, the garlic, salt, black and red peppers, and lemon zest. Whisk in just enough oil to make a thick paste.

Place a chicken, breast-side down, on a large cutting board. With your fingers, locate the backbone. Use a pair of poultry shears or sharp kitchen shears to cut through the chicken from top to bottom on either side of the backbone. Remove the backbone and turn the chicken over. Open it up and press down on the chicken with the flat of your hand to crack the rib bones and flatten the bird. Repeat the procedure with the second chicken.

With your fingers, carefully separate the skin from the breasts of one chicken and insert some of the paste under the skin of each breast. Repeat with the second chicken. Rub the remaining paste all over the exterior of both chickens. Place each chicken in a separate large zipper-lock bag and refrigerate for at least 4 hours or up to overnight.

Prepare a medium fire in a charcoal grill using hardwood coals (see Cook's Note, page 110), or preheat a gas grill to medium. If you are using a charcoal grill, spread the hot coals across ⅔ of the charcoal grate and leave the remaining portion clear to create a cooler zone. Lightly oil or spray the grill grate. If you are using gas, turn one of the burners to medium-low to create a cooler zone.

Place the chickens, skin-side down, directly over the charcoal or direct heat. Grill for 6 to 7 minutes, until the skin is nicely

CONTINUED ON NEXT PAGE . . .

... CONTINUED

seared; turn, and grill another 6 to 7 minutes. Move the chickens to indirect heat and continue to grill them, turning them carefully from time to time, for about 20 minutes, or until an instant-read thermometer registers 165°F and the juices run clear when pierced with a fork.

Remove the chickens to a cutting board and tent them loosely with foil. Let them rest for 5 to 10 minutes. Cut each chicken into 6 serving-size pieces. Arrange the pieces on a large serving platter and garnish with lemon slices and the remaining tablespoon of fresh herbs. Serve immediately.

DO AHEAD: The chickens may be marinated and kept in the refrigerator up to a day in advance of grilling. Remove them from the refrigerator about 30 minutes before grilling.

GOES WITH:

September Gratin, page 175

Squash Gratin, page 177

Tomato and Cheese Salad over Bruschetta, page 64

Bruschetta, page 31

Vegetarian Mixed Grill

MAKES 8 SERVINGS

Steak or burgers are usually what come to mind when we hear the word *grill*. But to be honest, one of my favorite things to grill is cheese. Semi-firm cheeses, such as Halloumi from Cyprus and queso blanco from Latin America, grill beautifully, searing on the outside and turning soft on the inside but keeping their shape. Several other cheeses also take well to the grill (see Cook's Note). Serve with fresh lemon wedges for squeezing, honey for drizzling, a bowlful of olives, and a Grilled Vegetable Salad on the side.

INGREDIENTS

1 (8-OUNCE) SLAB HALLOUMI CHEESE

1 (8-OUNCE) BLOCK QUESO BLANCO

8 OUNCES SCAMORZA, SMOKED SCAMORZA, OR PART-SKIM MOZZARELLA

8 OUNCES YOUNG MANCHEGO

VEGETABLE OIL OR HIGH-HEAT GRILL SPRAY FOR OILING THE GRILL GRATE

—

For serving:

2 LEMONS, CUT INTO THIN WEDGES

GRILLED VEGETABLE SALAD *(page 75)*

A SMALL BOWL OF CHESTNUT HONEY, WITH A HONEY DRIZZLER

A BOWL OF MIXED GREEN AND PURPLE OLIVES

Slice the cheeses into ½-inch-thick slabs.

Heat a gas grill to medium. Brush the grill grate with vegetable oil or spray with high-heat cooking spray. Set the cheese slices on the grill and grill for 2 to 3 minutes, until the bottom becomes browned and lightly charred (the browning will be uneven). Use a metal spatula to carefully flip the slices of cheese and grill for 1 or 2 minutes on the other side. Transfer the cheeses from the grill to a serving platter. Garnish the platter with lemon wedges and serve immediately with the grilled vegetable salad, honey, and olives.

COOK'S NOTE: Finding the right cheeses for grilling can be tricky. Fresh mozzarella has far too much moisture and not enough body to stand up to the heat of a grill. I have had luck with the following cheeses:

PART-SKIM MOZZARELLA: yes, the rubbery supermarket kind actually turns decent when grilled, though it can be a little oozy and hard to turn.

SCAMORZA AND SMOKED SCAMORZA: these low-moisture mozzarella-like cheeses are available at Italian delicatessens. Like mozzarella, they can get oozy.

MANCHEGO, a Spanish sheep's milk cheese, is especially good with honey drizzled over it. Choose a young manchego with a little moisture; the longer-aged cheese hardens when it is taken off the grill.

PECORINO TOSCANO: this cheese is similar to the more ubiquitous pecorino Romano but has slightly more moisture. I have tried grilling pecorino Romano but find that its texture becomes rock hard once it is taken off the flame. Pecorino Toscano is excellent with chestnut honey drizzled over it, which cuts the saltiness of the cheese.

GOES WITH:

Cold Curried Squash Soup, page 53

Mediterranean Composed Salad, page 66

Spinach and Apple Salad, page 59

Bruschetta, page 31

Pan-Grilled Clams

MAKES 8 SERVINGS

I like these clams best cooked over a hardwood charcoal fire because the smoke from the wood imbues the clams with a subtle smokiness. This is a great dish for a casual get-together as it encourages people to "dig right in."

INGREDIENTS

6 CLOVES GARLIC, FLATTENED WITH
THE BLADE OF A KNIFE

I TEASPOON CRUSHED RED PEPPER, OR TO TASTE

I CUP EXTRA-VIRGIN OLIVE OIL

8 DOZEN LITTLENECK OR OTHER SMALL CLAMS,
THOROUGHLY SCRUBBED

2 CUPS DRY WHITE WINE OR PROSECCO

KOSHER OR SEA SALT

⅓ CUP MINCED FRESH FLAT-LEAF PARSLEY

16 LARGE SLICES BRUSCHETTA *(page 31)*

Prepare the charcoal grill (see Cook's Note, page 110) or heat a gas grill on high. Put the garlic, red pepper, and olive oil in a large roasting pan that you don't mind tarnishing (the flames or heat from the grill will cause some blackening that usually can be washed off). Place the pan on the grill and heat until the garlic is sizzling but not browned, 2 to 3 minutes. Using an oven mitt to hold the pan, shake it from time to time to prevent the garlic from turning brown. Dump in the clams and pour the wine over them. Cover the grill and cook, shaking the pan frequently, until the clams open, 5 to 10 minutes. Transfer the clams and all of the liquid in the pan to a large serving bowl and sprinkle salt to taste and the parsley on top.

Give your guests each an individual shallow rimmed bowl with a slice of bruschetta placed on the bottom, and have them ladle the clams and their broth on top of the bread. Serve the remaining bread slices in a bread basket for those who want seconds.

GOES WITH:

Red, White, and Green Salad with Lemon-Balsamic Dressing, page 58

Italian Pot-Likker Greens, page 162

Sautéed Spinach with Garlic, page 167

September Gratin, page 175

Crepe Cannelloni with Zucchini and Cheese Stuffing
MAKES 8 MAIN-COURSE SERVINGS OR 12 FIRST-COURSE SERVINGS

Here might very well be the ultimate party recipe. Everything—crepes, stuffing, and sauce—can be made and assembled in advance and then baked right before serving. Using crepes rather than pasta dough yields cannelloni that are ethereally light. The result is comfort food at its finest.

INGREDIENTS

For the sauce:
2 TABLESPOONS EXTRA-VIRGIN OLIVE OIL

2 TABLESPOONS UNSALTED BUTTER

I CUP DICED YELLOW ONION

¾ CUP CHOPPED CARROTS

½ CUP CHOPPED CELERY

I (28-OUNCE) CAN WHOLE PEELED TOMATOES, CRUSHED

I (14-OUNCE) CAN STEWED TOMATOES, CRUSHED

I TEASPOON KOSHER OR SEA SALT, OR TO TASTE

FRESHLY GROUND BLACK PEPPER

¾ CUP HEAVY CREAM, AT ROOM TEMPERATURE

—

For the crepes:
8 LARGE EGGS, LIGHTLY BEATEN

2 CUPS GOAT'S MILK OR WHOLE COW'S MILK

¼ CUP MINCED FLAT-LEAF PARSLEY

I TEASPOON KOSHER OR SEA SALT

PINCH OF FRESHLY GROUND BLACK PEPPER

DUSTING OF FRESHLY GRATED NUTMEG

I½ CUPS UNBLEACHED ALL-PURPOSE FLOUR, SIFTED

2 TABLESPOONS UNSALTED BUTTER, OR AS NEEDED TO LIGHTLY GREASE PAN

INGREDIENTS

For the stuffing:
3 TABLESPOONS EXTRA-VIRGIN OLIVE OIL

¼ CUP MINCED SHALLOTS

I POUND ZUCCHINI (ABOUT 3 MEDIUM), SHREDDED AND SQUEEZED TO REMOVE EXCESS LIQUID

½ TEASPOON KOSHER OR SEA SALT, OR TO TASTE

FRESHLY GROUND BLACK PEPPER TO TASTE

⅔ CUP FINELY DICED RICOTTA SALATA

⅔ CUP SHREDDED AGED ASIAGO

I CUP FRESHLY GRATED PARMIGIANO-REGGIANO

½ CUP FRESHLY GRATED PECORINO ROMANO

I EGG, LIGHTLY BEATEN

—

For assembling:
I CUP FRESHLY GRATED PARMIGIANO-REGGIANO

To make the sauce:

Heat the oil and butter in a medium heavy-bottomed pot placed over medium heat. Add the onion, carrots, and celery and sauté, stirring often, until the vegetables are softened, about 15 minutes. Reduce the heat to medium low to prevent the vegetables from turning brown. Add the tomatoes, salt, and pepper. Cover partially and cook the sauce at a gentle simmer for 45 minutes, until the vegetables are tender. Remove from the heat and let the sauce cool for 10 minutes.

Purée the sauce in a blender or food processor, in two batches if necessary. Rinse out the pot and return the sauce to it. Add the heavy cream and bring the sauce just to a simmer over medium heat. Turn off the heat and set the sauce aside until you assemble the cannelloni.

To make the crepes:

In a large bowl, whisk together the eggs, milk, parsley, salt, pepper, and nutmeg. Gradually whisk in the flour, taking care to avoid lumps. Cover the crepe batter with plastic wrap and let stand for 30 minutes.

Melt a little butter in a 9-inch nonstick pan placed over medium heat (I use a well-seasoned cast-iron skillet). When the pan is hot, pour in a small ladleful of crepe batter (about ¼ cup) and quickly swirl it around so that it completely coats the bottom of the pan, forming a thin pancake. Cook for 30 to 45 seconds, until just set. Flip the crepe and cook for 20 to 30 seconds longer. Transfer the crepe to a plate. Continue making crepes until you have used all the batter, making sure to lightly grease the pan from time to time with a thin film of butter. You should end up with 24 crepes. Cover the crepes with plastic wrap until you are ready to assemble the cannelloni.

To make the stuffing:

Heat the oil in a large skillet or sauté pan placed over medium heat. Add the shallots and sauté, stirring, for 5 to 7 minutes, until softened and translucent. Add the zucchini and sauté for 12 to 15 minutes, until the liquid released by the squash has been absorbed and the squash has softened but still retains its texture. Season to taste with salt and pepper. Transfer the zucchini to a large bowl and let it cool for 10 minutes.

Add the cheeses and the egg to the bowl with the zucchini and gently fold the ingredients together.

To assemble and bake the cannelloni:

Heat the oven to 350°F.

Have the sauce, crepes, and stuffing at the ready. Spoon about ¼ cup of sauce into each of three 8-by-12-inch shallow baking dishes (see Cook's Note). Lay a crepe out on a clean work surface.

Spread 2 tablespoons of filling across the bottom third of the crepe. Roll it, jellyroll style, and place it seam-side down in the baking dish. Continue filling and rolling the crepes, arranging them side by side in a single layer in the baking dishes. You should be able to fit 8 crepes in each baking dish.

Spoon a thin layer of sauce over the stuffed crepes, covering them completely but not too heavily. Sprinkle ⅓ cup of Parmigiano cheese over each assembled dish. Bake the crepes for 15 to 20 minutes, until they are heated through and the cheese on top is melted and lightly golden.

COOK'S NOTE: If you are serving the cannelloni at a buffet table, use ceramic or other decorative baking dishes that you can bring straight from the oven to the table. If, however, you plan to dish out individual servings, you can bake the cannelloni in disposable aluminum baking pans. Serve the cannelloni, two per portion, in shallow rimmed pasta bowls.

A 9-inch pan will yield 24 crepes. A 10-inch pan will yield 18 slightly larger crepes. Either way, the amount of filling and sauce is enough to fill and sauce all of the crepes.

DO AHEAD: The sauce may be made in advance and refrigerated in a tightly lidded container for up to 3 days or frozen for up to 3 months. The crepes may be made in advance and refrigerated, tightly wrapped, for up to 3 days or frozen for up to 3 months. The stuffing may be made up to 2 days in advance and refrigerated in a tightly lidded container.

GOES WITH:

Artichokes alla Romana, page 160

Red, White, and Green Salad with Lemon-Balsamic Vinaigrette, page 58

Chicken, Eggplant, and Potato Torta

MAKES 12 SERVINGS

Here is a gem that my mother discovered in her collection of old Italian cooking magazines. Admittedly, it takes numerous steps to create this one-dish meal. But I can't emphasize enough how worth it the labor is. One bite and you will see why: creamy mashed potatoes, tender pieces of rosemary- and sage-scented chicken, and oozing mozzarella are all wrapped in a thin layer of eggplant. Much of the preparation can be done in advance, and the work is organized; the components can be prepared consecutively so that you aren't trying to juggle various pots and pans and cooking times all at once. Be ready to take a bow when you set this dish at the table; it is like no other.

INGREDIENTS

1 OR 2 EGGPLANTS (1½ POUNDS TOTAL)

KOSHER OR SEA SALT

2 CUPS UNBLEACHED ALL-PURPOSE FLOUR, FOR DREDGING

¼ CUP VEGETABLE OR OLIVE OIL (NOT EXTRA-VIRGIN) FOR FRYING

1½ POUNDS YUKON GOLD OR OTHER YELLOW-FLESHED POTATOES, SCRUBBED CLEAN

¼ CUP, PLUS 2 TABLESPOONS EXTRA-VIRGIN OLIVE OIL

FRESHLY GROUND BLACK PEPPER

1 TABLESPOON FINELY MINCED FRESH ROSEMARY

1 TABLESPOON FINELY MINCED FRESH SAGE

12 OUNCES THINLY SLICED BONELESS, SKINLESS CHICKEN BREASTS (CUTLETS)

12 OUNCES FRESH MOZZARELLA, THINLY SLICED

Trim off the ends of the eggplant and cut it lengthwise into thin (¼-inch-thick) slices. Sprinkle the slices on both sides with a little salt and layer them in a colander. Set a plate on top of the eggplant and weight it down with a heavy object. Let the eggplant drain for 30 to 60 minutes. Wipe the slices dry with paper towels.

Put the flour in a shallow baking dish or pie plate. Lightly dredge the slices of eggplant, shaking off any excess flour. Heat ¼ cup of vegetable oil in a large skillet or sauté pan placed over medium-high heat. When the oil is hot (375°F), add enough eggplant slices to fill the skillet without crowding it. Fry the eggplant slices until they are golden brown, taking care to turn them once so they brown on both sides, about 5 minutes total. Reduce the heat to medium if the eggplant seems to be browning too quickly. Use a large slotted spatula to remove the cooked eggplant to a platter lined with paper towels or a large brown paper shopping bag placed nearby. Continue to fry the eggplant slices, adding more oil as necessary, until you have cooked them all.

Place the potatoes in a large saucepan with water to cover by 1 inch. Generously salt the water, cover the pot, and set it over medium-high heat. Bring the water to a boil and boil the potatoes for 25 minutes, or until they are tender. Drain the potatoes in a colander and let them sit just until they are cool enough to handle. Peel the potatoes, return them to the pot, and mash them with a potato masher. Drizzle about ¼ cup of extra-virgin olive oil over the potatoes and season them with a little salt, pepper, and half of the rosemary and sage. Mix well with a wooden spoon or sturdy spatula. Cover and set aside.

Heat 2 tablespoons of extra-virgin olive oil in a large skillet placed over medium heat. Add the sliced chicken breasts to the skillet and sprinkle a little salt and pepper, and the remaining rosemary and sage, over them. Sauté the chicken for 3 to

4 minutes per side, or until lightly browned. Transfer the chicken to a plate and set aside.

Heat the oven to 475°F. Arrange the eggplant slices on the bottom and around the perimeter of a large round or rectangular oven-proof baking dish so that about a third of each slice placed around the perimeter drapes over the rim (you will be folding the slices over the top of the torta once you have finished filling it). Reserve a few slices of eggplant for the top of the torta.

Spread the mashed potatoes over the eggplant in one even layer, smoothing it out with a spatula. Arrange half of the mozzarella and all of the chicken slices over the potatoes. Top with the remaining eggplant and fold the overhanging pieces of eggplant from the bottom layer over the top. Arrange the remaining slices of mozzarella on top of the eggplant.

Place the torta in the oven and bake for about 20 minutes, or until the mozzarella is nicely browned and the torta is hot throughout. Remove the torta from the oven and let it rest for 15 to 20 minutes before serving.

DO AHEAD: The torta may be prepared and assembled a day in advance, covered tightly with plastic wrap, and refrigerated. You may transfer it straight from the refrigerator to the preheated oven, but be sure to let it bake for a few extra minutes.

GOES WITH:

Creamy Carrot Soup with Rice and Caramelized Carrots, page 57

Red, White, and Green Salad with Lemon-Balsamic Dressing, page 58

Farm Stand Sauté, page 159

Walnut Focaccia, page 46

Slow-Roasted Arctic Char with Sautéed Fennel and Pernod

MAKES 4 TO 6 SERVINGS

Arctic char is similar to salmon, with beautiful rosy flesh, a tender, flaky texture, and a sweet buttery flavor. It has the added bonus of being listed as a "best choice" selection by the Monterey Bay Aquarium's Seafood Watch program, which encourages consumers to buy fish and shellfish that are not endangered and that are environmentally friendly. I learned this superb slow-roasting technique from my friend Diane Morgan's book *Salmon.* Cooking the fillet slowly at a low temperature produces a wonderfully succulent, deeply pink fish. It is a perfect dinner party centerpiece.

INGREDIENTS

2 (1-POUND) FILLETS ARCTIC CHAR, PIN BONES REMOVED

3 TABLESPOONS EXTRA-VIRGIN OLIVE OIL

1 TEASPOON FENNEL POLLEN *(see Cook's Note, page 128)*

KOSHER OR SEA SALT

2 TABLESPOONS UNSALTED BUTTER

2 FENNEL BULBS, STEMS REMOVED (RESERVE THE FRONDS), BULBS QUARTERED LENGTHWISE, EACH QUARTER CUT CROSSWISE INTO 1/8-INCH-THICK SLICES

FRESHLY GROUND PEPPER

3 TABLESPOONS PERNOD *(see Cook's Note, page 128)*

2 TABLESPOONS CHOPPED FENNEL FRONDS

1/2 CUP HEAVY OR LIGHT CREAM

Heat the oven to 250°F.

Place the char fillets, skin side down, on a large rimmed baking sheet lined with parchment paper. In a small bowl, mix together 2 tablespoons of olive oil and the fennel pollen. Drizzle the oil mixture over the fish and rub it in gently with your fingertips. Season the fish with a little salt. Set the char in the oven to roast for 20 minutes.

While the char is roasting, sauté the fennel. Put the remaining tablespoon of oil and the butter in a large skillet and set the skillet over medium heat. When the butter is melted and begins to sizzle, add the sliced fennel and stir to coat it thoroughly with the butter and oil. Sauté the fennel for 8 to 10 minutes, or until it is just tender. Season to taste with salt and pepper. Raise the heat to medium-high and pour in the Pernod. Cook, stirring for a minute or so, until the Pernod has evaporated. Stir in the fennel fronds and cream. Boil briefly, until the sauce has thickened slightly. Turn off the heat and cover the pan to keep the fennel warm.

Check the fish for doneness. It is done when an instant-read thermometer inserted in the center registers between 125 and 130°F, and when the flesh is opaque pink and flakes slightly. The flesh should be barely firm to the touch and not at all hard or dry.

CONTINUED ON NEXT PAGE . . .

. . . CONTINUED

Using two wide spatulas, carefully transfer the char fillets to a large serving platter. Spoon the warm sautéed fennel over the fish and serve immediately.

✧✧·✧✧·✧✧

COOK'S NOTE: Fennel pollen is the pollen collected from wild fennel. It is harvested in Italy and in California and is quite expensive. However, it has a unique, heavenly aroma and distinct flavor, with hints of anise, saffron, and curry. Also, a little goes a long way, so if you do splurge, use it sparingly and it should last you awhile. You can substitute ½ teaspoon finely crushed fennel seeds and the tiniest pinch of curry powder.

Pernod is a liqueur produced in France that gets its flavor from star anise and the licorice plant. It is enjoyed as an aperitif but is also used in cooking and baking.

DO AHEAD: The fennel may be sautéed up to an hour in advance up to the addition of the Pernod. A few minutes before serving the fish, reheat the fennel over medium heat. When it is hot, turn the heat up and add the Pernod. Finish with the addition of the fennel fronds and cream as directed.

GOES WITH:

Truffled Mushrooms, page 165

Savory Carrot Crostata, page 171

Spinach and Apple Salad, page 59

Artichokes alla Romana, page 160

Sautéed Spinach with Garlic, page 167

Escarole and Swiss Chard Torte, page 163

Squash Gratin, page 177

Poached and Roasted Capon with Porcini Butter

MAKES 8 TO 10 SERVINGS

Years ago, when I lived in Detroit, I bought a lot of my food in the city's Eastern Market, a sprawling complex of low-slung warehouses occupied by wholesale meat processors, produce distributors, and retail storefronts. On Saturdays, the partially covered stalls were filled with fruit, vegetable, and flower vendors. Eastern Market was (and still is) the sort of place where, as a native Detroiter friend of mine put it, food *happens*; where you might find yourself, as I did once on a crisp fall morning, driving behind a flatbed truck piled high with sheep skins steaming in the chilly air. A lot of people don't like to be confronted with such realities of where our food comes from, but I loved the market for just that aspect.

I was especially fond of the poultry vendor who did business in one of the small storefronts. Inside, you could select the squawking bird of your choice from a cage and return an hour later to retrieve a still-warm wrapped package. One morning I told the poultry purveyor that I needed a good-size roaster for a dinner party. He replied: "What you want is a capon, the *Cadillac* of chickens!"

A capon, as I learned from the poultry man, is a young rooster that has been neutered, or *caponized,* to put it more euphemistically. It is larger than a roasting chicken, weighing between 9 and 14 pounds. In his book *Food,* food historian Waverly Root defines capon as "a domestic fowl with a villainous temper, out of resentment, one supposes, against the outrage practiced upon it to give it such tender, luxurious flesh." Indeed, a capon possesses a large, tender breast that is fattier and more succulent than the breast of chicken or turkey and thus remains moist during roasting. Italians serve capon at Christmas and use stock made from the bird as a base for soup with cappelletti (small stuffed pasta "hats").

This method of first poaching and then roasting the bird is a most useful trick that I learned a few years ago from Ariane Daguin, co-founder of D'Artagnan, Inc., who recommended it for a turkey as well. The poaching doubly insures that the meat will remain moist. It also means that the capon only needs about 30 minutes in the oven to achieve a perfect burnished finish, thus freeing up your oven for other dishes.

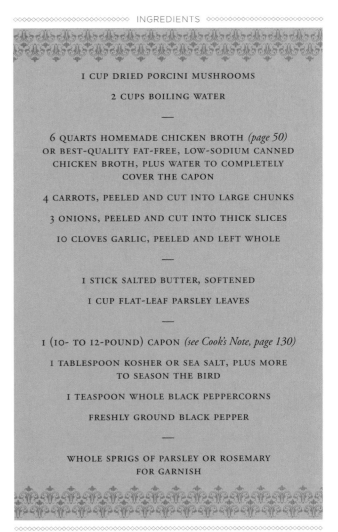

INGREDIENTS

I CUP DRIED PORCINI MUSHROOMS

2 CUPS BOILING WATER

—

6 QUARTS HOMEMADE CHICKEN BROTH *(page 50)* OR BEST-QUALITY FAT-FREE, LOW-SODIUM CANNED CHICKEN BROTH, PLUS WATER TO COMPLETELY COVER THE CAPON

4 CARROTS, PEELED AND CUT INTO LARGE CHUNKS

3 ONIONS, PEELED AND CUT INTO THICK SLICES

IO CLOVES GARLIC, PEELED AND LEFT WHOLE

—

I STICK SALTED BUTTER, SOFTENED

I CUP FLAT-LEAF PARSLEY LEAVES

—

I (IO- TO 12-POUND) CAPON *(see Cook's Note, page 130)*

I TABLESPOON KOSHER OR SEA SALT, PLUS MORE TO SEASON THE BIRD

I TEASPOON WHOLE BLACK PEPPERCORNS

FRESHLY GROUND BLACK PEPPER

—

WHOLE SPRIGS OF PARSLEY OR ROSEMARY FOR GARNISH

CONTINUED ON NEXT PAGE ...

... CONTINUED

Put the porcini mushrooms in a heat-proof bowl and pour the water over them. Let them sit for 30 minutes to soften.

Combine the chicken broth, carrots, onions, and garlic in a stockpot large enough to hold the capon. Bring to a boil over medium-high heat.

Drain the porcini through cheesecloth or damp paper towel, reserving the liquid. Pour the reserved liquid into the stock. Put the porcini and the butter and parsley in a food processor and process until a paste forms. Alternatively, finely chop the porcini and parsley and combine thoroughly with the softened butter.

Set the capon on a clean cutting board used for meat and poultry. Starting at the neck, carefully separate the skin from the breast and upper thighs of the capon with your fingers, taking care not to tear the skin. Rub the porcini butter between the skin and flesh, as well as all over the outside of the bird and inside the cavity. Fold the wings back to hold them securely, and tie the legs together with kitchen twine (this will make the bird easier to handle when transferring it from the pot to the roasting pan).

When the stock is boiling, season it with salt and whole peppercorns and carefully lower in the capon. Add just enough water to completely cover the bird, and adjust the heat so that the stock is gently simmering. Cover and simmer for 30 minutes, then turn off the heat and let the capon and stock cool to room temperature, up to 4 hours. Refrigerate overnight.

Preheat the oven to 475°F. Carefully lift the capon out of the pot (I use long slotted spoons and a helping hand from a family member) and place it on a rack set in a roasting pan (see Cook's Note). Sprinkle a little salt and pepper over the capon. Ladle a little of the stock around the bird. Roast the capon for 30 to 40 minutes, basting occasionally with some of the stock, until the skin is deeply golden. Turn the oven off and leave the bird inside for an additional 30 minutes or until you are ready to serve it. (Double-check that it is cooked to an internal temperature of 165° to 170°F.) Carve the capon and arrange the slices, wings, and legs on a serving platter. Spoon the pan juices over the meat and garnish with sprigs of parsley or rosemary. Serve immediately.

Cvɔ·Cvɔ·Cvɔ

COOK'S NOTE: Fresh and frozen capons are usually available at the meat department of well-stocked supermarkets at Christmastime. They are also available through special order, so ask your butcher or meat counter manager.

Don't discard the stock in which you poached the capon. After you remove the capon from the stockpot, set the pot over medium heat and simmer to further reduce the stock. Strain it through cheesecloth and use it as a base for soup.

GOES WITH:

Egg Ribbons in Homemade Broth, page 50

Crepe Cannelloni with Zucchini and Cheese Stuffing, page 122

Winter Endive and Orange Salad, page 61

Truffled Mushrooms, page 165

Squash Gratin, page 177

Roasted Squash Wedges with Maple Glaze, page 169

Roast Pork Loin with Carrots, Fennel, and Onions

MAKES 10 TO 12 MAIN-COURSE SERVINGS

INGREDIENTS

For the paste:

6 CLOVES GARLIC, PRESSED

3 TABLESPOONS FINELY MINCED FRESH ROSEMARY

3 TABLESPOONS MINCED FENNEL FRONDS
(RESERVE BULB FOR USE LATER IN RECIPE)

I TEASPOON CRUSHED FENNEL SEEDS
(see Cook's Note, page 132)

I TEASPOON KOSHER OR SEA SALT

FRESHLY GROUND BLACK PEPPER

GRATED ZEST OF I LEMON

I TABLESPOON EXTRA-VIRGIN OLIVE OIL

—

For the roast:

I (5-POUND) PORK LOIN ROAST, TIED

2 TABLESPOONS EXTRA-VIRGIN OLIVE OIL

¼ CUP COGNAC

½ CUP DRY WHITE WINE

I CUP FINELY DICED CARROTS

I CUP FINELY DICED FENNEL BULB

I CUP FINELY DICED YELLOW ONION

I CUP HOMEMADE CHICKEN BROTH *(page 50)*
OR BEST-QUALITY FAT-FREE, LOW-SODIUM
CANNED CHICKEN BROTH, PLUS
ADDITIONAL IF NECESSARY

—

WHOLE RADICCHIO LEAVES FOR GARNISH

The sweet flavor of fennel takes center stage in this simple but elegant roast, thanks to the triple combination of fennel bulb, crushed fennel seeds, and minced fennel fronds. During the roasting, the flavor of the finely diced vegetables intensifies as they absorb the juices from the herb- and spice-rubbed meat, creating a rich pan sauce. Get a head start by rubbing the pork with the paste the day before you plan to roast it and marinating it overnight in the refrigerator.

In a small bowl, mix together the ingredients for the paste, making sure they are thoroughly combined.

Set the roast in a baking dish. With a sharp paring knife, make numerous small, deep slits all around the roast and with your fingers press a little of the paste into the slits. Rub the remaining paste all over the exterior of the pork. Cover with plastic wrap and let sit at room temperature for 1 hour. Alternatively, cover and refrigerate overnight. Bring the roast back to room temperature before proceeding with cooking.

Heat the oven to 350°F. In a Dutch oven or other heavy-bottomed pot or deep-sided roasting pan large enough to fit the roast and vegetables comfortably, heat the olive oil over medium heat. Set the roast in the pot and sear it on all sides, allowing 3 to 4 minutes per side and turning the roast 3 or 4 times so that it is well browned all over. Sprinkle the cognac over the meat and let it bubble for a minute. Pour the wine over the roast and add the carrots, fennel, and onion to the pot. Add the broth and bring the liquid to a boil. Carefully

CONTINUED ON NEXT PAGE . . .

... CONTINUED

transfer the pot to the oven and roast, basting the meat every 15 to 20 minutes with the pan juices, for 1½ to 2 hours, adding more broth if necessary. The roast is done when the internal temperature of the meat reaches 155°F (the temperature will continue to rise to 160°F after the pork has been removed from the oven).

Cover the roast loosely with foil and let it rest for 10 to 15 minutes. Arrange the radicchio leaves on a large serving platter. Cut the roast into ½-inch slices and arrange them, overlapping slightly, on the platter. Spoon the vegetables and sauce from the roasting pan over the meat and serve immediately.

COOK'S NOTE: To crush fennel seeds, put them in a zipper-lock plastic bag and pound them gently but firmly with a meat pounder, heavy rolling pin, or bottom of a cast-iron skillet, or other similarly heavy object.

DO AHEAD: The roast may be rubbed with the aromatic paste a day ahead and refrigerated, tightly covered.

GOES WITH:

Artichokes alla Romana, page 160

Italian Pot-Likker Greens, page 162

Winter Endive and Orange Salad, page 61

Savory Carrot Crostata, page 171

Squash Gratin, page 177

Beef Tenderloin alla Bandiera Italiana

MAKES 12 OR MORE SERVINGS

❧·❀·❧

At upwards of $20 per pound, beef tenderloin is a financial splurge. And yet, for a special occasion there is nothing like it. Tenderloin is both easy and elegant, not to mention versatile. It can be served warm or at room temperature (and leftovers can be enjoyed cold in a sandwich). All three of these colorful sauces pair beautifully with the beef, and somehow, despite their many flavors, they also complement each other. Make all three for the colors of the Italian flag, or choose one and double the recipe.

INGREDIENTS

For the Salsa Verde:

3 RIZZOLI BRAND *ALICI IN SALSA PICCANTE (page 16)* OR BEST-QUALITY ITALIAN ANCHOVY FILLETS IN OLIVE OIL, DRAINED AND CHOPPED

2 CLOVES GARLIC, COARSELY CHOPPED

2 ½ PACKED CUPS FLAT-LEAF PARSLEY LEAVES

I PACKED CUP FRESH BREAD CRUMBS *(see Cook's Note, page 142)*

2 TABLESPOONS CAPERS, PREFERABLY IN SALT, RINSED AND DRAINED

2 TABLESPOONS WHITE WINE VINEGAR

I TEASPOON KOSHER OR SEA SALT

¼ TEASPOON FRESHLY GROUND BLACK PEPPER

¾ CUP EXTRA-VIRGIN OLIVE OIL

—

For the Salsa Bianca:

2 TABLESPOONS EXTRA-VIRGIN OLIVE OIL

¼ CUP FINELY MINCED SHALLOTS

I CUP CRUMBLED GORGONZOLA DOLCE

I CUP LIGHT CREAM

FRESHLY GROUND BLACK PEPPER

I TABLESPOON COGNAC

KOSHER OR SEA SALT

INGREDIENTS

For the Salsa Rossa:

2 TABLESPOONS EXTRA-VIRGIN OLIVE OIL

½ CUP CHOPPED RED ONION

¼ CUP CHOPPED SHALLOT

I LARGE, HEAVY RED BELL PEPPER, TRIMMED AND DICED

I SMALL CARROT, TRIMMED AND CUT INTO THIN COINS

I (14.5-OUNCE) CAN DICED TOMATOES

KOSHER OR SEA SALT

FRESHLY GROUND BLACK PEPPER

I TABLESPOON RED WINE VINEGAR

—

For the tenderloin:

I (5- TO 6-POUND) BEEF TENDERLOIN, TRIMMED OF SILVERSKIN AND EXCESS FAT AND TIED

2 TABLESPOONS EXTRA-VIRGIN OLIVE OIL

I TEASPOON COARSE KOSHER OR SEA SALT

FRESHLY GROUND BLACK PEPPER

I OR 2 BUNCHES ARUGULA FOR GARNISHING THE PLATTER

To make the Salsa Verde:
Place all of the ingredients except for the olive oil in the work bowl of a food processor. With the motor running, gradually pour in the olive oil until a thick coarse sauce has formed. Transfer the sauce to a bowl and cover tightly with plastic wrap until ready to use.

To make the Salsa Bianca:
Warm the olive oil in a saucepan placed over medium heat. Add the shallots and sauté, stirring frequently, until softened, about

CONTINUED ON NEXT PAGE ...

... CONTINUED

seven minutes. Add the gorgonzola, cream, and a few grindings of pepper and cook, stirring, until the cheese has melted. Stir in the cognac and cook for a minute or so. Taste and adjust the seasoning with a little salt if necessary. Turn off the heat, cover, and keep the sauce warm until ready to serve.

To make the Salsa Rossa:

Warm the oil in a medium-sized skillet or sauté pan placed over medium heat. Add the red onion and shallot and sauté, stirring frequently, until softened, about seven minutes. Add the peppers and carrots, cover, and cook at a gentle simmer for 15 minutes, reducing the heat to medium-low if necessary. Stir in the tomatoes, and salt and pepper to taste. Continue to cook at a gentle simmer for 30 minutes, or until all of the vegetables are very tender. Raise the heat to medium-high and stir in the vinegar. Cook for a minute. Remove from the heat. Purée the sauce in a blender or food processor. Return the sauce to the pot. Cover and keep warm until ready to serve, or refrigerate in a tightly lidded container and serve chilled.

To make the tenderloin:

Heat the oven to 500°F. Place the tenderloin on a large rimmed baking sheet. Rub it all over with the oil and season with the salt and pepper. Place in the oven and roast for 25 to 30 minutes, or until the internal temperature registers 120°F on an instant-read thermometer for medium-rare. Remove the tenderloin from the oven, cover it loosely with aluminum foil, and let it rest for 15 minutes before slicing. This will allow the juices to be reabsorbed into the meat before it is cut.

Remove the string and cut the tenderloin into ½-inch-thick slices. Lay the arugula on a large serving platter and arrange the slices of beef on top, slightly overlapping each other. Serve the meat with the sauces on the side.

COOK'S NOTE: Roasting beef tenderloin can create smoke in the oven, which will in turn seep into your kitchen. Be sure your oven is clean before roasting the meat to minimize smoke.

DO AHEAD: Roast the tenderloin 1 to 2 hours in advance if you plan to serve it at room temperature. Keep the meat covered in foil or plastic wrap until serving time. The Salsa Verde and Salsa Rossa can be made in advance and refrigerated in tightly lidded containers. Bring them to room temperature before serving, or reheat the Salsa Rossa if you want to serve it warm.

GOES WITH:

Truffled Mushrooms, page 165

Three-Cheese-Stuffed Red and Yellow Peppers, page 141

Sautéed Spinach with Garlic, page 167

Frank's Garlic Bread, page 45

Veal and Mushroom Stew in a Puff Pastry Crust

MAKES 8 MAIN-COURSE SERVINGS

INGREDIENTS

I CUP DRIED PORCINI MUSHROOMS

I CUP BOILING WATER

6 TABLESPOONS EXTRA-VIRGIN OLIVE OIL, PLUS
ADDITIONAL FOR GREASING A BAKING DISH

3 POUNDS BONELESS VEAL SHOULDER, CUT INTO
I ½-INCH PIECES

KOSHER OR SEA SALT

FRESHLY GROUND BLACK PEPPER

I ½ POUNDS MIXED FRESH MUSHROOMS, SUCH AS
PORTOBELLAS, SHIITAKES, AND CREMINI, CLEANED,
STEMS DISCARDED, AND CAPS THINLY SLICED

2 CLOVES GARLIC, PRESSED

I TEASPOON MINCED ROSEMARY

½ CUP DRY WHITE WINE

2 FRESH BAY LEAVES

I CUP BEST-QUALITY FAT-FREE, LOW-SODIUM
CANNED CHICKEN BROTH

¼ CUP DRY MARSALA

¼ CUP MINCED PARSLEY

½ CUP HEAVY CREAM

I SHEET FROZEN PUFF PASTRY, THAWED

I EGG, LIGHTLY BEATEN WITH I TABLESPOON WATER

This rich stew, topped with a flaky golden crust, makes an impressive entrée for a fall or winter sit-down dinner in the dining room. If it's elegance you are after, don't hesitate to break out the fine linens, silver, and china. You can get a head start by making the stew a day in advance and then baking it with its puff-pastry crust just before you plan to serve it (see Do Ahead).

Place the porcini mushrooms in a small heatproof bowl and pour the boiling water over them. Let them soak for 20 to 30 minutes, or until softened. Drain the porcini in a fine-mesh sieve lined with damp paper towels or cheesecloth, reserving the liquid. Chop the mushrooms finely and set the mushrooms and liquid aside separately.

In a large Dutch oven or other heavy-bottomed pot with a lid, heat 3 tablespoons of the olive oil over medium-high heat. When the oil is hot, brown the veal in 5 or 6 batches, taking care not to crowd the pot or the meat will steam rather than brown. Season each batch with a little salt and pepper when you put it in the pot. Turn the meat cubes from time to time as they cook for even browning. Each batch should take about 5 minutes. As each batch is ready, use a slotted spoon to remove it to a shallow bowl. Repeat until all the veal is browned.

Add the remaining 3 tablespoons of oil to the pot and add the mixed fresh mushrooms. In a small bowl, combine the garlic, rosemary, and 1 teaspoon of salt, and add this paste to the mushrooms. Sauté the mushrooms for about 5 minutes, until they are just beginning to soften. Stir in the reserved porcini mushrooms. Increase the heat to high and add the white wine. Let it bubble for a minute or so, and then add the reserved porcini liquid, the bay leaves, and the chicken broth to the pot. Return the veal to the pot. Bring the liquid to a boil, reduce the heat to medium-low, cover, and let the stew simmer for about 1¼ hours, or until the veal is tender (check by piercing the meat with a fork; it should slide in easily, with just the slightest resistance). The stew can be made ahead of time up to this point and refrigerated for up to 2 days.

While the stew is simmering, heat the oven to 400°F and oil a 9-by-13-inch rectangular oven-proof baking dish.

When the meat is tender, stir in the Marsala, parsley, and heavy cream. Spoon the stew into the baking dish.

On a lightly floured surface, roll out the puff pastry dough to fit over the baking dish. Moisten the rim of the baking dish with a little water. Cover the stew with the dough, and using the tines of a fork, press along the perimeter of the baking dish so that the pastry adheres to the rim. Brush the pastry with egg wash.

Bake the stew for 30 minutes, or until the stew is bubbly and the crust is puffed and golden brown. Serve immediately.

DO AHEAD: If you have made the stew in advance, be sure to reheat it on the stove top while you preheat the oven. About 30 minutes before you plan to serve the stew, proceed with the directions for finishing it with the puff pastry and baking it.

GOES WITH:

Creamy Carrot Soup with Rice and Caramelized Carrots, page 57

Winter Endive and Orange Salad, page 61

September Gratin, page 175

Eggplant Parmigiana Deluxe

MAKES 8 SERVINGS

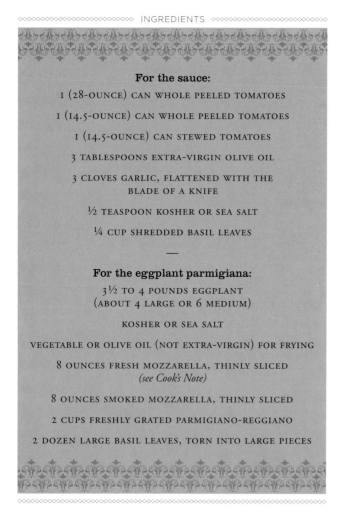

∞∞∞∞∞∞∞∞∞∞∞∞∞∞ INGREDIENTS ∞∞∞∞∞∞∞∞∞∞∞∞∞∞∞∞

For the sauce:

1 (28-OUNCE) CAN WHOLE PEELED TOMATOES

1 (14.5-OUNCE) CAN WHOLE PEELED TOMATOES

1 (14.5-OUNCE) CAN STEWED TOMATOES

3 TABLESPOONS EXTRA-VIRGIN OLIVE OIL

3 CLOVES GARLIC, FLATTENED WITH THE
BLADE OF A KNIFE

½ TEASPOON KOSHER OR SEA SALT

¼ CUP SHREDDED BASIL LEAVES

—

For the eggplant parmigiana:

3½ TO 4 POUNDS EGGPLANT
(ABOUT 4 LARGE OR 6 MEDIUM)

KOSHER OR SEA SALT

VEGETABLE OR OLIVE OIL (NOT EXTRA-VIRGIN) FOR FRYING

8 OUNCES FRESH MOZZARELLA, THINLY SLICED
(see Cook's Note)

8 OUNCES SMOKED MOZZARELLA, THINLY SLICED

2 CUPS FRESHLY GRATED PARMIGIANO-REGGIANO

2 DOZEN LARGE BASIL LEAVES, TORN INTO LARGE PIECES

For many Italian Americans, eggplant parmigiana is the ultimate comfort food and the ultimate party food wrapped into one rich, luscious dish. Extra layers of eggplant and cheese, and the addition of both fresh and smoked mozzarella, are what give my version here its "deluxe" status.

To make the sauce:
Pour the whole and stewed tomatoes into a bowl and break them up with a potato masher or with your hands.

In a large nonreactive saucepan, warm the oil and garlic over medium heat. Use a wooden spoon to press down on the garlic to release its aroma and swirl the pan to infuse the oil. Don't let the garlic brown or it will become bitter. Carefully pour in the tomatoes, taking care to avoid spatters, and stir to coat with the oil. Add the salt, raise the heat to medium-high and bring the tomatoes to a simmer. When the juices start bubbling, reduce the heat to medium and let the tomatoes cook, uncovered, stirring from time to time, for 30 to 35 minutes, or until the sauce has thickened and the oil has separated from the tomatoes. Remove from the heat and stir in the basil. Cover and set aside.

Cut the eggplant lengthwise into ½-inch-thick slices. Sprinkle them on both sides with a little salt and layer them in a colander. Set a plate on top of the eggplant and weight it down with a heavy object. Let the eggplant drain for 30 to 60 minutes. Wipe the slices dry with paper towels.

Heat ¼ cup vegetable or olive oil in a large skillet or sauté pan placed over medium-high heat. When the oil is hot (375ºF), add enough eggplant slices to fill the skillet without crowding it. Fry the eggplants until they are golden brown, taking care to turn them once so they brown on both sides, about 5 minutes total. Reduce the heat to medium if the eggplant seems to be browning too quickly. Use a large slotted spatula to remove the cooked eggplant to a platter lined with paper towels or a large brown paper shopping bag placed nearby. As the eggplant slices cool after draining, transfer them to a platter. Continue to fry the eggplant slices, adding more oil as necessary, until you have cooked them all.

To assemble and bake the parmigiana:
Heat the oven to 350ºF. Have the sauce, eggplant, cheeses, and basil nearby. Layer about ½ cup of sauce into a large rectangular baking dish. Arrange one layer of eggplant slices over the sauce. Top with some slices of fresh and smoked mozzarella and sprinkle with some Parmigiano cheese and basil. Add 2 more layers of sauce, eggplant, mozzarella and Parmigiano cheeses, and basil. Finish with a layer of eggplant, topped with a final layer of sauce and a generous sprinkling of Parmigiano cheese.

Bake the eggplant for 30 to 40 minutes, until it is bubbling and the top is nicely browned. Remove from the oven and let sit for about 20 minutes to firm up a bit. Serve the parmigiana warm or at room temperature.

COOK'S NOTE: Fresh mozzarella contains a lot of moisture, which will be released when you bake the parmigiana. If you like a parmigiana that is less juicy, use the drier part-skim mozzarella available in most supermarkets in place of the fresh mozzarella.

DO AHEAD: The eggplant can be fried several hours or up to a day in advance and stored in layers in a tightly lidded container in the refrigerator.

GOES WITH:

Red, White, and Green Salad with Lemon-Balsamic Dressing, page 58

Frank's Garlic Bread, page 45

Three-Cheese-Stuffed Red and Yellow Peppers

SERVES 4 AS A MAIN COURSE AND 8 AS A SIDE DISH

I know a lot of people who have never tasted a good stuffed pepper. They are usually made with unripe green peppers, filled with bland, pasty stuffing or gristly sausage, and doused with a heavy-duty sauce. These peppers are a revelation in comparison: sweet red and yellow peppers take the place of green, and the savory cheese-and-bread stuffing is at once substantial and light. Serve them as the entrée at a casual luncheon or supper party.

∞∞∞∞∞∞∞∞∞∞ INGREDIENTS ∞∞∞∞∞∞∞∞∞∞

¼ CUP PLUS 4 TABLESPOONS
EXTRA-VIRGIN OLIVE OIL

4 CUPS LIGHTLY PACKED FRESH BREAD CRUMBS
(see Cook's Note, page 142)

3 TABLESPOONS MINCED FLAT-LEAF PARSLEY

2 CLOVES GARLIC, MINCED

½ CUP FINELY CHOPPED MIXED
GIARDINIERA *(page 18)*

2 TABLESPOONS CAPERS, PREFERABLY IN SALT,
RINSED, DRAINED, AND COARSELY CHOPPED

½ CUP FRESHLY GRATED PARMIGIANO-REGGIANO

½ CUP FRESHLY GRATED PECORINO ROMANO

½ CUP FRESHLY SHREDDED ASIAGO

I TEASPOON KOSHER OR SEA SALT, OR TO TASTE

FRESHLY GROUND BLACK PEPPER

PINCH OF GROUND CAYENNE PEPPER (OPTIONAL)

2 LARGE RED BELL PEPPERS

2 LARGE YELLOW BELL PEPPERS

I (14.5-OUNCE) CAN STEWED TOMATOES, CRUSHED
WITH A POTATO MASHER OR COARSELY CHOPPED

Heat the oven to 375°F.

Heat ¼ cup of olive oil in a large skillet or sauté pan placed over medium heat. Add the bread crumbs, parsley, and minced garlic and sauté, stirring frequently, for 8 minutes, or until the bread crumbs are pale golden and starting to crisp. Transfer the bread crumbs to a large bowl. Add the giardiniera, capers, cheeses, salt, pepper, and cayenne, if using. Mix everything together with a large wooden spoon or silicone spatula. Set the stuffing aside while you prepare the peppers.

Cut the peppers in half lengthwise, cutting right through the stems so that each pepper half has a decorative stem end. With a paring knife, remove the seeds and the white pithy ribs. Spoon the filling into the hollowed-out pepper halves. Fill them generously but don't overstuff them. Reserve any leftover stuffing for sprinkling over the peppers before baking.

Coat the bottom of a baking dish that is just large enough to hold the peppers snugly with 2 tablespoons of olive oil. Pour about ¾ of the tomatoes into the dish and spread them out with a spatula. Arrange the peppers on top of the tomatoes. Spoon the remaining tomatoes over the tops of the peppers. Sprinkle with any remaining bread crumbs, and drizzle the remaining 2 tablespoons of olive oil over the peppers.

Bake the peppers for about 1 hour or slightly longer, until the tops are nicely browned and the peppers themselves are just tender. Turn off the oven and let the peppers sit inside for another 15 minutes to 30 minutes, until they are completely tender. Serve immediately.

CONTINUED ON NEXT PAGE . . .

. . . CONTINUED

❧·❧·❧·❧

COOK'S NOTE: To make fresh bread crumbs, cut away the crusts from a large chunk of ciabatta or other rustic Italian bread (about ⅓ of a 1-pound loaf). Tear the chunk into large pieces, place in a food processor, and pulse until coarse crumbs form. You should have about 2 cups worth.

❧·❧·❧·❧

DO AHEAD: The stuffing may be made several hours or up to a day in advance and stored in a tightly lidded container in the refrigerator. Bring it to room temperature before stuffing the peppers. The peppers may be cleaned and sliced in half several hours in advance, and stored in a zipper-lock plastic bag in the refrigerator. The stuffed peppers may be baked several hours in advance and served at room temperature or reheated in a low (300ºF) oven just until warmed through.

GOES WITH:

Caesar Salad, page 62

Vegetarian Mixed Grill, page 119

Grilled Caesar Flank Steaks with Lemon-Anchovy Butter, page 107

Spatchcocked Herbed Chickens alla Diavola, page 117

Beef Tenderloin alla Bandiera Italiana, page 133

Zuppa di Cozze

MAKES 6 TO 8 MAIN-COURSE SERVINGS

✦·✦·✦

Mussel stew is a staple in southern Italian cuisine, whether bathed in a rich tomato sauce or simmered in a white wine broth. Here is a nice version for summer, featuring ripe red and gold cherry tomatoes, fresh basil, and grilled bread for mopping up the garlicky juices.

∞∞∞∞∞∞∞∞∞∞∞∞ INGREDIENTS ∞∞∞∞∞∞∞∞∞∞∞∞

½ CUP PLUS 3 TABLESPOONS EXTRA-VIRGIN OLIVE OIL

6 CLOVES GARLIC, MINCED, PLUS 2 WHOLE CLOVES, FLATTENED WITH THE BLADE OF A KNIFE

3 QUARTS MIXED RED AND GOLD CHERRY TOMATOES

½ TEASPOON KOSHER OR SEA SALT

GENEROUS PINCH OF CRUSHED RED PEPPER

1 CUP COARSELY CHOPPED BASIL

6 POUNDS MUSSELS, DEBEARDED IF NECESSARY AND SCRUBBED CLEAN

⅔ CUP DRY WHITE WINE

6 SLICES BRUSCHETTA *(page 31)*, PLUS ADDITIONAL FOR THOSE WHO WANT MORE THAN ONE

Heat the ½ cup of oil and the minced garlic in a skillet or sauté pan placed over medium heat, stirring frequently so that the garlic softens but does not brown, 3 to 5 minutes. Add the tomatoes, salt, and red pepper and raise the heat to medium-high. When the sauce begins to bubble, reduce the heat and let it simmer, uncovered, for about 15 minutes, until thickened. Turn off the heat and stir in the basil. Cover to keep warm.

Put the remaining 3 tablespoons of olive oil and the flattened garlic cloves in a pot large enough to hold all of the mussels. Turn the heat to medium-high. When the garlic begins to sizzle, stir it around with a wooden spoon. Dump in the mussels and the wine, cover the pot, and cook for about 8 minutes, until the mussels have opened. You can uncover the pot once or twice and stir the mussels around a bit while they are cooking, but resist the urge to do this too often. When all of the mussels have opened (discard any that have not opened within 10 minutes at the most), pour the reserved sauce over them and mix everything together with a large spoon. Cook briefly, until everything is heated through.

Place a slice of bruschetta in each of 6 shallow rimmed bowls and ladle the mussel stew over the bread. Serve immediately, with additional slices of bruschetta on the side.

✦·✦·✦

DO AHEAD: The sauce for the mussel stew may be made several hours or even a day in advance and refrigerated until it is time to cook the mussels. If you do make it ahead, do not add the basil. Reheat the sauce until it comes to a simmer and then stir in the basil.

∞∞∞∞∞∞∞∞∞∞ GOES WITH: ∞∞∞∞∞∞∞∞∞∞

Escarole and Swiss Chard Torte, page 163

Vegetarian Mixed Grill, page 119

Red, White, and Green Salad with Lemon-Balsamic Dressing, page 58

∞∞∞∞∞∞∞∞∞∞∞∞∞∞∞∞∞∞∞∞∞∞∞∞∞∞∞∞∞∞

Fresh Tuna Stew with Olives and Herbs

MAKES 6 SERVINGS

I made a similar version of this fragrant fish stew in my first book, *The Glorious Soups and Stews of Italy,* using swordfish. It was a big hit in cooking classes, and I had a hunch that it would be just as good with tuna. My hunch turned out to be right. Tuna is a lean fish that usually calls for quick grilling to prevent it from drying out. Here, it is marinated overnight with a mix of herbs and vegetables and then simmered ever so gently on the stove. This slow cooking yields deliciously succulent and moist chunks of fish in a rich broth brightened by the fresh flavors of basil, mint, and oregano. Plus, it is completely hands-off, freeing you to tend to other tasks, or even socialize.

INGREDIENTS

¾ CUP EXTRA-VIRGIN OLIVE OIL

1 (2- TO 2½-POUND) PIECE OF GOOD-QUALITY (BUT NOT SUSHI-QUALITY) TUNA, SUCH AS YELLOWFIN, ABOUT 4 INCHES THICK

KOSHER OR SEA SALT

FRESHLY GROUND BLACK PEPPER

1 LARGE RED OR YELLOW ONION, HALVED AND THINLY SLICED

5 CLOVES GARLIC, LIGHTLY CRUSHED WITH THE FLAT SIDE OF A KNIFE BLADE

2 CUPS CHERRY TOMATOES, HALVED LENGTHWISE

1 CUP PITTED KALAMATA OLIVES

1 ROUNDED TABLESPOON MINCED FRESH BASIL, PLUS A COUPLE OF SPRIGS FOR GARNISH

1 ROUNDED TABLESPOON MINCED FRESH MINT, PLUS A COUPLE OF SPRIGS FOR GARNISH

1 ROUNDED TABLESPOON MINCED FRESH OREGANO

—

For serving:

8 SLICES BRUSCHETTA *(page 31)*

Choose a Dutch oven or other heavy-bottomed pot with a lid in which the tuna will fit comfortably but snugly. Coat the bottom of the pot with a little of the olive oil. Season the tuna generously on all sides with salt and pepper and place it in the pot. Cover the fish with the onion, garlic, tomatoes, olives, and herbs. Drizzle the remaining oil over everything, cover, and refrigerate overnight.

To cook the fish, remove the pot from the refrigerator and let it stand at room temperature for 60 minutes. Place the pot on the stove top over low heat and cook, covered, for 1 hour and 15 minutes to 1 hour and 40 minutes, depending on the size of the fish. To see if it is done, cut into the fish with a sharp paring knife; it should be opaque but still tender throughout. Taste the broth and adjust the seasoning with additional salt if necessary.

To serve, use a large serving spoon to scoop out chunks of tuna and arrange them in a deep ceramic or other decorative serving dish. Spoon the broth, onions, tomato, and olives over the fish and garnish it with some sprigs of fresh mint or basil. Serve with bruschetta on the side. Or to serve individually, place a slice of bruschetta at the bottom of each of 6 shallow rimmed bowls and spoon the stew over the bread.

COOK'S NOTE: In colder months, I sometimes like to serve this stew with Olive Oil–Roasted Potatoes (page 158) in place of the bruschetta.

GOES WITH:

Chef John Coletta's Calabrian Fennel Salad with Raisins and Red Finger Chiles, page 33

Red, White, and Green Salad with Lemon-Balsamic Dressing, page 58

Escarole and Swiss Chard Torte, page 163

Spicy Seafood Chowder with Sweet Fennel

SERVES 8 TO 10

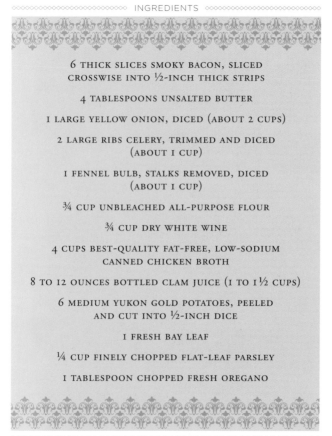

◇◇◇◇ INGREDIENTS ◇◇◇◇

6 THICK SLICES SMOKY BACON, SLICED CROSSWISE INTO ½-INCH THICK STRIPS

4 TABLESPOONS UNSALTED BUTTER

1 LARGE YELLOW ONION, DICED (ABOUT 2 CUPS)

2 LARGE RIBS CELERY, TRIMMED AND DICED (ABOUT 1 CUP)

1 FENNEL BULB, STALKS REMOVED, DICED (ABOUT 1 CUP)

¾ CUP UNBLEACHED ALL-PURPOSE FLOUR

¾ CUP DRY WHITE WINE

4 CUPS BEST-QUALITY FAT-FREE, LOW-SODIUM CANNED CHICKEN BROTH

8 TO 12 OUNCES BOTTLED CLAM JUICE (1 TO 1½ CUPS)

6 MEDIUM YUKON GOLD POTATOES, PEELED AND CUT INTO ½-INCH DICE

1 FRESH BAY LEAF

¼ CUP FINELY CHOPPED FLAT-LEAF PARSLEY

1 TABLESPOON CHOPPED FRESH OREGANO

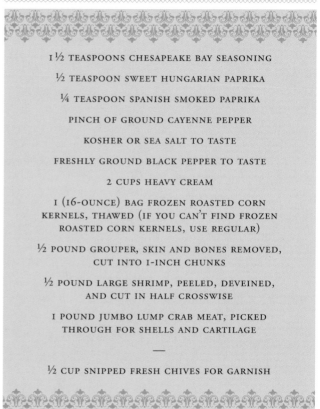

1½ TEASPOONS CHESAPEAKE BAY SEASONING

½ TEASPOON SWEET HUNGARIAN PAPRIKA

¼ TEASPOON SPANISH SMOKED PAPRIKA

PINCH OF GROUND CAYENNE PEPPER

KOSHER OR SEA SALT TO TASTE

FRESHLY GROUND BLACK PEPPER TO TASTE

2 CUPS HEAVY CREAM

1 (16-OUNCE) BAG FROZEN ROASTED CORN KERNELS, THAWED (IF YOU CAN'T FIND FROZEN ROASTED CORN KERNELS, USE REGULAR)

½ POUND GROUPER, SKIN AND BONES REMOVED, CUT INTO 1-INCH CHUNKS

½ POUND LARGE SHRIMP, PEELED, DEVEINED, AND CUT IN HALF CROSSWISE

1 POUND JUMBO LUMP CRAB MEAT, PICKED THROUGH FOR SHELLS AND CARTILAGE

—

½ CUP SNIPPED FRESH CHIVES FOR GARNISH

A good, hearty seafood chowder recipe is practically a requirement if you live in the mid-Atlantic. I created this one for a dinner party that my husband and I hosted one snowy night. As is my habit, I gave a classic American recipe an Italian touch by adding fennel and oregano. Our guests liked the result so much that they brought the leftovers home in containers.

Put the bacon in a large Dutch oven or heavy-bottomed pot and place it over medium-high heat. Cook, stirring, until the bacon begins to render its fat and turn brown, about 10 minutes. The bacon should be slightly crispy in places but still somewhat soft. Remove the bacon with a slotted spoon to a paper towel–lined plate.

Reduce the heat to medium and add the butter to the pot. When it has melted, add the onion, celery, and fennel. Cook, stirring frequently, until the onion is translucent and the vegetables have softened, 7 to 8 minutes. Reduce the heat to medium-low and sprinkle in the flour, stirring well with a wooden spoon until it is fully incorporated and the mixture is pasty.

Gradually pour in the wine, stirring until the mixture is well blended. Add the chicken broth and 1 cup of clam juice. Stir in the potatoes, bay leaf, parsley, oregano, and the seasonings.

Return the bacon to the pot. Cover partially with a lid and let the stew simmer gently over medium-low to low heat until the potatoes are tender, 20 to 30 minutes.

Stir in the cream and return the chowder to a simmer. Add the corn and the grouper and cook for 5 minutes. Add the shrimp and cook 5 minutes more, or until the shrimp have turned pink. Stir in the crab and cook until the chowder is heated through. Ladle the hot chowder into shallow rimmed bowls and garnish each serving with a sprinkling of chives. Serve immediately.

DO AHEAD: The chowder may be prepared up to 2 hours ahead up through the cooking of the potatoes. Remove from the heat and let sit at room temperature. A few minutes before serving time, reheat the chowder to a simmer over medium-low heat and finish the recipe as directed.

GOES WITH:

September Gratin, page 175

Winter Endive and Orange Salad, page 61

Frank's Garlic Bread, page 45

Smoky Ham and Corn Chowder

SERVES 8 MAIN COURSE SERVINGS OR UP TO 20 SMALL SERVINGS AS PART OF A BUFFET

INGREDIENTS

4 SLICES THICK SMOKY BACON, CUT CROSSWISE
INTO ½-INCH STRIPS

4 TABLESPOONS UNSALTED BUTTER

½ POUND GOOD-QUALITY SMOKED COOKED HAM,
CUT INTO ½-INCH DICE *(see Cook's Note, page 150)*

2 SMALL BONELESS SMOKED PORK CHOPS,
CUT INTO ½-INCH DICE

2 LARGE YELLOW ONIONS, DICED (ABOUT 4 CUPS)

2 TO 4 JALAPEÑO PEPPERS, MINCED, DEPENDING
ON HOW SPICY YOU LIKE YOUR CHOWDER

2 RED BELL PEPPERS, TRIMMED AND CUT
INTO ½-INCH PIECES

2 GREEN BELL PEPPERS, TRIMMED AND CUT
INTO ½-INCH PIECES

5 MEDIUM RED POTATOES (ABOUT 2 POUNDS), CUT
INTO ½-INCH DICE (PEELING IS OPTIONAL)

2 FRESH BAY LEAVES

5 SPRIGS FRESH THYME

1 TEASPOON KOSHER OR SEA SALT, OR TO TASTE

1 TEASPOON SWEET HUNGARIAN PAPRIKA

½ TEASPOON SMOKED SPANISH PAPRIKA

¼ TEASPOON CHIPOTLE POWDER (YOU MAY
SUBSTITUTE CAYENNE IF YOU DO NOT HAVE
CHIPOTLE POWDER, BUT YOU WILL LOSE THE
SMOKINESS OF THE CHIPOTLE)

½ CUP UNBLEACHED ALL-PURPOSE FLOUR

8 TO 10 CUPS BEST-QUALITY FAT-FREE, LOW-SODIUM
CANNED CHICKEN BROTH

1 (16-OUNCE) BAG FROZEN ROASTED CORN, THAWED
(IF YOU ARE UNABLE TO FIND FROZEN ROASTED CORN,
USE REGULAR)

1 CUP HEAVY CREAM

I served this chowder as part of a cocktail buffet party on a cold night in November. I was looking for one dish to serve as an anchor of sorts—something that was more than bite-sized, but not a full-blown main course. I ladled the finished chowder into my slow cooker, placed it on the buffet, and set it on "warm." Throughout the evening, guests helped themselves to bowls of chowder, which had the double effect of shaking off the late-fall chill and making everyone feel right at home. You will notice, as you read through the ingredient list, that the recipe calls not only for ham but also for bacon and smoked pork chop. As a resident of Virginia for more than a dozen years, I feel obligated to avail myself of the wonderful selection of pork products from my adopted home state.

Place the bacon in a large Dutch oven or other heavy-bottomed pot and cook it over medium heat until it begins to brown and render its fat, about 10 minutes. Add the butter, ham, and pork chops and cook, stirring frequently, for 5 to 7 minutes, until the meat is lightly browned. Stir in the onions and jalapeño peppers and sauté, stirring often, until the onions are softened and translucent, about 8 minutes. Stir in the red and green bell peppers, potatoes, bay leaves, and thyme. Sauté until the peppers and potatoes are slightly softened, about 5 minutes. Add the salt, sweet and smoked paprika, and the chipotle powder and stir to combine. Sprinkle in the flour, stirring all the while to prevent lumps from forming.

Pour in a cup of chicken broth and stir well to combine it with the flour. Gradually add an additional 7 to 9 cups of broth, depending on how thick you like your chowder. Cover the pot partially and simmer the chowder gently over low heat for 25 to 30 minutes, until all of the vegetables are tender. Stir in the corn and cream and bring the chowder to a simmer. Serve immediately.

CONTINUED ON NEXT PAGE...

... CONTINUED

ℰⅅ·ℰⅅ·ℰⅅ

COOK'S NOTE: For a three-letter word, ham is a complicated subject, as I learned when I moved to Virginia. There is dry-cured ham and wet-cured ham, country ham and city ham, baked ham and smoked ham, salt-cured and sugar-cured. And that is only the beginning. For this recipe you want a good-quality basic cooked ham that has been smoked. You should be able to find it in the deli department of your supermarket.

ℰⅅ·ℰⅅ·ℰⅅ

DO AHEAD: You can make the chowder a day in advance, up to the adding of the corn and cream. Refrigerate the chowder in a tightly lidded container. When you are ready to finish the chowder, bring it to a simmer in a large pot. Add the corn and cream and heat through until it is just bubbling.

GOES WITH:

Spinach and Apple Salad, page 59

Italian Pot-Likker Greens, page 162

Roasted Cherry Tomato Gratin, page 176

Tomato and Cheese Tart, page 170

Popovers, page 213

Beef Brisket Chili over Polenta

MAKES 6 TO 8 SERVINGS

~·§·~

INGREDIENTS

For the chili:

6 THICK SLICES SMOKY BACON, CUT CROSSWISE INTO ½-INCH SLICES

4 POUNDS BEEF BRISKET, CUT INTO ½-INCH CUBES

I LARGE RED ONION, CHOPPED

6 CLOVES GARLIC, MINCED

I TO 2 TABLESPOONS VEGETABLE OIL, IF NEEDED

3 TABLESPOONS ANCHO CHILI POWDER
(see Cook's Note, page 152)

2 TABLESPOONS GROUND CUMIN

¾ TEASPOON GROUND CINNAMON

3 TEASPOONS DRIED MEXICAN OREGANO

2 TEASPOONS SMOKED PAPRIKA

¼ TO ½ TEASPOON CHIPOTLE POWDER
(see Cook's Note, page 152)

I (14-OUNCE) CAN DICED TOMATOES

3 CUPS BEST-QUALITY FAT-FREE, LOW-SODIUM CANNED BEEF BROTH

WATER

KOSHER OR SEA SALT

FRESHLY GROUND BLACK PEPPER

—

For the polenta:

8 CUPS WATER

I ½ TEASPOONS KOSHER OR SEA SALT

2 CUPS POLENTA

4 TABLESPOONS UNSALTED BUTTER

—

Optional garnishes:

SLICED SCALLIONS

SHREDDED CHEDDAR CHEESE

SOUR CREAM

MINCED CILANTRO

It doesn't matter whether your people are from Austin or Abruzzo. If you live in the United States, you need a good chili recipe, either for your Super Bowl party or, as in my case, on Oscar night. This is a bean-free chili, with plenty of meat, heat, and spice. It is ladled over polenta, which takes the place of cornbread. Be sure to start the polenta about an hour before you plan to serve the chili. Or for a surprisingly delicious alternative, serve the chili over fragrant basmati rice (see Variation).

To make the chili:

Brown the bacon in a Dutch oven or heavy-bottomed pot placed over medium heat, stirring frequently, until the bacon begins to render its fat, about 10 minutes. Using a slotted spoon, remove the bacon to a paper towel–lined plate and set aside.

Put some of the beef into the pot, taking care not to crowd the cubes or they will steam rather than brown. Sear the beef in the bacon fat, turning the cubes with tongs once or twice, so that they brown on at least two sides, about 4 minutes total. Using the slotted spoon, remove the cubes to a bowl or deep plate. Continue to sear the beef in batches until it is all browned.

Put the onion and garlic into the pot and reduce the heat to medium-low. Add a little vegetable oil if not enough fat from the meat is left in the pot. Sauté the onion and garlic, stirring frequently, until they are softened, about 8 minutes. Stir in the ancho chili powder, cumin, cinnamon, oregano, paprika, and chipotle powder and cook for 1 minute. Return the bacon and beef to the pot and add the tomatoes. Stir to combine everything thoroughly. Pour in the beef broth and just enough water to barely cover the meat. Raise the heat to medium-high and bring the chili to a boil. Reduce the heat, cover partially, and cook the chili at a very gentle simmer for 3 to 4 hours, until the meat is fork-tender and some chunks have begun to

CONTINUED ON NEXT PAGE . . .

... CONTINUED

fall apart. (Add an additional splash of water during cooking if the chili seems too thick.) Season to taste with salt and pepper.

To make the polenta:

In a heavy-bottomed saucepan, combine the water and salt and bring to a boil over medium-high heat. Very carefully sprinkle in the polenta in a slow, steady stream, stirring constantly with a whisk as you add it. When all of the polenta has been mixed in, reduce the heat to medium and continue to cook the polenta, stirring frequently with a wooden spoon, for 40 to 45 minutes, or until it is very thick and comes away cleanly from the sides and bottom of the pan.

Stir in the butter and mix vigorously until the butter is melted and completely incorporated into the polenta. Taste and adjust the seasoning with salt if needed.

To serve, spoon some hot polenta into individual shallow rimmed bowls and top with a generous ladleful or two of chili. Set out the optional garnishes and allow your guests to help themselves.

COOK'S NOTE: Using a variety of mild, hot, and smoked chili powders deepens the flavor of the chili. If you stock up on several kinds you will find that they are also good for seasoning steaks and other cuts of meat, as well as vegetables, dips, and soups.

VARIATION: I have found that this chili is delicious served over fragrant rice, such as basmati. For this version, bring 8 cups of chicken broth to a boil in a large pot over medium-high heat; add 4 cups of white basmati rice. When the broth returns to a boil, reduce the heat to medium-low, cover the pot, and cook the rice at a gentle simmer for 17 to 18 minutes, or until the grains are tender but not at all mushy. Remove from the heat and let the rice sit, covered, for a minute or so. Fluff with a fork. Serve the rice in individual shallow rimmed bowls topped with the chili and garnishes.

DO AHEAD: The chili may be made up to 3 days in advance and stored in a tightly lidded container in the refrigerator, or in the freezer for up to 1 month. Reheat it, partially covered, over medium-low heat until it is simmering. Add a splash of broth or water if necessary to loosen it.

Lamb alla Cacciatore

MAKES 4 TO 6 MAIN-COURSE SERVINGS

The same ingredients that comprise the classic dish Chicken alla Cacciatore—woodsy rosemary and earthy mushrooms—also pair beautifully with lamb.

INGREDIENTS

½ CUP (½ OUNCE) DRIED PORCINI MUSHROOMS

½ CUP BOILING WATER

3 TABLESPOONS EXTRA-VIRGIN OLIVE OIL

2 POUNDS BONELESS LAMB STEW MEAT
(LEG OR SHOULDER), CUT INTO 2-INCH CUBES

KOSHER OR SEA SALT

FRESHLY GROUND BLACK PEPPER

I CARROT, FINELY CHOPPED

I RIB CELERY, FINELY CHOPPED

I MEDIUM YELLOW ONION, FINELY CHOPPED
(ABOUT ¾ CUP)

I CLOVE GARLIC, FINELY MINCED

4 OUNCES FRESH SHIITAKE MUSHROOMS, SLICED

6 SUN-DRIED TOMATOES IN OIL, COARSELY CHOPPED

2 TEASPOONS MINCED FRESH OREGANO

2 TEASPOONS MINCED FRESH ROSEMARY

I CUP DRY WHITE WINE

I CUP BEST-QUALITY FAT-FREE, LOW-SODIUM CANNED
CHICKEN BROTH OR WATER

Heat the oven to 325°F.

Place the porcini mushrooms in a small bowl and pour the boiling water over them. Let them soak for 20 to 30 minutes, or until softened. Drain the porcini in a fine-mesh sieve lined with damp paper towels or cheesecloth, reserving the liquid.

Chop the mushrooms coarsely and set the mushrooms and liquid aside separately.

In a large Dutch oven or other heavy-bottomed pot, warm the olive oil over medium-high heat. When the oil is hot, arrange some of the pieces of lamb in the pot. Sprinkle the pieces with a little salt and pepper and sear, turning as needed, for 8 to 10 minutes, or until browned on all sides. Be careful not to crowd the pot or the lamb will steam rather than brown. Remove the browned lamb to a bowl or platter. Continue until you have browned all of the lamb.

Reduce the heat to medium and add the carrots, celery, and onion to the pot. Cook them for about 7 minutes or until the vegetables are softened. Stir in the garlic and sauté briefly, until it has released its fragrance. Add the shiitake mushrooms and cook, stirring frequently, until they have softened, about 10 minutes. Add the reserved porcini mushrooms, tomatoes, herbs, and 1 teaspoon of salt. Cook for 2 minutes. Raise the heat to medium-high and pour in the wine. Let it boil, stirring, for a couple of minutes until it is almost evaporated. Pour in the broth or water and return the lamb to the pot.

Cover and put the pot in the oven. Braise the stew for 1 ¼ hours, or until the meat is fork-tender and the sauce is reduced and richly flavored. Taste and adjust the seasoning with additional salt and pepper if necessary.

DO AHEAD: The stew may be made up to 2 days in advance and refrigerated in a tightly lidded container.

GOES WITH:

Polenta, page 151

Olive Oil–Roasted Potatoes, page 158

Red, White, and Green Salad with Lemon-Balsamic Dressing, page 58

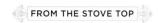
Beef and Chestnut Stew with Marsala

MAKES 6 SERVINGS

My sister, Maria, a gifted home cook, created this recipe on the fly one weekend when my family was visiting. It contains two of my favorite ingredients—chestnuts and dried cherries—both of which gradually fall apart and become one with the sauce during the slow simmering of the stew. Serve this stew as an entrée at a small fall or winter dinner party.

INGREDIENTS

¼ CUP PLUS 2 TABLESPOONS EXTRA-VIRGIN OLIVE OIL

3½ TO 4 POUNDS BONELESS CHUCK ROAST,
CUT INTO 2-INCH CUBES

KOSHER OR SEA SALT

FRESHLY GROUND BLACK PEPPER

3 LARGE CARROTS, SLICED INTO THIN COINS

1 LARGE YELLOW ONION, THINLY SLICED

2 CUPS DRY MARSALA

2 CUPS BEST-QUALITY FAT-FREE, LOW-SODIUM
CANNED BEEF BROTH

2 BAY LEAVES

2 SPRIGS FRESH THYME

1½ CUPS PEELED, COOKED CHESTNUTS *(page 17)*

⅔ CUP DRIED TART CHERRIES

Heat ¼ cup of the olive oil in a large Dutch oven or other heavy-bottomed pot placed over medium heat. Working in batches, add some of the meat and sear, turning the pieces with tongs as needed, for about 5 minutes, or until evenly browned on all sides. Sprinkle the meat with a little salt and pepper as you brown it. Take care not to crowd the pot or the meat will steam rather than brown. As the meat is browned, use a slotted spoon to remove it to a bowl. Continue until you have browned all of the meat.

Add the remaining 2 tablespoons of oil to the pot and stir in the carrots and onion. Sauté, stirring frequently, until the carrots have begun to soften, about 15 minutes. Return the meat to the pot, raise the heat to medium-high, and pour in the Marsala. Let the liquid bubble for 1 to 2 minutes, then add the broth and herbs. When the liquid begins to boil, reduce the heat to low, cover, and cook at a gentle simmer for 1 hour. Stir in the chestnuts and cherries. Recover and simmer gently for 2 hours. Uncover and simmer for an additional 30 to 40 minutes, until the meat is fork-tender and the sauce is thick. Taste, and adjust the seasoning with additional salt and pepper if necessary. Remove the herbs and serve immediately.

DO AHEAD: The stew may be made up to 2 days in advance and kept in a tightly lidded container in the refrigerator.

GOES WITH:

Pear Salad with Walnuts, Pecorino, and Chestnut Honey, page 68

Roasted Squash Wedges with Maple Glaze, page 169

Olive Oil–Roasted Potatoes, page 158

Stuffed Veal Involtini with a Crumbled Sausage Sauce

MAKES 4 MAIN-COURSE SERVINGS

This is a recipe I usually reserve for a special family dinner or small dinner party, for the simple reason that while the veal rolls may be assembled in advance, they are best when cooked and served at the last minute. Having said that, let me add that these little bundles are well worth the inconvenience of last-minute cooking; they are packed with flavor, and as you sauté them, a little of the fontina cheese oozes out and becomes part of the sauce.

INGREDIENTS

8 (2-OUNCE) SLICES BONELESS VEAL CUTLETS (SCALLOPINE), POUNDED TO ⅛-INCH THICKNESS

8 THIN SLICES OF PROSCIUTTO COTTO, ABOUT 4 OUNCES TOTAL *(page 18)*

6 OUNCES IMPORTED FONTINA VAL D'AOSTA CHEESE, THINLY SLICED

16 FRESH WHOLE SAGE LEAVES, PLUS I TABLESPOON FINELY CHOPPED FRESH SAGE LEAVES

KOSHER OR SEA SALT TO TASTE

FRESHLY GROUND BLACK PEPPER

2 TABLESPOONS UNSALTED BUTTER

2 TABLESPOONS EXTRA-VIRGIN OLIVE OIL

I (¼-POUND) LINK SWEET ITALIAN SAUSAGE

¼ CUP DRY MARSALA

½ CUP BEST-QUALITY FAT-FREE, LOW-SODIUM CANNED CHICKEN BROTH

¼ CUP HEAVY CREAM

Place one of the veal cutlets on a clean work surface. Lay a slice of prosciutto cotto on top of the meat, trimming it to fit if necessary. Lay 2 or 3 slices of cheese on top of the prosciutto, and top with 2 sage leaves. Starting at the short side nearest you, roll up the cutlet, jellyroll style, and secure it with a toothpick.

Continue until you have stuffed and rolled all eight scallopine. Season the rolls all over with a sprinkle of salt and a grinding of pepper.

Heat the butter and the oil in a large skillet or sauté pan placed over medium heat. When the butter has melted and is sizzling, set the veal rolls in the pan. Add only as many rolls as will fit without crowding the pan. Let the veal brown without turning for 2 to 3 minutes, until nicely colored on the bottom. Using tongs, turn the rolls and continue to sear until they are well browned all over. Remove the veal rolls to a platter.

Remove the casing from the sausage and crumble it into the skillet, stirring the meat to prevent it from sticking to the bottom of the pan. Cook the sausage until it is no longer pink and just starting to brown, about 5 minutes. Increase the heat to high and pour in the Marsala. Let the wine bubble for about a minute, and then reduce the heat to medium and return the veal rolls to the pan. Pour in the chicken broth, cover, and cook just until the sauce begins to boil. Uncover and cook, turning the rolls from time to time, for 6 to 8 minutes, until there is no trace of pink remaining in the veal.

Transfer the rolls to a decorative serving platter and cover loosely with aluminum foil to keep warm. Raise the heat to high and add the cream and chopped sage to the pan. Cook on high for 3 to 5 minutes, until the sauce is reduced and thickened. Pour the sauce over the meat and serve immediately.

GOES WITH:

Italian Pot-Likker Greens, page 162

Truffled Mushrooms, page 165

Roasted Squash Wedges with Maple Glaze, page 169

Walnut Focaccia, page 46

Yes, salads make a fine accompaniment to a meal, but don't forget there is a whole world of side dishes out there. Despite their name, side dishes are an integral part of a meal.

For one thing, they have a practical function: imagine a large dinner plate with nothing on it but a slice or two of meat—make it good meat even, beef tenderloin. Now imagine that same plate with the beef tenderloin and next to it a gorgeous mound of Truffled Mushrooms (page 165) and a bright orange wedge of Savory Carrot Crostata (page 171).

Side dishes add visual and textural appeal to a meal. They allow a cook to get creative. And they are an expression of the season. The Tomato and Cheese Tart on page 170 is only worth making when big, beefy slicing tomatoes are at their peak. And what finer adornment could you ask for at a fall table than a platter of golden Roasted Squash Wedges with Maple Glaze (page 169)?

CH. 5 VEGETABLES & SIDE DISHES

Olive Oil–Roasted Potatoes

SERVES 8 AS A SIDE DISH

Don't balk at the idea of briefly boiling the potatoes before you roast them. This little trick yields potatoes that are beautifully golden brown and crisp on the outside and creamy and tender on the inside.

INGREDIENTS

KOSHER OR SEA SALT

4 POUNDS (ABOUT 12 MEDIUM) YUKON GOLD OR OTHER YELLOW POTATOES, PEELED AND QUARTERED LENGTHWISE *(see Cook's Note)*

EXTRA-VIRGIN OLIVE OIL

FRESHLY GROUND BLACK PEPPER

1 SPRIG FRESH ROSEMARY (OPTIONAL), PLUS SEVERAL ADDITIONAL SPRIGS FOR GARNISH

Heat the oven to 425°F.

Bring a large pot of salted water to a boil. Put in the potatoes and return the water to a boil. Boil the potatoes for 3 to 4 minutes; they should still be fairly crisp. Drain the potatoes and spread them in one layer on a large roasting pan.

Drizzle a generous amount of olive oil (⅓ to ½ cup) over the potatoes and grind black pepper to taste over them. Pull the leaves off the sprig of rosemary, if using, and scatter them over the potatoes. Toss the potatoes gently with a spatula to coat them thoroughly. Roast the potatoes in the oven for 30 minutes. Turn them carefully with a spatula and roast them another 20 to 30 minutes, until they are crispy and golden brown on the outside. Remove the potatoes from the oven and sprinkle them with salt. Transfer the potatoes to a warmed serving platter or bowl and garnish with a couple of sprigs of rosemary. Serve immediately.

COOK'S NOTE: If you have baby Yukon Golds at your disposal or other such new potatoes, you can cook them in the same way but leave them whole, with their skins on.

DO AHEAD: You can boil the potatoes several hours in advance and leave them, loosely covered with foil or plastic wrap, until you are ready to roast them. Even roasted they keep well, so if you need to free up your oven for another dish, roast the potatoes in advance, and then pop them back into a 425°F oven for a few minutes before serving time, just until they are heated through.

Farm Stand Sauté

MAKES 4 SERVINGS

INGREDIENTS

2 MEDIUM ZUCCHINI, QUARTERED
LENGTHWISE AND THEN CUT CROSSWISE
INTO ½-INCH PIECES

1 LARGE OR 2 SMALL CUCUMBERS, QUARTERED
LENGTHWISE, SEEDED, AND CUT INTO
½-INCH PIECES

KOSHER OR SEA SALT

3 TABLESPOONS UNSALTED BUTTER

1 BUNCH SMALL RADISHES, PREFERABLY
IN A VARIETY OF COLORS, TRIMMED
AND QUARTERED

4 SCALLIONS, WHITE AND GREEN PARTS,
THINLY SLICED

2 TEASPOONS CHOPPED FRESH DILL OR
FENNEL FRONDS

FRESHLY GROUND BLACK PEPPER

¼ CUP HEAVY CREAM

This dish always comes as a revelation to those who believe cucumbers and radishes were meant only for salads. Sautéed with a little cream and dill, the vegetables lose their sharp edges and become mellow and velvety. This recipe is easily doubled.

Put the zucchini and cucumber pieces in a colander and sprinkle a little salt over them. Let them drain for 30 minutes; pat dry.

Melt the butter in a large skillet or sauté pan placed over medium heat. Add the zucchini, cucumbers, and radishes, tossing to coat them well with butter. Sauté for a minute or two and then stir in the scallions. Sauté the vegetables for 5 to 8 minutes, or until they are crisp-tender. Sprinkle in the dill and season the vegetables with a little salt and pepper. Pour in the cream and sauté for another minute or so, until slightly thickened. Remove from the heat and serve immediately.

Artichokes alla Romana

MAKES 4 GENEROUS SERVINGS

My mother used to make stuffed artichokes often when I was growing up; it was one of my all-time favorite dishes and still is. Sometimes she would serve the artichokes as a first course, and sometimes as a second course after a dish of pasta. As a child, I thought there was nothing more fun than pulling the artichoke leaves out with my fingers and using my teeth to scrape off the delicious bread-crumb stuffing. The smaller the artichoke got as I ate, the closer I knew I was getting to the true prize: the tender artichoke bottom. I like serving these artichokes to friends because it requires them to literally dig in with their fingers, which somehow puts everyone at ease.

INGREDIENTS

1 CUP DRY BREAD CRUMBS

¾ CUP FRESHLY GRATED PARMIGIANO-REGGIANO

1 CLOVE GARLIC, PRESSED

2 TABLESPOONS MINCED FLAT-LEAF PARSLEY

½ TEASPOON KOSHER OR SEA SALT

FRESHLY GROUND BLACK PEPPER

1 TO 2 TABLESPOONS EXTRA-VIRGIN OLIVE OIL, PLUS ADDITIONAL FOR DRIZZLING

JUICE OF 1 LEMON

4 LARGE ARTICHOKES

In a medium bowl, mix together the bread crumbs, Parmigiano, garlic, and parsley. Season with salt and pepper to taste. Add 1 to 2 tablespoons of oil to moisten the mixture but not so much that it clumps together. Set aside.

Place a large bowl of cold water near your work surface and pour the lemon juice into it. Cut the stem off the bottom of one artichoke. With a paring knife, trim the end off of the artichoke stem and peel off the tough outer layer. Put the stem in the water. Pull off the tough leaves on the very bottom of the artichoke. Set the artichoke upside-down on your cutting board and press on it with the palm of your hand, rolling it around slightly to help open up the leaves. With a sharp knife, cut the top third off of the artichoke. With your fingers or a small spoon, open up the leaves of the artichoke and tuck in one-fourth of the crumb mixture, dividing it between the leaves. Set the artichoke in a large Dutch oven or other heavy-bottomed pot. Continue until you have trimmed all of the artichoke stems and stuffed all of the artichokes. The artichokes should fit upright, snugly, in the pot. If there are any leftover bread crumbs, sprinkle them on top of the artichokes. Add the stems to the pot. Carefully pour the lemon water around the artichokes but not over them. The water should come about halfway up the sides of the artichokes. Add additional water if necessary. Sprinkle a little salt and pepper over the artichokes, and drizzle a little olive oil over them.

Set the pot on a burner and turn the heat to medium-high. Bring the liquid to a boil. Reduce the heat to medium-low, cover the pot, and braise the artichokes at a gentle simmer for 2 to 3 hours, depending on their size.

Heat the oven to 375°F. Check the artichokes from time to time as they cook. The artichokes are done when they are tender enough that you can easily pull out a leaf. When the artichokes are tender, uncover the pot and set it in the oven. Bake for 20 minutes, or until the tops of the artichokes are crisp and browned and the liquid is reduced.

Place an artichoke and a stem in each of four shallow rimmed soup plates. Spoon some of the sauce over the artichokes and serve. Make sure you set empty bowls on either side of your table so that your diners can discard their artichoke leaves. To eat, pull a leaf from the artichoke and with your teeth scrape off the stuffing. As you get nearer to the choke, the leaves will become more tender. When the leaves start to get prickly, remove them, as well as the fuzzy choke, to expose the delicious artichoke bottom. This is your prize for all of your hard work getting through the leaves. Enjoy.

ఴ·ఴ·ఴ

DO AHEAD: The stuffing may be made several hours in advance and kept, covered, at room temperature.

Italian Pot-Likker Greens

MAKES 6 TO 8 SERVINGS

I feel compelled to disclose that these hearty bitter greens produce a strong aroma when braised, especially with lots of wine and garlic. However, because they pair so well with roasts, including Roast Pork Loin with Carrots, Fennel, and Onions (page 131) and Poached and Roasted Capon with Porcini Butter (page 129), I also feel compelled to share the recipe with you. The savory juices from the pot are also great for sopping up with bread. Since the aroma is not nearly as pungent when the greens are reheated, I recommend cooking them a day or two in advance and then reheating them on the stove right before serving time. This has the added advantage of putting you ahead of schedule.

INGREDIENTS

4 POUNDS RAPINI, WASHED, TOUGH
LOWER STEMS REMOVED AND LARGE LEAVES
TORN INTO LARGE PIECES

6 TO 8 CLOVES GARLIC, HALVED

¾ TO 1 CUP EXTRA-VIRGIN OLIVE OIL

1 TO 1½ CUPS DRY WHITE WINE

KOSHER OR SEA SALT

GENEROUS PINCH CRUSHED RED PEPPER

Put two or three large handfuls of rapini, with water still clinging to them, into a large, high-sided saucepan or kettle and set the pan over medium heat. Add several half-cloves of garlic to the pot and pour in about ⅓ cup of oil and ½ cup of wine. Season generously with salt and some of the red pepper. Cover the pot and let the greens cook for 5 to 7 minutes, or until they have begun to wilt. Continue to add fresh greens as those in the pan cook down, adding more garlic, oil, wine, and red pepper. When all of the rapini have been added, use a long, two-pronged serving fork to turn the greens in the pot. Add a splash more oil and wine, and any remaining garlic. Cover and let the greens simmer for 30 to 40 minutes, stirring them from time to time. The greens are done when they are very dark and tender. Taste, and adjust the seasoning with additional salt if necessary.

Transfer the hot greens, along with their juices, to a decorative bowl and serve immediately.

Escarole and Swiss Chard Torte

SERVES 6 AS A MAIN COURSE OR 10 AS A SIDE DISH

INGREDIENTS

For the filling:

4 TABLESPOONS EXTRA-VIRGIN OLIVE OIL

8 CLOVES GARLIC, MINCED

3 LEEKS, TRIMMED AND THOROUGHLY RINSED, WHITE AND PALE GREEN PARTS CUT INTO ¼-INCH ROUNDS

2 HEADS ESCAROLE (1½ POUNDS TOTAL), WASHED, TRIMMED, AND LEAVES COARSELY SHREDDED

2 BUNCHES SWISS CHARD (1½ POUNDS TOTAL), WASHED, TOUGH LOWER STALKS REMOVED, AND LEAVES COARSELY SHREDDED

1½ CUPS COARSELY CHOPPED, PITTED GAETA OR KALAMATA OLIVES

1 TEASPOON KOSHER OR SEA SALT, OR TO TASTE

FRESHLY GROUND BLACK PEPPER TO TASTE

½ POUND FRESH RICOTTA

½ POUND RICOTTA SALATA, SHREDDED ON THE LARGE HOLES OF A BOX GRATER

1 CUP FRESHLY GRATED PARMIGIANO-REGGIANO

4 EGGS, LIGHTLY BEATEN

———

To assemble the torte:

1 BATCH OF SAVORY PASTRY DOUGH *(page 96)*

UNBLEACHED FLOUR FOR DUSTING THE WORK SURFACE

1 EGG YOLK, LIGHTLY BEATEN WITH 2 TABLESPOONS WATER

As with so many Italian recipes, this torte is at once rustic and elegant. A dense filling of bitter greens, olives, and three kinds of cheese is baked between two layers of flaky golden pastry. This makes a fine vegetarian entrée for an early spring luncheon or supper. But it is also superb paired with Slow-Roasted Arctic Char with Sautéed Fennel and Pernod (page 127) or Zuppa di Cozze (page 143). You can serve it warm or at room temperature, and if you have leftovers you can enjoy them cold straight out of the fridge.

Heat the oven to 350°F.

Warm the oil in a large skillet or sauté pan placed over medium heat. Add the garlic and leeks and cook, stirring frequently, for about 10 minutes, until the leeks are softened. Pile the greens into the pan by the handful, adding as much as you can. You will not be able to add them all at once. Cover and cook briefly until the greens have begun to wilt. Continue to add greens as those in the pan cook down, stirring as you go to make room for more. Once you have added all the greens, cover the pan again and continue to cook over medium heat until the vegetables are completely wilted and softened, about 20 to 30 minutes. Uncover, turn the heat up to medium-high, and cook until the greens are greatly reduced in volume and most of the liquid in the pan has evaporated.

Stir in the olives and salt, and pepper to taste. Remove the greens from the heat and let the mixture come to room temperature.

While the greens are cooling, combine the fresh ricotta, ricotta salata, and Parmigiano cheeses in a large bowl. Stir in the eggs,

CONTINUED ON NEXT PAGE ...

and then the reserved greens, taking care to incorporate everything thoroughly. Cover the filling with plastic wrap and set it aside while you roll out the dough.

Divide the dough into two pieces, one slightly larger than the other. On a lightly floured work surface, roll the larger piece into a disk large enough to cover the bottom and sides of a 10-inch-by-2-inch round cake pan with some overhang. The dough should be about ⅛ inch thick. Place your rolling pin on the edge of the dough closest to you and gently wrap the dough around the rolling pin. Lift the dough over the pan and carefully unroll it, gently pressing it into the pan. Trim the overhang to about ¾ inch, and prick the bottom of the dough with the tines of a fork.

Spoon the filling into the pastry-lined pan, smoothing out the top. Roll the remaining piece of dough into a disk large enough to cover the top of the torte with a little overhang. Place your rolling pin on the edge of the dough closest to you and gently wrap the dough around the rolling pin. Lift the dough over the pan and carefully unroll it to cover the filling. Gently press the overhanging edges of the top and bottom crusts together. Use a little water to moisten the dough to help seal it if necessary. Using your fingers, begin rolling the crust in toward the pan to create a rolled seam. Continue to roll along the circumference of the pan until you have fully sealed the crust.

Brush the top of the torte with the egg wash. With a sharp paring knife, cut three 2-inch slits across the top of the torte.

Bake the torte for 1 hour, or until the crust is golden brown and the filling is set. Remove the torte from the oven and let it cool for at least 10 minutes on a rack. The torte can be served warm or at room temperature. To serve, run a knife around the inside border of the pan and carefully invert the torte onto a rack. Place a serving plate on top of the upside-down torte and gently re-invert it onto the plate.

DO AHEAD: The dough can be made a day in advance and refrigerated, wrapped tightly in plastic, or frozen for up to 1 month. Bring the dough to slightly cooler than room temperature before rolling it out. The filling can be made a day in advance and refrigerated in a tightly lidded container. Bring it to room temperature before assembling the torte. The torte can be baked several hours in advance and served at room temperature or reheated in a low (275ºF) oven until it is warmed through.

Truffled Mushrooms

MAKES 6 SERVINGS

The term "truffled" mushrooms comes from the Italian *funghi trifolati*; that is, mushrooms prepared in the style of truffles—sautéed in olive oil with garlic and parsley. Serve these mushrooms as a side dish, or chop them into small pieces and spoon them onto Crostini (page 22).

INGREDIENTS

2 CLOVES GARLIC, SLICED
PAPER-THIN

2 TABLESPOONS BUTTER

2 TABLESPOONS EXTRA-VIRGIN
OLIVE OIL

2 POUNDS MIXED MUSHROOMS,
SUCH AS PORTOBELLAS, SHIITAKES,
AND CREMINI, TRIMMED AND
THINLY SLICED

KOSHER OR SEA SALT

FRESHLY GROUND BLACK PEPPER

½ CUP DRY WHITE WINE

2 TABLESPOONS MINCED FRESH
FLAT-LEAF PARSLEY

Put the garlic, butter, and oil in a large skillet or sauté pan and place the pan over medium heat. When the butter has melted, reduce the heat to medium-low and sauté the garlic until softened but not browned, about 5 minutes. Add the mushrooms and sprinkle with a little salt and pepper. Stir the mushrooms with a wooden spoon or a spatula to coat them with the oil and butter. Sauté over medium-low heat until the mushrooms are tender and the liquid that they release has evaporated, about 20 minutes. Raise the heat to high and pour in the wine. Stir, and let the wine bubble for a minute or two. Taste and adjust the seasoning with additional salt or pepper. Remove from the heat and stir in the parsley.

DO AHEAD: The mushrooms may be sautéed up to a day in advance and refrigerated in a tightly lidded container. Do not add the parsley at the end of cooking. Reheat the mushrooms in a skillet placed over medium heat and stir in the parsley just before serving.

Sautéed Spinach with Garlic

MAKES 4 SERVINGS

Spinach sautéed with garlic is a classic Italian preparation. This is one of my favorite side dishes to make. It literally takes 5 minutes or less to cook, and there is something about spinach that makes me feel virtuous when I serve it, even if it is sharing the plate with a large wedge of Pizza Rustica (page 97).

INGREDIENTS

¼ CUP EXTRA-VIRGIN OLIVE OIL

3 CLOVES GARLIC, SLICED PAPER-THIN

1 POUND BABY SPINACH LEAVES

KOSHER OR SEA SALT

Put the oil and garlic in a large skillet or sauté pan and set it over medium heat. Cook the garlic, stirring frequently, until it is soft and translucent but not at all browned, about 5 minutes. Reduce the heat to medium-low if necessary to prevent the garlic from browning.

When the garlic is soft, begin to add the spinach by the handful, using tongs or a wooden spoon to coat the spinach with the oil. Raise the heat to medium-high and sauté the spinach, tossing it frequently. Continue to add spinach by the handful as the leaves in the pan wilt. When you have added the last of the spinach—this should take no more than 5 minutes total—remove the pan from the heat and toss well so that the last leaves wilt from the residual heat. Season the spinach to taste with salt and serve immediately.

Roasted Squash Wedges with Maple Glaze

MAKES 8 TO 10 SERVINGS

ɛ৩·🌼·ɛ৩

A large platter of bright, burnished orange squash wedges makes a gorgeous side dish for a fall dinner party. Using a mix of winter squashes adds to the appeal; the subtle differences in flavor, texture, and color of the various squashes really stand out when you serve them side by side. The varieties listed below are just suggestions; use whichever ones appeal to you or are available at the market. I like to use Grade B maple syrup here because it has a pronounced maple flavor that enhances the sweetness of the squash.

◇◇◇◇◇◇◇◇◇◇◇◇◇◇◇◇◇◇◇ INGREDIENTS ◇◇◇◇◇◇◇◇◇◇◇◇◇◇◇◇◇◇◇

I ACORN SQUASH

I DELICATA SQUASH

I SWEET DUMPLING SQUASH

I BUTTERCUP OR KABOCHA SQUASH

½ CUP (I STICK) UNSALTED BUTTER

½ CUP PURE MAPLE SYRUP,
PREFERABLY GRADE B

KOSHER OR SEA SALT

FRESHLY GROUND BLACK PEPPER

◇◇◇

Heat the oven to 400°F.

With a large, sharp knife, cut the acorn squash in half lengthwise and scoop out and discard the seeds and stringy fibers. Cut each half in half lengthwise to make 4 quarters.

Cut the delicata squash in half lengthwise and scoop out and discard the seeds and stringy fibers. Cut each half in half crosswise to make 4 pieces.

Cut the sweet dumpling squash in half and scoop out and discard the seeds and stringy fibers.

Cut the buttercup or kabocha squash in half lengthwise and scoop out and discard the seeds and stringy fibers. Cut each half lengthwise into 3 wedges.

Put the butter and maple syrup in a heavy-bottomed pot and place over medium heat. Heat the mixture until the butter has completely melted. Sprinkle a little salt into the maple-butter mixture, just enough to cut the sweetness a little.

Place the squash wedges on a large rimmed baking sheet or shallow roasting pan and brush them evenly with the maple butter. Grind a little pepper over the wedges. Roast, basting every 15 minutes with syrup, until the squash is golden brown and tender, about 45 minutes total.

Remove from the oven and carefully pile the wedges on a large, deep serving platter. Serve immediately.

ɛ৩·ɛ৩·ɛ৩

DO AHEAD: The squashes may be cut several hours in advance and stored in zipper-lock bags in the refrigerator.

Tomato and Cheese Tart

MAKES ONE 9-INCH TART

This tart is adapted from a recipe by Marian Morash, author of *The Victory Garden* cookbook, one of my all-time favorite cookbooks. I've made a few changes here and there, but the recipe remains the same at heart: simple and yet very satisfying.

INGREDIENTS

For the tart dough:

1 CUP UNBLEACHED ALL-PURPOSE FLOUR, PLUS ADDITIONAL FOR ROLLING OUT THE DOUGH

½ TEASPOON KOSHER OR SEA SALT

½ CUP FRESH RICOTTA OR SMALL-CURD COTTAGE CHEESE

8 TABLESPOONS (1 STICK) COLD UNSALTED BUTTER, CUT INTO ½-INCH DICE

—

For the filling:

2 TEASPOONS SMOOTH DIJON MUSTARD

2 TO 3 RIPE BEEFSTEAK TOMATOES, SLICED THICKLY

¾ CUP SHREDDED SWISS CHEESE

¼ CUP SHREDDED FONTINA

2 TABLESPOONS COARSELY CHOPPED FRESH BASIL

2 TABLESPOONS MINCED FRESH FLAT-LEAF PARSLEY

KOSHER OR SEA SALT

FRESHLY GROUND BLACK PEPPER

½ CUP SHREDDED PART-SKIM MOZZARELLA (NOT FRESH)

¼ CUP FRESHLY GRATED PARMIGIANO-REGGIANO

To make the tart dough:

Combine 1 cup of flour and the salt in the work bowl of a food processor fitted with the metal blade. Pulse briefly to combine. Distribute the ricotta or cottage cheese and butter around the bowl and process just until a dough starts to form.

Turn the dough out onto a clean work surface and pat into a disk. Wrap tightly in plastic and refrigerate for 30 minutes.

On a lightly floured surface, roll the dough out into a 12-inch round. Carefully wrap the dough around the rolling pin and drape it over a 9-inch fluted tart pan with a removable bottom. Gently press the dough into the bottom and up the sides of the pan. Trim the overhang to about ½ inch and fold it in, pressing it against the inside rim to reinforce the sides of the tart shell. Use the rolling pin or the flat of your hand to press around the perimeter of the pan to cut off any excess dough. Put the lined tart pan in the refrigerator to chill for 30 minutes.

Heat the oven to 425ºF. Remove the tart shell from the refrigerator and line it with a piece of heavy-duty aluminum foil (or 2 pieces of regular aluminum foil to create a double thickness). Fill the lined shell with pie weights or dried beans and bake for 8 minutes. Remove the aluminum foil and the beans and bake for 2 more minutes; the crust will not be fully cooked. Set the tart shell on a rack to cool for about 10 minutes.

Reduce the heat to 350ºF. Brush the bottom of the cooled tart shell with the mustard—a thin coating is all you need. Arrange a layer of tomato slices, Swiss and fontina cheeses, and herbs over the bottom of the crust and sprinkle with a little salt and pepper. Repeat with a second layer. Sprinkle the mozzarella and Parmigiano over the top of the tart and bake for 25 to 30 minutes, or until it is melted and golden on top. Serve the tart warm.

DO AHEAD: The tart dough may be made up to 2 days in advance and kept, tightly wrapped in plastic, in the refrigerator. Remove the dough from the refrigerator and let it come to slightly cooler than room temperature before rolling it out.

Savory Carrot Crostata

MAKES ONE 11-INCH TART

ఆ/ీ·€}ీ·ఆ/ీ

This stunning tart is based on a recipe in a 1968 issue of Italy's premier cooking magazine, *La Cucina Italiana*. My mother, who subscribed to the magazine for years, has saved many of the issues, including that one, and she has been making the tart since the recipe was first published. It makes a lovely, elegant side dish for a sit-down dinner party, but my mother and I have also made it for Thanksgiving. The recipe is a little labor-intensive by today's standards but is, without a doubt, worth the time and the effort.

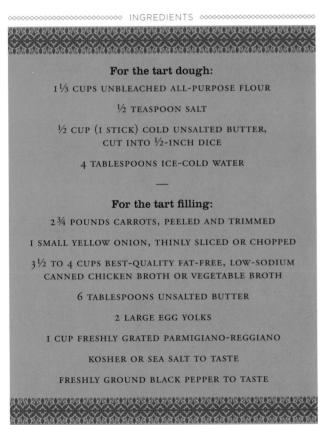

INGREDIENTS

For the tart dough:

1⅓ CUPS UNBLEACHED ALL-PURPOSE FLOUR

½ TEASPOON SALT

½ CUP (1 STICK) COLD UNSALTED BUTTER,
CUT INTO ½-INCH DICE

4 TABLESPOONS ICE-COLD WATER

—

For the tart filling:

2¾ POUNDS CARROTS, PEELED AND TRIMMED

1 SMALL YELLOW ONION, THINLY SLICED OR CHOPPED

3½ TO 4 CUPS BEST-QUALITY FAT-FREE, LOW-SODIUM
CANNED CHICKEN BROTH OR VEGETABLE BROTH

6 TABLESPOONS UNSALTED BUTTER

2 LARGE EGG YOLKS

1 CUP FRESHLY GRATED PARMIGIANO-REGGIANO

KOSHER OR SEA SALT TO TASTE

FRESHLY GROUND BLACK PEPPER TO TASTE

To make the tart dough:
Place the flour and salt in the work bowl of a food processor and pulse briefly to combine. Distribute the pieces of butter around the work bowl and process until the mixture is crumbly. Add just enough water through the feed tube to bring the dough together. Turn the dough out onto a lightly floured surface and pat it into a disk. Wrap in plastic and refrigerate for 30 minutes.

On a lightly floured surface, roll the dough out into a 14-inch circle. Carefully wrap the dough around the rolling pin and drape it over an 11-inch fluted tart pan with a removable bottom. Gently press the dough into the bottom and up the sides of the pan. Trim the overhang to about ½ inch and fold it in, pressing it against the inside rim to reinforce the sides of the tart shell. Use the rolling pin or the flat of your hand to press around the perimeter of the pan to cut off any excess dough. Put the lined tart pan in the refrigerator to chill for 30 minutes.

Heat the oven to 400ºF. Remove the tart shell from the refrigerator and line it with a piece of heavy-duty aluminum foil (or 2 pieces of regular aluminum foil to create a double thickness). Fill the lined shell with pie weights or dried beans and bake for 20 minutes. Remove the aluminum and the beans and bake for 10 to 15 more minutes, until the crust is light golden. Transfer the pan to a rack to cool. Reduce the oven heat to 375ºF.

To make the filling:
Select half of the carrots (choose the least attractive) and cut them into thick coins. Reserve the remaining carrots for the top layer. Place the cut carrots into a large saucepan with the onion and just enough broth to cover. Bring the broth to a simmer

CONTINUED ON NEXT PAGE . . .

. . . CONTINUED

over medium-high heat, reduce the heat to medium-low, cover the pan, and gently cook the carrots for 30 minutes. Uncover and cook for an additional 15 to 20 minutes, or until the carrots are very tender and almost all of the liquid has evaporated. Let cool for 10 minutes.

Transfer the cooked carrots to a blender and purée until smooth, adding a splash of broth if necessary to loosen the mixture just enough to purée it. Transfer the purée to a skillet or sauté pan placed over medium-low heat. Cook briefly, stirring frequently with a wooden spoon or a spatula, until the purée is thick and any liquid has evaporated. Remove from the heat and stir in 2 tablespoons of butter. Whisk in the egg yolks and Parmigiano cheese, and season to taste with salt and pepper.

Make the top layer: Cut the remaining carrots into thin, uniform coins. Melt 2 tablespoons of butter in a large skillet or wide sauté pan placed over medium-low heat. When the butter has melted, add the carrots and sprinkle with a little salt and pepper. Cook the carrots over medium-low to low heat for about 30 minutes, or until they are just tender. While they are cooking, moisten them from time to time with a splash of broth to prevent them from sticking to the bottom of the pan. Remove from the heat and let sit until cool enough to touch.

Spread the carrot purée into the baked tart shell. Arrange the carrot coins on top of the purée in slightly overlapping concentric circles, beginning at the outer edge of the tart and ending at the very center. Gently brush the top of the tart with any liquid remaining in the pan in which the carrot coins were sautéed and dot with the remaining 2 tablespoons of butter.

Bake the tart for about 20 minutes, until the filling is completely heated through and the top is lightly browned. Transfer the tart to a rack to cool for 10 minutes. Remove the tart ring and set the tart on a serving platter. Serve warm.

❧·❧·❧

DO AHEAD: The tart dough may be made up to 2 days in advance and refrigerated. Remove it from the refrigerator and let it come to slightly cooler than room temperature before rolling out. This tart is best on the day it is made, but it may be baked several hours in advance and kept at room temperature. Reheat it in a 350°F oven until it is just warmed through.

September Gratin

MAKES 6 SERVINGS

◇◇◇◇◇◇◇◇◇◇◇◇◇◇◇◇◇ INGREDIENTS ◇◇◇◇◇◇◇◇◇◇◇◇◇◇◇◇◇

For the vegetables:

3 SWEET RED PEPPERS, OR 2 RED AND I YELLOW,
TRIMMED AND SEEDED, SLICED LENGTHWISE
INTO THIN RIBS

I YELLOW SUMMER SQUASH, ENDS TRIMMED,
HALVED LENGTHWISE, AND CUT CROSSWISE INTO
THIN HALF-COINS

I ZUCCHINI SQUASH, ENDS TRIMMED, HALVED
LENGTHWISE, AND CUT CROSSWISE
INTO THIN HALF-COINS

I LARGE YELLOW ONION, PEELED, HALVED, AND
SLICED INTO THIN HALF-RINGS

¼ CUP TOMATO SAUCE *(page 138)* OR ¼ CUP CHOPPED
SUN-DRIED TOMATOES MARINATED IN OIL

¼ CUP EXTRA-VIRGIN OLIVE OIL

I TABLESPOON CHOPPED FRESH BASIL

I TEASPOON CHOPPED FRESH THYME

KOSHER OR SEA SALT TO TASTE

FRESHLY GROUND BLACK PEPPER TO TASTE

½ TEASPOON SWEET HUNGARIAN PAPRIKA,
OR TO TASTE

—

For the bread crumb coating:

2 CUPS FRESH BREAD CRUMBS *(page 142)* MADE
WITH SOURDOUGH BREAD

3 TABLESPOONS FRESHLY GRATED PARMIGIANO-REGGIANO

3 OR 4 TABLESPOONS EXTRA-VIRGIN OLIVE OIL

KOSHER OR SEA SALT

BUTTER FOR THE BAKING DISH

The vegetables for this colorful side dish are available year-round in supermarkets. But my favorite time to make it is toward summer's end, when farmers market stalls are brimming with fleshy red and yellow peppers and squashes of all kinds. This recipe is easily doubled to feed a crowd.

Heat the oven to 400°F.

In a large bowl, toss the vegetables and tomato sauce or sundried tomatoes with the olive oil, basil, thyme, salt, pepper, and paprika until thoroughly combined. Turn the mixture into a large baking dish or roasting pan and roast in the oven for 45 minutes to 1 hour, stirring every 15 minutes or so, until the vegetables are tender and lightly browned in spots.

While the vegetables are cooking, prepare the bread crumb topping: Mix the bread with the Parmigiano, olive oil, and salt to taste. Set aside.

Butter an oven-proof ceramic or Pyrex baking dish. Turn the vegetables into the baking dish. Top with the bread crumb mixture. Return the vegetables to the oven for 20 minutes or so, until the top is golden brown. Remove from the oven and allow the gratin to sit for a few minutes before serving.

DO AHEAD: The vegetables may be roasted up to a day in advance and refrigerated in a tightly lidded container. Bring to room temperature before assembling the gratin. The topping may be made several hours in advance and kept, covered, at room temperature.

Roasted Cherry Tomato Gratin

MAKES 6 TO 8 SERVINGS

Roasting cherry tomatoes intensifies their flavor. I sometimes use a mix of red and golden cherry tomatoes to give this gratin extra visual appeal.

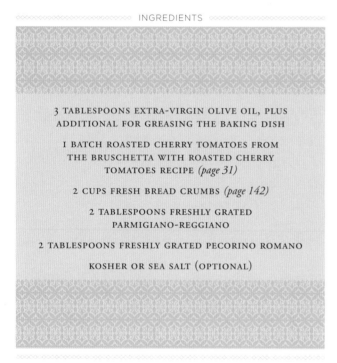

INGREDIENTS

3 TABLESPOONS EXTRA-VIRGIN OLIVE OIL, PLUS ADDITIONAL FOR GREASING THE BAKING DISH

I BATCH ROASTED CHERRY TOMATOES FROM THE BRUSCHETTA WITH ROASTED CHERRY TOMATOES RECIPE *(page 31)*

2 CUPS FRESH BREAD CRUMBS *(page 142)*

2 TABLESPOONS FRESHLY GRATED PARMIGIANO-REGGIANO

2 TABLESPOONS FRESHLY GRATED PECORINO ROMANO

KOSHER OR SEA SALT (OPTIONAL)

Heat the oven to 425ºF.

Lightly coat a round or rectangular ceramic baking dish with a little oil. Spread the roasted cherry tomatoes in the dish.

In a small bowl, mix together the bread crumbs and cheeses. Drizzle in 3 tablespoons of olive oil and toss. Taste and add salt if necessary. Sprinkle the bread crumb mixture over the tomatoes. Bake for 20 to 25 minutes, or until the topping is golden brown. Remove the gratin from the oven and let it stand for 10 minutes to cool slightly. Serve warm.

DO AHEAD: The cherry tomatoes may be roasted and the gratin assembled 2 hours in advance. Keep covered with plastic wrap until ready to bake.

Squash Gratin

MAKES 6 TO 8 SERVINGS

ε∕ɔ·ξ☼ξ·ε∕ɔ

Spaghetti squash has an appealing golden color, a mild flavor, and flesh that separates into strands when scraped with a fork. Here, the strands are folded into a gratin of aromatic rice, onions, and three cheeses.

◇◇◇◇◇◇◇◇◇◇◇◇◇◇◇◇◇◇◇◇ INGREDIENTS ◇◇◇◇◇◇◇◇◇◇◇◇◇◇◇◇◇◇◇◇

I SPAGHETTI SQUASH

6 TABLESPOONS EXTRA-VIRGIN OLIVE OIL,
PLUS ADDITIONAL FOR GREASING A GRATIN DISH

KOSHER OR SEA SALT

FRESHLY GROUND BLACK PEPPER

2 CUPS HOMEMADE VEGETABLE BROTH *(page 55)*
OR BEST-QUALITY LOW-SODIUM CANNED
VEGETABLE BROTH

I CUP AROMATIC LONG-GRAIN RICE, SUCH
AS BASMATI OR JASMINE

2 CLOVES GARLIC, SLICED PAPER-THIN

½ POUND CREMINI OR BUTTON MUSHROOMS,
CLEANED, TRIMMED, AND THINLY SLICED

I SMALL YELLOW ONION, HALVED AND SLICED
INTO THIN HALF-RINGS

2 SMALL-TO-MEDIUM ZUCCHINI, SLICED INTO
THIN ROUNDS

I TABLESPOON MINCED FLAT-LEAF PARSLEY

⅓ CUP SHREDDED DRY JACK CHEESE

⅓ CUP CUBED FRESH MOZZARELLA

⅓ CUP FRESHLY GRATED PARMIGIANO-REGGIANO

Heat the oven to 375ºF. Cut the spaghetti squash in half lengthwise and scoop out the seeds. Brush the flesh with 2 tablespoons of olive oil and sprinkle with a little salt and pepper. Place the squash, cut side down, on a rimmed baking sheet and bake until tender, about 45 minutes. Remove the squash from the oven and let it stand until it is cool enough to handle. Scrape the flesh into a bowl and set aside. Leave the oven on.

While the squash is baking, bring the vegetable broth to a boil in a saucepan placed over medium-high heat. Carefully pour in the rice. When the liquid returns to a boil, reduce the heat to medium-low and cover. Cook the rice for about 15 minutes, until the grains are slightly underdone and the liquid has been absorbed. Transfer the rice to a large bowl and toss with 1 tablespoon of olive oil.

Put the remaining 3 tablespoons of oil and the garlic in a large skillet or sauté pan and set the pan over medium-low heat. Sauté the garlic until it is softened but not at all browned, about 5 minutes. Add the mushrooms, onion, and zucchini and sprinkle with a little salt and pepper. Sauté the vegetables for about 10 minutes, until they are tender and the liquid they release has been reabsorbed. Stir in the parsley. Remove from the heat and transfer to a bowl. Let cool for a few minutes.

Add the reserved spaghetti squash and the mushroom-zucchini mixture to the bowl with the rice. Add the dry Jack and mozzarella cheeses and gently but thoroughly fold everything together.

Grease an 8-by-12-inch or similar-sized gratin dish with a little olive oil. Pour the rice-vegetable mixture into the dish and sprinkle the Parmigiano on top. Bake the gratin for 20 to 25 minutes, or until the top is golden brown and the edges are crusty. Remove the gratin from the oven and let it rest for 5 to 10 minutes before serving.

ε∕ɔ·ε∕ɔ·ε∕ɔ

DO AHEAD: The spaghetti squash and the mushroom-zucchini mixture may be cooked a day in advance and refrigerated in tightly lidded containers. Bring it to room temperature before proceeding with the recipe. The gratin may be assembled several hours in advance and kept, covered, at room temperature until baking time.

I always profess not to have a sweet tooth, and yet when I'm entertaining I can't help but feel that the evening is not complete if it doesn't include dessert. Whether it is a bowl of Drunken Strawberries (page 182) in late spring or an ultra-rich Bittersweet Mocha Grappa Torte with Walnuts (page 193) on a winter's eve, let there be something to end the meal on a sweet note.

Fruit often takes center stage in Italian desserts, and in these pages you will find more than a few worthy contenders, from Blood Orange Granita (page 183) to Sour Cherry Gelato with Bittersweet Chocolate-Cherry Sauce (page 185).

I happen to be partial to desserts with cream and custard (okay, so I may have a sweet tooth), and if you are as well, let me point you in the direction of Chestnut-Cognac Bavarese (page 190) and Pandoro Trifle with Vin Santo (page 197). For the best of both worlds, look no further than the cool comfort of Apricot Semifreddo (page 181). And for sheer fun, treat your company to Cheesecake Sundaes with Raspberry Sauce (page 187), an especially popular choice among children.

CH. 6 DESSERTS

Apricot Semifreddo

MAKES 10 SERVINGS

The word *semifreddo* literally translates to "half-cold" and refers to a variety of chilled or partially frozen Italian confections including Bavarian creams, cakes, and frozen mousses and light custards. The version here is essentially a frozen apricot mousse, made light and airy thanks to the careful incorporation of whipped cream. Unlike ice cream, a semifreddo such as this does not need to be churned; instead, it is frozen in a loaf pan or a mold. When sliced it is beautifully flecked with golden bits of apricot. Smooth and light, it has just the right amount of tartness.

INGREDIENTS

I CUP DRIED CALIFORNIA APRICOTS

⅔ CUP FRESHLY SQUEEZED ORANGE JUICE

1½ CUPS HALF-AND-HALF

½ TEASPOON PURE VANILLA EXTRACT

4 LARGE EGG YOLKS

½ CUP SUGAR

⅛ TEASPOON KOSHER OR SEA SALT

1½ CUPS HEAVY WHIPPING CREAM

¼ CUP CONFECTIONERS' SUGAR

½ PINT FRESH RED RASPBERRIES

½ PINT FRESH GOLDEN RASPBERRIES

FRESH MINT LEAVES FOR GARNISH

Place the apricots and orange juice in a small saucepan and set the pan over medium-high heat. Bring to a boil; reduce the heat to medium-low and cover. Simmer the apricots for 10 to 15 minutes, until they are softened. Remove them from the heat and let stand until cool. Puree the apricots and the juice in a food processor or blender until smooth.

Combine the half-and-half and vanilla extract in a medium-sized heavy-bottomed saucepan and set over medium heat. Bring the mixture just to the boiling point but take care not to let it boil. In a bowl, whisk together the egg yolks, sugar, and salt until light and thick. Pour a little of the hot half-and-half mixture into the egg yolks, whisking rapidly to prevent the yolks from cooking. Pour the egg yolks back into the pan with the half-and-half and cook over medium-low heat until the custard is thick enough to lightly coat the back of a wooden spoon, about 5 minutes. Remove the custard from the heat and stir in the apricot puree. Transfer the custard to a bowl and cover tightly with plastic wrap. Press the wrap right onto the surface of the custard to prevent a skin from forming. Refrigerate for several hours or overnight, until the apricot custard is thoroughly chilled.

In a large bowl, whip the heavy cream with the confectioners' sugar until just stiff. Gently fold in the chilled apricot custard.

Line an 8½-by-4½-inch loaf pan with plastic wrap, leaving an overhang of wrap on both sides and each end of the pan. Pour the apricot mixture into the loaf pan and smooth the top with a spatula. Cover the top of the semifreddo with the overhang. Freeze the semifreddo for at least 6 hours, until it is completely frozen.

To serve, remove the semifreddo from the freezer and unmold it onto a platter or cutting board. Let it stand for no more than 5 minutes to soften slightly. Cut the semifreddo into ¾-inch-thick slices and set the slices on dessert plates. Scatter a few of the red and golden raspberries over each slice and garnish each with a mint leaf or two.

DO AHEAD: The semifreddo may be made up to 3 days in advance and kept frozen until serving time.

Drunken Strawberries

MAKES 6 TO 8 SERVINGS

You may be surprised that such a simple preparation can yield such a luscious result. The secret is to use just-ripe strawberries—not the gigantic, pithy ones from the super-market—and a good-quality, sturdy but fruity wine.

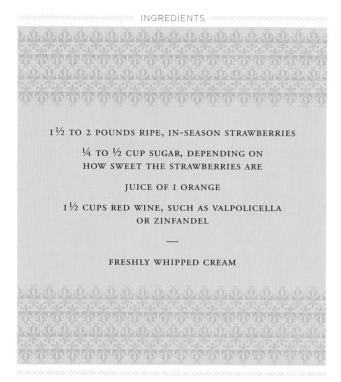

INGREDIENTS

1 ½ TO 2 POUNDS RIPE, IN-SEASON STRAWBERRIES

¼ TO ½ CUP SUGAR, DEPENDING ON
HOW SWEET THE STRAWBERRIES ARE

JUICE OF 1 ORANGE

1 ½ CUPS RED WINE, SUCH AS VALPOLICELLA
OR ZINFANDEL

—

FRESHLY WHIPPED CREAM

Trim the strawberries and cut the large ones in half. Place them in a bowl and sprinkle with the sugar. Pour in the orange juice and wine and fold everything together gently but thoroughly. Cover tightly with plastic wrap and refrigerate for 2 hours. To serve, spoon the strawberries into bowls or glasses and spoon some of the juices over them. Top each serving with a dollop of whipped cream. Pour any extra juices into wine glasses and enjoy as a beverage.

DO AHEAD: You can steep the strawberries in the liquid up to 12 hours in advance, but be aware that the fruit will soften. Although some people prefer it this way, I like this dessert best when the berries are still firm.

Blood Orange Granita

MAKES 6 SERVINGS

I like the dramatic color and somewhat tart flavor of blood oranges, which is why I chose them for this recipe. But really, any good juicing orange will yield a deliciously refreshing granita.

INGREDIENTS

I WHOLE CARDAMOM POD

I CUP SUGAR

1 ¾ CUPS FRESHLY SQUEEZED BLOOD ORANGE JUICE (USE VALENCIA OR NAVEL ORANGES OR TANGERINES IF YOU ARE UNABLE TO FIND BLOOD ORANGES)

I TABLESPOON FRESHLY SQUEEZED LEMON JUICE

ZEST OF ONE ORANGE

GRAND MARNIER OR A SIMILAR ORANGE-FLAVORED LIQUEUR (OPTIONAL)

6 SMALL SPRIGS FRESH MINT

Place a large rectangular metal baking pan in the freezer to chill it.

In a small saucepan, bring 1 cup of water and the cardamom pod to a boil. Pour in the sugar and cook just until the sugar has dissolved completely. Remove the syrup from the heat and let cool to room temperature. Refrigerate in a tightly lidded container until completely chilled (leave the cardamom pod in the syrup).

In a bowl, combine the orange and lemon juice, and the orange zest. Discard the cardamom pod from the syrup and stir the syrup into the orange juice mixture. Retrieve the metal baking pan from the freezer and pour the orange mixture into it. Return the pan, uncovered, to the freezer. Freeze the mixture for 30 minutes. Remove it from the freezer and use a fork to scrape the crystals away from the sides of the pan and turn the mixture. Continue to freeze, scraping every 30 minutes, until the mixture is completely frozen, about 2 hours. Transfer the granita to a container with a tight lid and freeze until ready to serve.

To serve, divide the granita among 6 ice cream bowls or custard cups. Drizzle a few drops of Grand Marnier, if using, over each bowl and garnish each with a sprig of mint.

DO AHEAD: The syrup may be made up to 3 days in advance and refrigerated. The granita may be made up to 3 days in advance and frozen. Use a fork to break up the crystals before serving.

Espresso Granita

MAKES 8 SERVINGS

My mother's three older sisters, Gilda, Elsa, and Adriana—all independent working women who never married—shared an apartment in Rome near beautiful Villa Ada. Around the corner from their house was a neighborhood *gelateria.* It was a small place, but the quality of the ice cream and other treats was top-notch. As much as I loved the velvety *gianduja* (chocolate and hazelnut) gelato, I absolutely could not resist the *granita di caffè con panna* with its sweet, strong coffee ice sandwiched between two layers of dense, freshly whipped cream. The icy granita was very sweet, and the smooth whipped cream was unsweetened; together they were perfection in a glass.

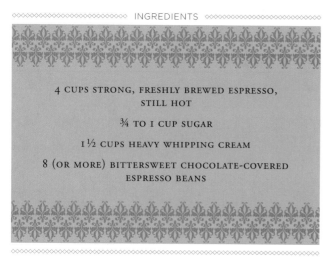

∞∞∞∞∞∞∞∞∞∞∞∞∞∞∞∞ INGREDIENTS ∞∞∞∞∞∞∞∞∞∞∞∞∞∞∞∞

4 CUPS STRONG, FRESHLY BREWED ESPRESSO, STILL HOT

¾ TO 1 CUP SUGAR

1½ CUPS HEAVY WHIPPING CREAM

8 (OR MORE) BITTERSWEET CHOCOLATE-COVERED ESPRESSO BEANS

Place a large rectangular metal baking pan in the freezer to chill it.

In a bowl, combine the coffee and sugar, stirring until the sugar is dissolved. Let the coffee cool to room temperature. Retrieve the metal baking pan from the freezer and pour the sweetened coffee into it. Freeze the mixture for 30 minutes. Remove it from the freezer and use a fork to scrape the crystals away from the sides of the pan and turn the mixture. Continue to freeze, scraping every 30 minutes, until the mixture is completely frozen, about 2 hours. Transfer the granita to a container with a tight lid and freeze until ready to serve.

At serving time, whip the cream to stiff peaks. Spoon a couple of tablespoons of whipped cream into each of 8 small tumblers or wine glasses. Spoon the granita into the glasses and mound each serving generously with more whipped cream. Place a chocolate-covered coffee bean on top of each serving. Serve immediately.

DO AHEAD: The granita may be made and frozen up to 3 days in advance. Use a fork to break up the crystals before serving.

Sour Cherry Gelato with Bittersweet Chocolate-Cherry Sauce

MAKES ABOUT 1 QUART ICE CREAM, TO SERVE 6

☙·❧·☙

My maternal grandmother, Maria Tomassoni, used to sun-dry sour cherries and preserve them in an alcohol-laden syrup. Whenever my sister or I were feeling under the weather she would feed us a small spoonful of the intensely flavored fruit. That usually put us right and no doubt accounts for why sour cherries are one of my favorite fruits, whether they are steeped in liquor or straight off the tree. This ice cream churns to a creamy blush and is studded with garnet cherries. It is delicious on its own or with a spoonful of the rich, bittersweet chocolate sauce drizzled over it.

∞∞∞∞∞∞∞∞∞∞∞ INGREDIENTS ∞∞∞∞∞∞∞∞∞∞∞

For the gelato:

1½ CUPS WHOLE MILK

1½ CUPS HEAVY CREAM

1 WHOLE VANILLA BEAN, SPLIT

6 LARGE EGG YOLKS

¾ CUP SUPERFINE SUGAR

PINCH OF KOSHER OR SEA SALT

4½ PACKED CUPS PITTED SOUR CHERRIES (PIE CHERRIES), CUT IN HALF

½ CUP GRANULATED SUGAR

—

For the Bittersweet Chocolate-Cherry Sauce:

2 TABLESPOONS UNSWEETENED COCOA

⅓ CUP HEAVY CREAM

1 CUP LIGHT CORN SYRUP

8 OUNCES BEST-QUALITY BITTERSWEET CHOCOLATE, CHOPPED

3 TABLESPOONS SALTED BUTTER

1 TABLESPOON KIRSCH *(see Cook's Note, page 186)*

To make the gelato:

Place the milk and heavy cream into a large saucepan. Scrape the seeds from the vanilla bean into the pan and add the pod to the pan as well. Bring the milk and cream just to a boil but take care not to let the mixture boil over. Remove the pan from the heat.

In a medium-sized bowl, beat the egg yolks with the superfine sugar and the salt until light and thick. Whisk a small ladleful of the hot milk and cream into the eggs, whisking quickly to prevent the eggs from cooking. Add 4 or 5 more ladlefuls of the milk mixture, one at a time, whisking all the while. Pour the egg-milk mixture into the saucepan with the remaining milk and cream and whisk to combine thoroughly. Cook the custard on medium-low to medium heat, stirring constantly, for about 20 minutes or until it is thick enough to lightly coat the back of a wooden spoon. Do not let the custard boil. Remove from the heat and pour the custard into a heat-proof bowl. Remove and discard the vanilla bean pod. Cover the custard with plastic wrap, making sure to press the wrap right onto the surface to prevent a skin from forming. Refrigerate until thoroughly chilled.

Place 3 cups of the cherries and the granulated sugar in a medium-sized saucepan. Bring the cherries to a simmer over medium heat and cook until the sugar has melted and the cherries are soft, 10 to 15 minutes. Pass the cooked cherries through a food mill fitted with the disk with the smallest holes. Strain the purée through a fine-mesh sieve and discard the solids. You should have about 1¼ cups of liquid. Put the liquid in a small saucepan and bring it to a simmer over medium heat. Simmer gently for 10 to 15 minutes, until it is slightly thickened and reduced to about 1 cup. Remove the cherry syrup from the heat and let it cool to room temperature.

CONTINUED ON NEXT PAGE ...

. . . CONTINUED

Stir the cherry syrup into the cold custard and refrigerate until the mixture is thoroughly chilled.

Freeze the cherry custard in an ice cream machine according to the manufacturer's instructions. When the ice cream is just about done, mix in the reserved 1 ½ cups cherries. Transfer the ice cream to a tightly lidded container and freeze until hard.

To make the sauce:

In a medium-sized saucepan whisk together the cocoa and heavy cream until smooth. Place the pan over medium heat and stir in the corn syrup, chocolate, and butter. Gently stir or whisk frequently until the chocolate has melted. Bring the sauce to a boil, reduce the heat to medium-low, and let boil gently for 5 minutes, or until thickened to a sauce consistency. Remove the sauce from the heat and let cool 5 minutes. Stir in the Kirsch.

To serve, scoop the ice cream into glass bowls and top with a drizzle of warm chocolate-cherry sauce.

✧·✧·✧

COOK'S NOTE: Kirsch is a clear, potent cherry brandy manufactured primarily in Germany. Use cognac as a substitute.

✧·✧·✧

DO AHEAD: The gelato may be made up to a week in advance and stored in the freezer. Remove it from the freezer and let it soften slightly before serving. The chocolate-cherry sauce may be made a week (or more) in advance and stored in a tightly lidded container in the refrigerator. To serve, heat the sauce gently in a double boiler until it is warm and has returned to sauce consistency.

Cheesecake Sundaes with Raspberry Sauce

MAKES 12 TO 15 SERVINGS

For the crust:

⅔ CUP SLICED ALMONDS

24 GINGERSNAP COOKIES, BROKEN INTO LARGE PIECES

1 TABLESPOON SUGAR

PINCH OF KOSHER OR SEA SALT

4 TABLESPOONS UNSALTED BUTTER, MELTED, PLUS
ADDITIONAL FOR GREASING THE BAKING PAN

—

For the cheesecake:

1 POUND CREAM CHEESE, AT ROOM TEMPERATURE

1 ⅓ CUPS SUGAR

4 LARGE EGGS

2 TABLESPOONS FRESHLY SQUEEZED LEMON JUICE

ZEST OF 1 LEMON

1 TEASPOON PURE VANILLA EXTRACT

¼ TEASPOON KOSHER OR SEA SALT

1 POUND MASCARPONE

1 CUP SOUR CREAM

BOILING WATER FOR BAKING THE CAKE IN A WATER BATH

—

For the raspberry sauce:

1 QUART RASPBERRIES

1 ½ CUPS CONFECTIONERS' SUGAR

1 TABLESPOON FRESHLY SQUEEZED LEMON JUICE

½ TEASPOON PURE VANILLA EXTRACT

—

1 PINT RASPBERRIES FOR GARNISH

Here, cheesecake is treated to a clever makeover, presented not as a slice but scooped into a bowl like ice cream. I came across this ingenious idea at a small music club and café called Iota, in nearby Arlington, Virginia. I immediately figured it would make an excellent party dessert. And in fact it is always a hit, both with kids and adults. For this version, I offer my mascarpone cheesecake, which is rich and creamy and the perfect consistency for scooping. But if you have a favorite cheesecake recipe, try it sometime as a sundae.

To make the crust:
Heat the oven to 350°F. Spread the almonds on a small rimmed baking sheet and bake for 5 minutes, or until lightly golden. Let cool for 10 minutes. Leave the oven on.

Put the cooled almonds and the gingersnaps in the work bowl of a food processor fitted with the metal blade. Add the sugar and salt and process until the cookies and almonds are reduced to fine crumbs. Drizzle in the butter and process until everything is combined.

Butter a 13-by-9-inch rectangular baking pan and press the cookie crumbs into the bottom and up the sides of the pan. The crust does not have to go all the way up the sides. Set aside.

To make the cake:
Using an electric mixer, beat the cream cheese until it is smooth. Add the sugar and beat until well blended. Add the eggs, one at a time, and beat until well incorporated, scraping down the sides of the bowl as necessary. Beat in the lemon juice and zest, the vanilla, and the salt. Add the mascarpone and sour cream and beat until everything is smooth and well blended. Pour the batter into the prepared pan.

CONTINUED ON NEXT PAGE . . .

. . . CONTINUED

Place the cake pan in a larger roasting pan. Carefully pour enough boiling water into the roasting pan to reach halfway up the sides of the cake pan. Bake the cheesecake for 45 minutes. Turn off the heat but do not open the oven. Let the cake sit in the oven for 1 hour. Remove the cake to a rack to cool to room temperature, then cover tightly with plastic wrap and refrigerate overnight, or until completely chilled.

To make the raspberry sauce:
Put 1 quart of raspberries in a medium-sized saucepan and mash them with a potato masher. Stir in the confectioners' sugar. Set the pan over medium-high heat and bring the berries to a boil. Reduce the heat to medium and simmer for 5 minutes, stirring frequently. Remove the sauce from the heat and stir in the lemon juice and vanilla. Strain the sauce through a fine-mesh sieve and discard the seeds. Let cool to room temperature and then transfer to a tightly lidded container. Refrigerate for several hours or overnight, until completely chilled.

To serve the cheesecake:
Use an ice cream scoop to scoop out balls of cheesecake into ice cream bowls or custard cups, making sure to get some of the crust with each scoop. Drizzle some of the chilled raspberry sauce over each serving and top each with a few of the whole raspberries. Serve cold.

DO AHEAD: The cheesecake and raspberry sauce may be made up to 2 days in advance and refrigerated. The cheesecake may be scooped into the individual bowls, covered tightly with plastic wrap, and refrigerated several hours or up to a day in advance. Garnish the bowls with the sauce and fresh berries right before serving.

Chestnut-Cognac Bavarese

MAKES 8 SERVINGS

Dense, sticky, tooth-achingly sweet chestnut jam was a favorite childhood treat of mine. Every so often, after my mother returned from one of her trips to the Italian delicatessen in Trenton, New Jersey, a small jar of it would turn up on the breakfast table, and my sister and I would spread it thickly on buttered toast. Here, the jam gets a more sophisticated treatment in a rich cognac-tinged Bavarian cream (*Bavarese* in Italian), to which it imparts its uniquely luscious yet earthy flavor. Be sure to generously shower the *Bavarese* with bittersweet chocolate shavings just before serving; the combination of chestnut and chocolate is an unforgettable one.

INGREDIENTS

1 ¼ CUPS PLUS 5 TABLESPOONS WHOLE MILK

3 LARGE EGG YOLKS

⅓ CUP SUGAR

½ TEASPOON PURE VANILLA EXTRACT

I CUP CHESTNUT JAM (*see Cook's Note*)

2 TABLESPOONS COGNAC

I TABLESPOON UNFLAVORED POWDERED GELATIN

I CUP HEAVY WHIPPING CREAM

VEGETABLE OIL OR COOKING SPRAY FOR GREASING A GELATIN MOLD

—

To serve:

½ CUP HEAVY CREAM

8 *MARRONS GLACÉS* (*see Cook's Note*)

I (I-OUNCE) SQUARE BEST-QUALITY BITTERSWEET CHOCOLATE

Put 1 ¼ cups milk in a saucepan and bring it just to a boil over medium heat. Remove it from the heat just as the milk starts to rise.

Bring a separate pot of water to a simmer over medium-high heat, keeping it at a gentle simmer.

Whisk the egg yolks and sugar together in a medium-sized heat-proof bowl until the yolks are light and thick (about 100 strokes). Pour a few drops of the hot milk into the egg mixture, whisking briskly as you pour to prevent the eggs from cooking. Continue to slowly whisk the milk into the eggs until you have added it all.

Set the bowl with the milk-egg mixture over the pot of simmering water, taking care that the bottom of the bowl does not touch the water. Cook, stirring constantly with a wooden spoon or heat-proof silicon spatula, until the custard has thickened enough to lightly coat the back of the spoon, 15 to 20 minutes. Remove the custard from the heat and stir in the vanilla extract.

In a small bowl, stir together the chestnut jam, 2 tablespoons of milk, and the cognac. Whisk this into the custard, mixing until it is thoroughly incorporated.

In a small saucepan, combine the gelatin with the remaining 3 tablespoons of milk. Cook, over very low heat, stirring constantly, just until the gelatin is dissolved. Stir the gelatin into the chestnut custard, making sure it is fully incorporated.

Cover the custard with plastic wrap and refrigerate it for 30 to 40 minutes, until it has thickened considerably but is not yet set. Check the mixture every 15 minutes, stirring to prevent the edges from setting.

Whip 1 cup of heavy cream to soft peaks and gently fold it into the thickened custard. Lightly grease a 5- to 6-cup gelatin or pudding mold or 1½-quart soufflé dish with vegetable oil or cooking spray. Spoon the chestnut cream into the mold, cover tightly with plastic wrap, and refrigerate for at least 6 hours, preferably overnight. Alternatively, you can spoon the chestnut cream into 8 individual dessert glasses, cover with plastic wrap, and refrigerate 6 hours to overnight.

To serve, carefully unmold the *Bavarese* onto a serving platter (you may need to dip the base of the mold or soufflé dish briefly in hot water to make unmolding easier). Whip the ½ cup of heavy cream until stiff. Spoon it into a pastry bag fitted with a star tip. Pipe 8 whipped cream stars around the top or base of the *Bavarese* (where you place them will depend on the design of your mold) and press a *marron glacé* into each star. If you are using individual dessert glasses, spoon a dollop of whipped cream or pipe a whipped-cream star onto each dessert and top with a *marron glacé*. Using the large holes on a box grater, grate a shower of chocolate over the *Bavarese*. Serve immediately.

❦·❦·❦·❦

COOK'S NOTE: Chestnut jam is available at gourmet food shops and supermarkets, and from online food purveyors. *Marrons glacés* are whole chestnuts that have been poached in vanilla-scented sugar syrup. They are available at gourmet food shops and supermarkets, and from online food purveyors.

❦·❦·❦·❦

DO AHEAD: Make the *Bavarese* a day in advance to give it adequate time to set.

Bittersweet Mocha Grappa Torte with Walnuts

MAKES 12 TO 16 SERVINGS

I can't even count the number of times that chocolate tortes have been a source of disappointment to this chocolate lover. So elegant and beautiful, yet more often than not they fail to deliver. They are either too liquored up, too jammy, too nutty, too dry, or too dense (giant chocolate truffle, anyone?). That's why I am so in love with this recipe; it delivers everything it promises. It is luscious, and every mouthful is packed with the decadent flavor of ultra-bittersweet chocolate and a good shot of grappa. Whipped egg whites lighten the torte and give it a distinctive, sophisticated appearance: the torte rises, soufflé-like, in the oven, and then gently falls as it cools, creating cracks on the surface. Dusted with confectioners' sugar, it is a marvel to behold, and even better to eat.

INGREDIENTS

1 CUP (2 STICKS) UNSALTED BUTTER, CUT INTO PIECES, PLUS MORE FOR GREASING CAKE PAN

¾ CUP SHELLED WALNUTS

¼ CUP UNBLEACHED ALL-PURPOSE FLOUR

1 POUND BITTERSWEET CHOCOLATE, COARSELY CHOPPED

1½ CUPS GRANULATED SUGAR

⅔ CUP STRONG BREWED COFFEE

⅓ CUP GRAPPA (*see Cook's Note, page 194*)

6 LARGE EGGS, SEPARATED

⅛ TEASPOON KOSHER OR SEA SALT

¼ TEASPOON CREAM OF TARTAR

CONFECTIONERS' SUGAR FOR SERVING

Heat the oven to 350°F.

Generously butter the inside of a 9-inch springform pan, including the top rim. Cut a circle of parchment paper to fit the bottom of the pan. Line the pan with the parchment paper and butter it. Though the batter for the torte is thick, you may also want to line the outside of the pan with a piece of aluminum foil to prevent any batter from leaking.

Place the walnuts and the flour in the work bowl of a food processor fitted with the metal blade. Process for 10 to 20 seconds, until the nuts are finely ground and the mixture has a mealy consistency. Set aside.

Put the chocolate, butter pieces, ¾ cup of sugar, and the coffee in a large saucepan and place the pan over medium heat. Cook, stirring constantly, until the chocolate and butter are completely melted and the mixture is glossy and registers about 130°F on a candy thermometer.

Remove the chocolate mixture from the heat and gradually whisk in the grappa, stirring until it is completely incorporated. Gradually whisk in the egg yolks and the salt. Using a rubber or silicone spatula, transfer the chocolate mixture to a large mixing bowl. Stir in the ground walnut-flour mixture.

In a large, clean, dry metal bowl, beat the egg whites and the cream of tartar with an electric mixer on medium speed until the egg whites are foamy. Increase the speed to high and gradually sprinkle in the remaining ¾ cup of sugar, beating until the egg whites are shiny and hold glossy peaks.

CONTINUED ON NEXT PAGE . . .

...CONTINUED

With a clean rubber or silicone spatula, scoop about ⅓ of the egg whites into the chocolate-nut mixture and gently fold them in. Carefully fold in the remaining egg whites with as light a hand as possible so as not to deflate them. Pour the batter into the prepared cake pan, gently smoothing out the top.

Bake the torte for 45 minutes, or until the border is puffed and set but the very center of the torte still jiggles slightly.

Set the torte on a rack and let it cool in the pan for 30 minutes. The torte will deflate some as it cools, and cracks will appear on the surface.

If you put foil around the exterior of the pan, remove it. Run a knife around the inside border and remove the ring from around the torte. Let the torte cool completely. To serve, place the torte on a cake stand or serving platter (see Cook's Note). Dust the top liberally with confectioners' sugar.

✧·✧·✧

COOK'S NOTE: Grappa is a colorless Italian brandy distilled from the pulpy mass of grape skins, pits, and stems left in the wine press after the juice has been extracted. It has a high alcohol content (40 percent). Italians sometimes add a shot of grappa to their espresso, or enjoy it as an after-dinner drink on its own.

Removing the bottom of the cake pan from under the torte is optional, and it involves some risk as the delicate crackled top that forms during cooling may crumble further. However, I have done it successfully, so I offer these instructions as an option: to remove the bottom of the pan, very gently place a rack or plate over the top of the cooled torte and invert the torte. Gently remove the bottom of the pan and peel off the piece of parchment. Then, re-invert the torte onto a stand or a serving platter. Dust liberally with confectioners' sugar.

✧·✧·✧

DO AHEAD: The torte may be made up to 2 days in advance and refrigerated, tightly covered in plastic wrap. Bring the torte to room temperature before dusting with confectioners' sugar and serving.

✧·✧·✧

SERVING SUGGESTION: Offer your guests—what else—a shot of grappa to accompany this torte. A dollop of freshly whipped cream atop each slice would be completely unnecessary. And yet, who could resist such a lovely final flourish?

Baked Farro Pudding

MAKES 4 TO 6 SERVINGS

Slow and sweet is how I like to describe this luscious pudding. It takes a good 3½ hours to bake in a low-temperature oven, but all it requires of you is a gentle stirring now and again. The pudding may be served warm or chilled, but I like it best chilled, especially on a hot day in summer.

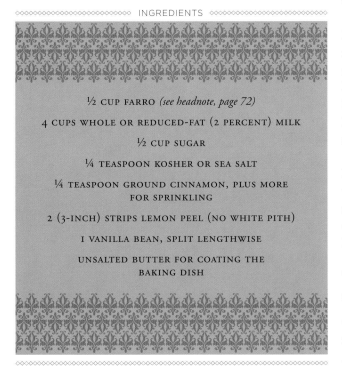

◇◇◇◇◇◇◇◇◇◇◇◇◇◇◇◇◇◇◇ INGREDIENTS ◇◇◇◇◇◇◇◇◇◇◇◇◇◇◇◇◇◇◇

½ CUP FARRO *(see headnote, page 72)*

4 CUPS WHOLE OR REDUCED-FAT (2 PERCENT) MILK

½ CUP SUGAR

¼ TEASPOON KOSHER OR SEA SALT

¼ TEASPOON GROUND CINNAMON, PLUS MORE
FOR SPRINKLING

2 (3-INCH) STRIPS LEMON PEEL (NO WHITE PITH)

1 VANILLA BEAN, SPLIT LENGTHWISE

UNSALTED BUTTER FOR COATING THE
BAKING DISH

Place the farro in a medium-sized saucepan and add water to cover by 2 inches. Bring to a boil and boil for 2 minutes. Remove the pan from the heat, cover, and let sit for 15 minutes. Drain the farro in a colander and transfer it to the work bowl of a food processor fitted with the metal blade. Pulse the farro just until the grains are coarsely ground, 30 to 45 seconds.

Heat the oven to 275°F. In a large bowl, combine the farro, milk, sugar, salt, cinnamon, and lemon peel. Scrape the seeds from the vanilla bean into the mixture and add the pod as well. Mix well. Coat a 2-quart oven-proof baking dish with a little butter. Pour the mixture into the dish and place in the oven. Bake the pudding for 3½ hours, stirring every hour to prevent a skin from forming.

Remove the pudding from the oven. Discard the vanilla pod and the lemon strips if you can locate them. Transfer the pudding to a clean ceramic vessel with a cover. Place a sheet of plastic wrap directly over the top of the pudding, and then cover with the lid. Refrigerate until thoroughly chilled.

To serve, spoon the pudding into individual custard cups and sprinkle each serving with a little cinnamon.

DO AHEAD: The pudding may be baked a day in advance and refrigerated, tightly covered with plastic wrap.

Pandoro Trifle with Vin Santo

MAKES 12 TO 15 SERVINGS

Pandoro, which means "golden bread" in Italian, is a tall, star-shaped leavened sweet bread that is produced in Verona. It is similar to the Italian holiday bread *panettone,* but is lighter in texture and does not contain the candied fruit typically found in *panettone.* Pandoro's airy texture and delicate, buttery sweetness make it a perfect base for this luscious, billowy strawberries-and-cream trifle. Pandoro's distinct sweet flavor is echoed in the flavor of the vin santo, the sweet dessert wine that is used to moisten the cake layers in the trifle. Both are most definitely worth searching out for this shamelessly extravagant dessert.

INGREDIENTS

For the pastry cream:

2 CUPS WHOLE MILK

I VANILLA BEAN

6 LARGE EGG YOLKS

⅔ CUP PLUS 2 TABLESPOONS SUGAR

¼ CUP UNBLEACHED ALL-PURPOSE FLOUR

I CUP HEAVY CREAM, CHILLED

8 OUNCES MASCARPONE

Pour the milk into a medium-sized heavy-bottomed saucepan. With a paring knife, split open the vanilla bean and scrape the seeds into the milk. Add the pod to the milk and place over medium heat. Bring to a boil and immediately remove the pot from the heat so that the milk does not boil over.

In a bowl, whisk together the egg yolks and ⅔ cup sugar until the mixture is pale yellow. It should form a "ribbon" when lifted with the whisk as it falls back into the bowl. Stir in the flour.

Ladle a little of the hot milk into the egg mixture, stirring vigorously as you do so to prevent the eggs from cooking. Continue to gradually ladle milk into the eggs until you have added about half of the milk. Pour this mixture back into the pan with the remaining hot milk, whisking as you go. Bring the milk and egg mixture to a boil over medium heat, stirring continuously with a whisk or wooden spoon. It will thicken as it begins to boil. Immediately turn the heat to low and continue to cook for 3 to 4 more minutes, stirring continuously to avoid scorching.

Pour the custard into a bowl and cover the top with plastic wrap. Press the wrap right onto the surface of the custard; this will prevent a tough skin from forming. Let the pastry cream come to room temperature, and then refrigerate it.

Whip the heavy cream and mascarpone together with the 2 remaining tablespoons of sugar until it just holds its shape. Gently fold the whipped-cream mixture into the chilled pastry cream. Refrigerate while you prepare the strawberries for the trifle.

INGREDIENTS

For the strawberry filling:

I POUND STRAWBERRIES, HULLED AND SLICED LENGTHWISE INTO QUARTERS

2 TABLESPOONS SUGAR

JUICE OF ½ LEMON

Place the strawberries in a bowl and toss them with the sugar and lemon juice. Cover the bowl with plastic wrap and let the strawberries macerate at room temperature for 30 to 60 minutes.

CONTINUED ON NEXT PAGE...

For the trifle:

1 WHOLE PANDORO CAKE *(see Sources, page 218)*

½ CUP VIN SANTO *(see Cook's Note)*

1 ½ CUPS HEAVY CREAM, CHILLED

2 TABLESPOONS SUGAR

4 TO 5 LARGE RIPE STRAWBERRIES, HULLED
AND CUT LENGTHWISE INTO THIN SLICES

½ CUP BLANCHED SLIVERED ALMONDS

Remove the cake from its box and cellophane wrapper. Use a serrated knife to cut a thin slice off the bottom to remove the bottom crust. Slice off the top of the cake in a piece about ¾ inch thick and set it aside. You will use this star-shaped piece to garnish the trifle.

Starting from the wider bottom end of the pandoro, cut the cake into ¾-inch-thick slices (you may not use all of the cake for the trifle; the leftovers can be stored in the cellophane wrapper). Place a slice in the bottom of an 8-inch-wide by 5-inch-deep trifle bowl or other large glass bowl of similar size. The star shape of the slice of cake will leave gaps in the layer; fill these in by tearing up another slice of cake and fitting the pieces into the gaps.

Using a pastry brush, moisten the layer of cake with one-third of the vin santo. Spoon one-third of the macerated strawberries over the cake and drizzle a little of the juice over them. Spread one-third of the chilled pastry cream over the moistened cake, smoothing it out with a spatula.

Set another layer of cake on top of the pastry cream layer. Brush with another one-third of the vin santo and spoon another third

of the strawberries and their juices over the cake. Top with a second layer of pastry cream.

Make a third, final layer of cake, vin santo (reserve 1 tablespoon), strawberries and juice, and pastry cream. Whip the 1 ½ cups heavy cream with the 2 tablespoons of sugar and the remaining tablespoon of vin santo until it is just stiff. Spread the whipped cream over the top layer of pastry cream. Arrange the strawberry slices in a circle around the rim of the trifle. Set the reserved top of the cake, cut side up, in the center of the trifle. Cover the trifle tightly with plastic wrap and refrigerate for at least 4 hours, or overnight.

Heat the oven to 400°F. Spread the slivered almonds in one layer on a small baking sheet and bake for 5 to 7 minutes, until they are fragrant and lightly toasted. Let them cool completely.

When you are ready to serve the trifle, remove the plastic wrap and sprinkle the toasted almonds over the top. Bring the trifle to the table and use a large serving spoon to scoop the trifle into individual custard cups or ice cream bowls.

COOK'S NOTE: Vin santo, "sainted wine," is a sweet (or sometimes dry) dessert wine that is produced in several regions in Italy, including Tuscany, Umbria, and the Veneto. It is made from late-harvested grapes that are also air-dried before being pressed. The fermented juice is aged for 3 to 5 years in small barrels, traditionally made from chestnut but now made mostly from oak.

DO AHEAD: Although numerous steps are required to make the trifle, they are all simple. In fact, this is a perfect dessert for a crowd, as it feeds many people and is best when assembled a day ahead. The pastry cream may be made up to 2 days in advance.

Sour Cherry–Mascarpone Pound Cake

MAKES 10 TO 12 SERVINGS

Sour cherries are popular in Italy, where they are turned into preserves or partially dried in the sun and then steeped in liquor and spooned over cake or ice cream. Having lived for a number of years in Michigan, which grows the majority of the U.S. sour cherry crop, I have become especially fond of fresh ones. I eat them the way most people eat their sweeter cousins, Bing and Rainier cherries—by the handful. The crimson fruit adds bursts of bright color and a welcome tartness to this rich pound cake.

INGREDIENTS

1½ CUPS (3 STICKS) UNSALTED BUTTER, AT ROOM TEMPERATURE, PLUS MORE TO GREASE THE PAN

3 CUPS UNBLEACHED ALL-PURPOSE FLOUR, PLUS MORE TO FLOUR THE PAN

2 CUPS FRESH SOUR CHERRIES, PITTED AND HALVED

3½ CUPS SUGAR

1 TEASPOON KOSHER OR SEA SALT

6 LARGE EGGS

2 TEASPOONS PURE VANILLA EXTRACT

8 OUNCES MASCARPONE OR SOUR CREAM, AT ROOM TEMPERATURE

CONFECTIONERS' SUGAR, FOR DUSTING

Heat the oven to 325°F. Lightly butter and flour a 10-inch Bundt or tube pan and set it aside.

In a small bowl, mix the cherries with ½ cup of the sugar. Let the mixture steep while you prepare the batter for the cake.

In a medium bowl, mix together the flour and salt. Set aside.

Put the 1½ cups butter in the bowl of a standing mixer and beat briefly on medium speed to soften. Add the remaining 3 cups of sugar, ½ cup at a time, and beat at high speed until light and airy, 5 full minutes. Add the eggs, one at a time, beating after each addition and scraping down the sides of the bowl with a rubber spatula as needed. Beat in the vanilla. Change the speed to medium and alternately add the flour-salt mixture and the mascarpone or sour cream, beginning and ending with the flour mixture. Mix until incorporated.

Drain the cherries, reserving the syrup that collects in the bowl. With a rubber or silicone spatula, fold the cherries into the batter.

Pour the batter into the prepared pan and shake lightly to even out the top. Bake until the cake is golden brown and a cake tester inserted in the center comes out clean, about 1 hour 15 minutes.

While the cake is baking, put the reserved cherry syrup in a small saucepan and boil for about 5 minutes, or until slightly thickened. Strain and reserve the liquid.

When the cake is done, place the pan on a cooling rack and cool for 20 minutes. Remove the cake from pan. While it is still warm, brush the top and sides with the warm cherry syrup. The cake will absorb the syrup. Let the cake cool to room temperature.

To serve, transfer the cake to a decorative platter or cake stand. Dust with confectioners' sugar.

DO AHEAD: The cake may be made several hours and up to 1 day in advance and kept, tightly wrapped in plastic, at room temperature. Dust with confectioners' sugar just before serving.

Three Rustic Tarts and a Batch of Butter Cookies

The same basic dough (with a variation in one recipe) is used to create three luscious
rustic tarts *(crostate)* and a delicious batch of butter cookies.

꽁옥·◊·옥꽁

Sweet Pastry Dough
MAKES ENOUGH DOUGH FOR ONE 9-INCH LATTICE-TOP TART
OR ONE SINGLE-CRUST 11-INCH TART

This tender dough is known as *pasta frolla* in Italian. It is rich
and buttery, with a hint of lemon. It has a crumbly shortbread
texture when baked. Be sure to chill the dough thoroughly—
for at least 1 hour—after mixing it (overnight is fine). Remove
it from the refrigerator about 45 minutes before rolling it out,
so that the butter softens and the dough becomes pliable. Use
a lightly floured surface to roll out the dough and do not over-
work it; too much flour and handling will yield a tough crust.

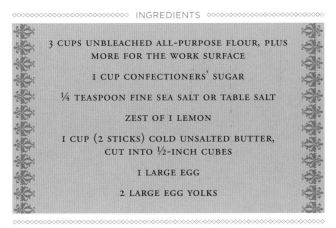

INGREDIENTS

3 CUPS UNBLEACHED ALL-PURPOSE FLOUR, PLUS
MORE FOR THE WORK SURFACE

1 CUP CONFECTIONERS' SUGAR

¼ TEASPOON FINE SEA SALT OR TABLE SALT

ZEST OF 1 LEMON

1 CUP (2 STICKS) COLD UNSALTED BUTTER,
CUT INTO ½-INCH CUBES

1 LARGE EGG

2 LARGE EGG YOLKS

Put the flour, sugar, salt, and lemon zest in the work bowl of a
food processor fitted with a metal blade. Pulse briefly to combine the ingredients. Distribute the butter around the bowl and
pulse until the mixture is crumbly. Add the egg and egg yolks
and process until the dough just begins to come together.

Turn the dough out onto a lightly floured work surface and gather
it together. Knead it briefly and shape it into a disk. Wrap tightly
in plastic and refrigerate for at least 1 hour, until well chilled.

VARIATION:
Almond Pastry Dough for Toasted Coconut Crostata
Substitute ½ cup almond flour or almond meal for ½ cup of
the flour and omit the lemon zest.

Lemon Crostata
MAKES ONE 11-INCH TART

I am convinced that a lemon tart can successfully follow just
about any meal. There is something about its freshness that
makes it thoroughly welcome at the end of dinner. This one
is especially nice because it is so easy to make—no messing
around with cooking a lemon curd on the stove top, no risk
of curdling.

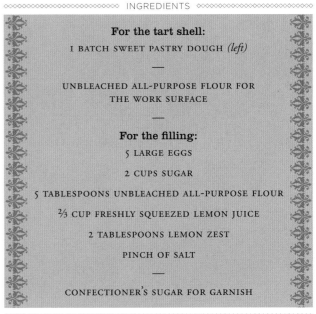

INGREDIENTS

For the tart shell:
1 BATCH SWEET PASTRY DOUGH *(left)*

—

UNBLEACHED ALL-PURPOSE FLOUR FOR
THE WORK SURFACE

—

For the filling:
5 LARGE EGGS

2 CUPS SUGAR

5 TABLESPOONS UNBLEACHED ALL-PURPOSE FLOUR

⅔ CUP FRESHLY SQUEEZED LEMON JUICE

2 TABLESPOONS LEMON ZEST

PINCH OF SALT

—

CONFECTIONER'S SUGAR FOR GARNISH

CONTINUED ON NEXT PAGE . . .

... CONTINUED

To make the tart shell:

Cut the dough disk into 2 portions, one slightly larger than the other. Rewrap the smaller portion and set aside. On a lightly floured work surface, roll out the larger portion into a 13-inch round about ⅛ inch thick or slightly thicker. Carefully wrap the dough around the rolling pin and drape it over an 11-inch fluted tart pan with a removable bottom. Gently press the dough into the bottom and up the sides of the pan. Trim the overhang to about ½ inch and fold it in, pressing it against the inside rim to reinforce the sides of the tart shell. Use the rolling pin or the flat of your hand to press around the perimeter of the pan to cut off any excess dough. Put the lined tart pan in the refrigerator to chill for 30 minutes.

Heat the oven to 350ºF.

Remove the tart shell from the refrigerator and line it with a piece of heavy-duty aluminum foil (or 2 pieces of regular aluminum foil to create a double thickness). Fill the lined shell with pie weights or dried beans and bake for 20 minutes. Remove the foil and the beans and bake for 15 more minutes, until the crust is light golden.

While the shell is baking, roll out the remaining piece of dough to ⅛-inch thickness. Use a cookie cutter to cut out decorative shapes (stars, moons, or whatever you like) to adorn the top of the tart. Or use a sharp paring knife to cut out a lemon shape about 4 inches long and 3 inches wide, and a pair of oval leaves. Score the leaves lightly with the blade of the knife to resemble the ribs. Place the dough cut-outs on a rimmed baking sheet and refrigerate until the tart shell has finished baking.

Remove the tart shell from the oven and let cool slightly on a rack. Set the cut-outs in the oven and bake for 10 to 12 minutes, until the edges are lightly browned. Transfer the cut-outs to a rack to cool.

To make the filling and bake the crostata:

Whisk together the eggs, sugar, flour, lemon juice and zest, and salt until well blended. Pour the filling into the baked tart shell. Set the *crostata* in the oven and bake for 30 to 35 minutes, until the filling is just set. Remove from the oven and let cool to room temperature on a rack. Carefully remove the fluted ring from around the *crostata* and transfer the *crostata* to a decorative serving plate. Dust the tart with confectioners' sugar. Arrange the cookie cut-outs as you please on top of the tart and serve.

DO AHEAD: The pastry dough may be made up to 2 days in advance and refrigerated or up to 1 month in advance and frozen. Bring the pastry to room temperature or slightly cooler before rolling it out.

For presentation purposes more than anything, this *crostata* is best served on the day it is made. But it may be made early in the day and left at room temperature until serving time. Leftovers keep beautifully in the refrigerator for at least 2 days without the crust getting soggy (I have never had leftovers hang around any longer than that).

Harvest Crostata
MAKES ONE 9-INCH LATTICE-TOP TART

Of the many desserts I have made or enjoyed over the years—chocolate-laden, cream-filled, liquor-soaked, constructed, deconstructed, and flambéed—this rustic tart still ranks as one of my very favorites. It is simple and homey and yet at the same time elegant. It tastes of fall's sweet flavors and, like fall's brilliant colors, disappears all too quickly.

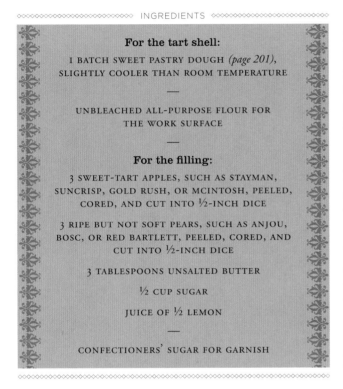

For the tart shell:

1 BATCH SWEET PASTRY DOUGH *(page 201),*
SLIGHTLY COOLER THAN ROOM TEMPERATURE

—

UNBLEACHED ALL-PURPOSE FLOUR FOR
THE WORK SURFACE

—

For the filling:

3 SWEET-TART APPLES, SUCH AS STAYMAN,
SUNCRISP, GOLD RUSH, OR MCINTOSH, PEELED,
CORED, AND CUT INTO ½-INCH DICE

3 RIPE BUT NOT SOFT PEARS, SUCH AS ANJOU,
BOSC, OR RED BARTLETT, PEELED, CORED, AND
CUT INTO ½-INCH DICE

3 TABLESPOONS UNSALTED BUTTER

½ CUP SUGAR

JUICE OF ½ LEMON

—

CONFECTIONERS' SUGAR FOR GARNISH

To make the tart shell:

Cut the dough disk into 2 portions, one slightly larger than the other. Rewrap the smaller portion and set aside. On a lightly floured work surface, roll out the larger portion into a 12-inch round about ⅛ inch thick. Carefully wrap the dough around the rolling pin and drape it over an 11-inch fluted tart pan with a removable bottom. Gently press the dough into the bottom and up the sides of the pan. Trim the overhang to about ½ inch and fold it in, pressing it against the inside rim to reinforce the sides of the tart shell. Use the rolling pin or the flat of your hand to press around the perimeter of the pan to cut off any excess dough. Put the lined tart pan in the refrigerator to chill for 30 minutes.

To make the filling:

In a heavy-bottomed saucepan, combine the apples, pears, butter, sugar, and lemon juice and bring to a simmer over medium-high heat, stirring to prevent the fruit from scorching. Cook, stirring frequently, for about 15 minutes, or until the fruit has broken down and the mixture has thickened. Remove from the heat and let cool to room temperature.

To assemble and bake the crostata:

Heat the oven to 350°F. Remove the tart shell from the refrigerator. Spoon the cooled filling into the shell and smooth it with a spatula. Roll out the remaining dough portion into a 10-inch round about ⅛ inch thick or slightly thicker, and cut it into ¾-inch-wide strips with a fluted pastry wheel. Carefully place the strips over the filling in a lattice pattern, gently pressing the ends of the strips into the metal rim of the tart pan to cut off the excess.

Bake the *crostata* for 30 to 40 minutes, or until the crust is golden. Remove the *crostata* from the oven and place it on a wire rack to cool for about 20 minutes. Remove the fluted rim of the tart pan and let the *crostata* cool completely on the rack. To serve, transfer the *crostata* to a decorative serving platter. Dust the top liberally with confectioners' sugar.

DO AHEAD: The pastry dough may be made up to 2 days in advance and kept, tightly wrapped in plastic, in the refrigerator, or up to 1 month in advance and kept frozen. Bring the dough to slightly cooler than room temperature before rolling it out. The filling may be made 1 day in advance and kept in a tightly lidded container in the refrigerator. Bring it to room temperature before assembling and baking the *crostata*.

CONTINUED ON NEXT PAGE . . .

CONTINUED

Toasted Coconut Crostata

MAKES ONE 11-INCH TART

My sister, Maria, adores coconut in any form. When we were young she was always on the lookout for the guy who would walk by on the beach in Italy, carrying a bucket of fresh coconut in water and calling out, *"Coccoooooo! Cocc'Americano!"*—the Italian term for coconut. I made this *crostata* for her birthday recently. It is adapted from a recipe that my next-door neighbor and friend Anne shared with me.

INGREDIENTS

For the tart shell:

1 BATCH ALMOND PASTRY DOUGH
(Sweet Pastry Dough variation, page 201)

—

UNBLEACHED ALL-PURPOSE FLOUR FOR
THE WORK SURFACE

—

1 ½ CUPS SHREDDED UNSWEETENED COCONUT

—

For the filling:

2 CUPS HALF-AND-HALF

2 CUPS COCONUT MILK

1 CUP SUGAR

⅔ CUP CORNSTARCH

½ TEASPOON KOSHER OR SEA SALT

3 LARGE EGGS, LIGHTLY BEATEN

1 TEASPOON PURE COCONUT EXTRACT

½ TEASPOON PURE VANILLA EXTRACT

—

FRESHLY WHIPPED CREAM FOR SERVING

To make the tart shell and toast the coconut:
Cut the dough disk into 2 portions, one slightly larger than the other. Rewrap the smaller portion and refrigerate or freeze for another use. On a lightly floured work surface, roll out the larger portion into a 13-inch round about ⅛ inch thick or slightly thicker. Carefully wrap the dough around the rolling pin and drape it over an 11-inch fluted tart pan with a removable bottom. Gently press the dough into the bottom and up the sides of the pan. Trim the overhang to about ½ inch and fold it in, pressing it against the inside rim to reinforce the sides of the tart shell. Use the rolling pin or the flat of your hand to press around the perimeter of the pan to cut off any excess dough. Put the lined tart pan in the refrigerator to chill for 30 minutes.

Heat the oven to 350°F. Remove the tart shell from the refrigerator and line it with a piece of heavy-duty aluminum foil (or 2 pieces of regular aluminum foil to create a double thickness). Fill the lined shell with pie weights or dried beans and bake for 20 minutes. Remove the foil and the beans and bake for 15 more minutes, until the crust is light golden. Remove from the oven and transfer to a wire rack. Let the tart shell cool to room temperature. Remove the fluted ring from around the tart shell.

Spread the shredded coconut on a baking sheet and toast in the oven for 5 to 7 minutes, until golden brown. Be sure to check the oven frequently, as the coconut can burn easily. Remove the toasted coconut from the oven and transfer it to a bowl.

To make the filling:
Combine the half-and-half, coconut milk, sugar, cornstarch, salt, and eggs in a medium-sized saucepan and set the pan over medium-low heat. Stirring constantly with a whisk, cook the mixture until it just begins to boil and has achieved a pudding-like consistency. This will take up to 30 minutes, but please be patient and continue to stir; rushing this step could cause the eggs to "cook" and curdle.

Remove the thickened custard from the heat and stir in the coconut and vanilla extracts, mixing until well incorporated. Fold in half of the toasted coconut. Scrape the custard into a bowl and cover it with plastic wrap, pressing the wrap directly onto the surface of the custard to prevent a skin from forming. Let the custard cool to room temperature.

To assemble the crostata:

Spread the custard into the cooled tart shell. Cover the *crostata* with plastic wrap and refrigerate until thoroughly chilled. To serve, place the chilled *crostata* on a decorative platter. Sprinkle the reserved toasted coconut on top of the *crostata*. Cut into wedges and garnish each slice with a dollop of freshly whipped cream.

DO AHEAD: The pastry dough may be made up to 2 days in advance and kept, tightly wrapped in plastic, in the refrigerator, or up to 1 month in advance and kept frozen. Bring the dough to slightly cooler than room temperature before rolling it out. The filling may be made a day in advance and kept in a tightly lidded container in the refrigerator. Be sure to cover the surface of the custard with a layer of plastic wrap to prevent a skin from forming. To serve, spoon the chilled custard into the baked tart shell and use an angled spatula to smooth out the top. Garnish with the toasted coconut right before serving.

Butter Cookies
MAKES SEVERAL DOZEN COOKIES

This recipe is nothing more than my sweet pastry dough, rolled and cut into shapes and baked. A plate of these lemon-scented cookies makes for a nice light dessert after a rich meal.

INGREDIENTS

I BATCH SWEET PASTRY DOUGH *(page 201)*, SLIGHTLY COOLER THAN ROOM TEMPERATURE

UNBLEACHED ALL-PURPOSE FLOUR FOR DUSTING THE WORK SURFACE

CONFECTIONERS' SUGAR FOR DUSTING

Heat the oven to 350°F.

On a clean, lightly floured work surface, roll the dough out to ¼-inch thickness. Using cookie cutters, cut out a variety of shapes. Place the cookies on an ungreased baking sheet and chill for 30 minutes.

Gather up the scraps of dough, re-roll, and continue to cut out cookies until you have used all of the dough.

Bake the cookies in batches for 10 to 15 minutes, until the edges are lightly browned. Transfer the baking sheet to a wire rack and let cool 5 minutes. With an angled spatula, remove the cookies from the baking sheet and let them cool completely on the rack.

To serve, arrange the cookies on a decorative plate and dust with confectioners' sugar.

COOK'S NOTE: I sometimes like to serve these cookies with other treats, such as a bowl of clementines in winter, berries and whipped cream in summer, or some chocolate-covered espresso beans or *torrone*, Italian nougat candy, at Christmas.

Brunch is an all-American tradition, one of my favorites. I love it all—the eggs (poached, scrambled, fried, or souffléd), thick slices of smoky bacon and sage-laced breakfast sausages, custardy French toast, light-as-air pancakes doused with maple syrup, and sour-cream coffee cake with its crumbly topping.

So I surprised even myself when I created this menu and found it veering in a slightly different direction. But really, it makes perfect sense. It reflects my love for both Italian and American classics and offers something just a bit different to set out for friends and family.

Yogurt Parfaits (page 209), made with ultra-creamy and dense Greek yogurt, fresh blueberries, and tart dried cherries, are a cool, refreshing start.

In place of coffee cake there is Ciambellone (page 210), a vanilla-scented ring cake that was truly made for dunking. The ethereally light Heavenly Eggs (page 211) are a variation of a wonderful recipe given to me years ago by a dear family friend. They make a superb entrée accompanied by Asparagus with Olive Oil and Lemon (page 214).

I didn't grow up with Popovers (page 213), but I have been baking them since I was a teenager and first came across a recipe in my mother's old Betty Crocker cookbook. My kids adore them and so I make them often. These bake up beautifully brown and tall and are divine with butter and jam.

Bacon and sausage are optional, but I wouldn't think of not serving at least one as part of a brunch. Choose high-quality meats; it makes a difference. Strawberry Jam Crostata (page 215) could be considered a dessert of sorts, but one that is perfectly at home on the brunch table, to be enjoyed with a cup of coffee—or a glass of champagne.

CH. 7
BUON GIORNO: BRUNCH MENU FOR A BIG MORNING IN

Yogurt Parfaits

MAKES 8 SERVINGS

Greek yogurt, which has become widely available in the United States in recent years, is much thicker, creamier, and richer than American yogurt. Its consistency is just right for these colorful parfaits. If you are unable to find Greek yogurt, look for Lebanese yogurt, which is similarly rich and creamy. Or use American yogurt, but set it in a cheesecloth-lined sieve or colander to drain for several hours in the refrigerator before using.

INGREDIENTS

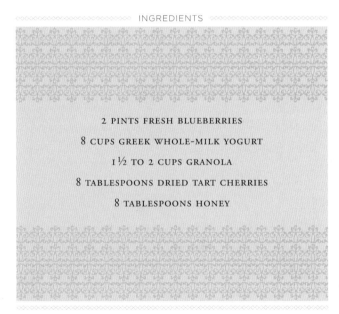

2 PINTS FRESH BLUEBERRIES

8 CUPS GREEK WHOLE-MILK YOGURT

1½ TO 2 CUPS GRANOLA

8 TABLESPOONS DRIED TART CHERRIES

8 TABLESPOONS HONEY

Spoon a few blueberries into the bottoms of 8 parfait glasses or tumblers. Spoon ½ cup of yogurt into each glass and sprinkle some granola and a few dried cherries over the yogurt. Add more yogurt to each glass and top with more blueberries, a drizzle of honey, and an additional sprinkle of granola. Serve cold.

DO AHEAD: The parfaits may be assembled and refrigerated up to 2 hours in advance. However, if you like your granola crunchy, I recommend assembling them right before serving. Or set out the ingredients on a table and have your guests assemble their own parfaits.

Ciambellone

MAKES ONE 9-INCH RING CAKE

A dunking cake if ever there was one, this is my mother's absolutely fool-proof recipe; our family has been devouring it for at least three generations. The secret ingredient is a sweet, citrus-infused liqueur from Abruzzo (see Cook's Note). Perhaps it is what makes this cake such a big hit with children.

〰〰〰〰〰 INGREDIENTS 〰〰〰〰〰

3 CUPS UNBLEACHED ALL-PURPOSE FLOUR,
PLUS ADDITIONAL FOR DUSTING THE BAKING PAN

1½ CUPS SUGAR

2 TEASPOONS BAKING POWDER

1 TEASPOON BAKING SODA

⅛ TEASPOON KOSHER OR SEA SALT

½ CUP (1 STICK) UNSALTED BUTTER, CUT
INTO ½-INCH PIECES, PLUS ADDITIONAL FOR
GREASING THE BAKING PAN

3 LARGE EGGS, LIGHTLY BEATEN

¼ CUP PLUS 2 TABLESPOONS LIGHT CREAM OR
HALF-AND-HALF

1 TEASPOON PURE VANILLA EXTRACT

1 TEASPOON PURE ALMOND EXTRACT

2 TABLESPOONS *PUNCH ABRUZZESE* LIQUEUR
OR DARK RUM *(see Cook's Note)*

2 TABLESPOONS PEARL SUGAR FOR SPRINKLING
(see Cook's Note; you may substitute granulated sugar)

Heat the oven to 350ºF. Butter and flour a 9-inch tube pan and set aside.

In the work bowl of a food processor fitted with the metal blade, place the flour, sugar, baking powder, baking soda, and salt. Pulse briefly to combine. Distribute the butter around the bowl and process briefly until the butter is incorporated. In a medium bowl, whisk together the eggs, ¼ cup cream, vanilla and almond extracts, and liqueur. With the food processor running, pour the liquid mixture through the feed tube and process until everything is well blended and a thick and sticky batter has formed. With a large spatula, scoop the batter (it will be almost as thick as a ball of dough) into the prepared baking pan and spread it around evenly.

Bake the cake for 30 minutes. Remove the pan from the oven and brush the cake with the 2 remaining tablespoons of cream and sprinkle with the pearl or granulated sugar. Return the cake to the oven for 5 more minutes, or until a cake tester inserted into the center of the cake comes out clean and the top of the cake is golden brown. Transfer the pan to a rack to cool for 20 to 30 minutes. Remove the cake from the pan and let it cool completely on the rack. Transfer the cake, sugar-side-up, to a decorative platter before serving.

COOK'S NOTE: *Punch Abruzzese* is produced outside of Chieti, my mother's hometown. It is a sweet, potent liqueur made from caramelized sugar and the zest of lemons and oranges. *Punch* is not easy to find, and I am still searching for a good Internet source for it; but it is well worth knowing about, which is why I mention it here. It is considered a good after-dinner digestive and is delicious drizzled over vanilla ice cream. If you are unable to find it, substitute Cointreau, Grand Marnier, or dark rum mixed with a little orange and lemon zest.

Pearl sugar consists of bright white, irregularly shaped granules of sugar. It is often used as a decorative touch in European baked goods (see Sources, page 218).

DO AHEAD: The cake may be made a day in advance and kept, tightly wrapped, at room temperature.

Heavenly Eggs

MAKES 8 SERVINGS

This recipe was given to me years ago by a dear friend of my mother's, Marie Speciale. Eggs and cheese are combined in the top of a double boiler and gently simmered without stirring until they are just firm. This hands-off cooking technique yields the lightest, fluffiest scrambled eggs I have ever had. What is more, they are perfect to serve at a brunch buffet because they keep well in a chafing dish. The original recipe calls for cream cheese, but I often use mascarpone, which imparts a creamy sweetness to the eggs. You won't go wrong either way.

INGREDIENTS

8 OUNCES MASCARPONE OR CREAM CHEESE

½ CUP LIGHT CREAM

I DOZEN LARGE EGGS

2 TABLESPOONS FINELY MINCED FRESH
FLAT-LEAF PARSLEY

KOSHER OR SEA SALT

FRESHLY GROUND BLACK PEPPER

Fill the lower pan of a large double boiler with just enough water so that when you place the top pan over it, the water does not touch the bottom of the top pan. Put the mascarpone or cream cheese and the light cream into the top pan and set the top pan over the lower pan. Turn the heat to medium-high and bring the water in the lower pan to a simmer. Stir the mixture as it heats up to incorporate the cheese into the cream. Reduce the heat to medium if the water in the bottom of the pan is boiling too much; it should be at a lively simmer but not a rolling boil.

In a large bowl, lightly beat the eggs with the parsley. Sprinkle in a little salt and pepper. When the cheese in the top pan of the double boiler has melted, pour the eggs into the pan and stir to combine them with the cheese mixture. Let the eggs cook, without stirring them, for 20 to 30 minutes, or until they are almost set. With a rubber spatula, gently fold the eggs to move the top, uncooked portion toward the bottom of the pan. Cook for a minute or two more, until the eggs are just firm. Remove the pan from the heat and serve. Or, if you are serving the eggs as part of a brunch buffet, transfer them to a chafing dish and keep warm until serving time.

Popovers

MAKES 8 POPOVERS

The simple pleasure of a freshly baked popover is not to be missed. My version boasts a crisp golden brown crust and a moist, custardy interior. Among the many virtues of popovers is that they can be made with ingredients that most of us nearly always have on hand—eggs, flour, milk, and butter. They are exceptionally versatile: they make a great accompaniment to soup for a light supper, but are just as at home nestled next to a roast for Sunday dinner. I like to serve popovers for breakfast and brunch, with bacon and sliced fresh fruit on the side.

Use individual 6-ounce (¾-cup) Pyrex baking cups rather than muffin tins if you want your popovers to bake up nice and high (like a soufflé, they will deflate once removed from the oven). Be sure to very generously grease the cups before filling them with batter to prevent the popovers from sticking. I find cooking spray works best.

Heat the oven to 425ºF.

Generously coat eight 6-ounce Pyrex baking cups with cooking spray. Place the cups on a rimmed baking sheet and set aside.

Place the flour, milk, salt, eggs, and butter in the pitcher of a blender. Blend together on high speed until smooth. Pour the batter in equal amounts into the greased cups (they will be about ¾ full).

Bake the popovers for about 35 minutes, until they have puffed up high and their tops are golden brown. Carefully remove the hot popovers from the cups and place them in a cloth-lined basket or a serving plate. Serve at once with fresh butter and jam.

DO AHEAD: The batter for popovers may be made several hours in advance and refrigerated in a tightly lidded container. Be sure to remove it from the refrigerator 20 to 30 minutes before baking and mix it thoroughly before filling the custard cups.

⁓⁓⁓ INGREDIENTS ⁓⁓⁓

COOKING SPRAY

2 CUPS UNBLEACHED ALL-PURPOSE FLOUR

2 CUPS WHOLE MILK

1¼ TEASPOONS KOSHER OR SEA SALT

4 LARGE EGGS

4 TABLESPOONS UNSALTED BUTTER, MELTED
AND SLIGHTLY COOLED

Asparagus with Olive Oil and Lemon

MAKES 8 SERVINGS

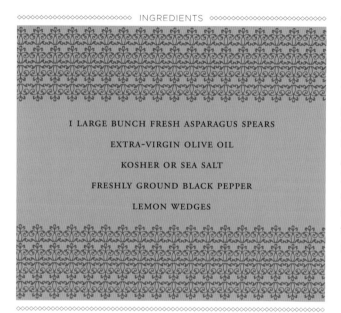

I LARGE BUNCH FRESH ASPARAGUS SPEARS

EXTRA-VIRGIN OLIVE OIL

KOSHER OR SEA SALT

FRESHLY GROUND BLACK PEPPER

LEMON WEDGES

This is hardly a recipe, but it is always welcome at brunch, when there tends to be an excess of carb-laden sweets and rich meats but not much in the way of greens.

With a sharp knife, trim the tough bottom ends off the asparagus. Place a large pot on the stove and set a steamer basket in it. Fill the pot with enough water to reach just below the steamer. Cover and bring the water to a boil over medium-high heat. Arrange the asparagus spears in the steamer basket, cover, and let steam for about 3 minutes, or until they are bright green and crisp-tender. Turn off the heat, and using tongs, remove the asparagus from the steamer basket to a serving platter. Drizzle with olive oil and sprinkle with a little salt and pepper. Garnish the platter with lemon wedges and serve.

Strawberry Jam Crostata

MAKES 1 9-INCH LATTICE-TOP TART

Strawberry seems to me the appropriate jam to choose for a brunch tart, but of course you can use whatever fruit jam you like best. Just make sure it is of good quality, dense, and with lots of chunks of fruit in it.

INGREDIENTS

For the tart shell:

I BATCH SWEET PASTRY DOUGH *(page 201)*, SLIGHTLY COOLER THAN ROOM TEMPERATURE

—

UNBLEACHED ALL-PURPOSE FLOUR FOR DUSTING THE WORK SURFACE

—

For the filling:

I TO I ½ CUPS STRAWBERRY JAM OR PRESERVES

—

CONFECTIONERS' SUGAR FOR DUSTING

To make the tart shell:

Cut the dough disk into 2 portions, one slightly larger than the other. Rewrap the smaller portion and set it aside. On a lightly floured surface, roll out the larger portion into a 12-inch round about ⅛ inch thick. Carefully wrap the dough around the rolling pin and drape it over a 9-inch fluted tart pan with a removable bottom. Gently press the dough into the bottom and up the sides of the pan. Trim the overhang to about ½ inch and fold it in, pressing it against the inside rim to reinforce the sides of the tart shell. Use the rolling pin or the flat of your hand to press around the perimeter of the pan to cut off any excess dough. Put the lined tart pan in the refrigerator to chill for 30 minutes.

To assemble and bake the tart:

Heat the oven to 350°F. Remove the tart shell from the refrigerator. Spoon the jam into the shell and smooth it with a rubber spatula. Roll out the remaining dough portion into a 10-inch round about ⅛ inch thick and cut it into ¾-inch-wide strips with a fluted pastry wheel. Carefully place the strips over the filled tart shell in a lattice pattern, gently pressing the ends of the strips into the sides of the tart shell.

Bake the *crostata* for 30 to 40 minutes, or until the crust is golden. Remove the *crostata* from the oven and place it on a wire rack to cool for 20 minutes, or until cool enough to handle. Remove the fluted rim of the tart pan and let the *crostata* cool completely on the rack before transferring it to a decorative serving platter. Dust with confectioners' sugar.

DO AHEAD: The pastry dough may be made up to 2 days in advance and kept, tightly wrapped in plastic, in the refrigerator, or up to 1 month in advance and kept frozen. Bring the dough to slightly cooler than room temperature before rolling it out. The *crostata* may be assembled and baked a day in advance. Once it has cooled, cover it tightly with plastic wrap and store at room temperature. Dust with confectioners' sugar just before serving.

Suggested Menus

For me, much of the enjoyment of throwing a party or having friends over for dinner comes from planning the menu. Even before I've set a date I'm already thinking about what sort of gathering it will be, what's in season, and how I can have the most fun with it in the kitchen. I spend lots of time flipping through cookbooks and magazines new and old, looking for inspiration and ideas—not because I have to find the *perfect* side to accompany a particular roast but because I love figuring out what goes together. Devising a good menu is like solving a puzzle: there's a nice feeling of accomplishment when it all comes together. Following are a dozen menus featuring the recipes in this book. There are many, many more combinations and themes, but I will leave that to you. After all, I don't want to be the only one having fun in the kitchen.

Menu Mediterraneo: A Mediterranean Menu for 8

Spinach and Yogurt Dip, page 41

Mixed Olives

Pistachio Nuts

Vegetarian Mixed Grill, page 119

Farro Salad, page 72, *or* Grilled Vegetable Salad, page 75

Espresso Granita, page 184

La Rosticceria: A Rustic Summer Menu for 12

Bruschetta with Roasted Cherry Tomatoes, page 31

Spatchcocked Chickens alla Diavola, page 117

Insalata di Riso, page 69

Sliced Fresh Tomatoes Drizzled with Olive Oil

2 batches Sour Cherry Gelato with Bittersweet Chocolate-Cherry Sauce, page 185

Arriva l'Autunno: An Early Fall Dinner for 8

Crostini with a Selection of Colorful Toppings, page 22

Rosemary-Rubbed Butterflied Leg of Lamb, page 112

September Gratin, page 175, *or* Caponata, page 34

Olive Oil–Roasted Potatoes, page 158

Harvest Crostata, page 202

Anno Nuovo: An Elegant New Year's Dinner for 6

Stuffed Olives, page 27

Egg Ribbons in Homemade Broth, page 50

Beef Tenderloin alla Bandiera Italiana, page 133

Savory Carrot Crostata, page 171

Winter Endive and Orange Salad, page 61

Bittersweet Mocha Grappa Torte with Walnuts, page 193

Antipasti: A Cocktail Party for 20

Mini Rice Croquettes, page 25

Stuffed Olives, page 27

Italian Cheese Platter, page 39

Sea Salt and Rosemary Sweet Potato Chips, page 43

Caponata, page 34

Chef John Coletta's Calabrian Fennel Salad with Raisins and Red Finger Chiles, page 33

Smoky Ham and Corn Chowder, page 149, served in small cups

Gorgonzola-Stuffed Dates, page 29

Butter Cookies, page 205

Chocolate-Covered Espresso Beans

Una Cenetta per L'Inverno: A Midwinter Supper for 8

Spicy Seafood Chowder with Sweet Fennel, page 146

Popovers, page 213

Escarole and Swiss Chard Torte, page 163

Fresh Clementines

La Primavera: An Early Spring Dinner for 6

Creamy Carrot Soup with Rice and Caramelized Carrots, page 57

Slow-Roasted Arctic Char with Sautéed Fennel and Pernod, page 127

Farm Stand Sauté, page 159

Walnut Focaccia, page 46

Baked Farro Pudding, page 195

La Domenica: Sunday Dinner for 10

Crepe Cannelloni with Zucchini and Cheese Stuffing, page 122

Roast Pork Loin with Carrots, Fennel, and Onions, page 131

Truffled Mushrooms, page 165

Winter Endive and Orange Salad, page 61

Toasted Coconut Crostata, page 204

La Famiglia: Comfort Food for the Family

Double Carbonara, page 84

Caesar Salad, page 62

Strawberry Jam Crostata, page 215

Menu di Mare: Seafaring Dinner for 6

Seaside Salad, page 37

Bruschetta, page 31

Fresh Tuna Stew with Olives and Herbs, page 145

Red, White, and Green Salad with Lemon-Balsamic Dressing, page 58

Apricot Semifreddo, page 181

Menu Magro: A Vegetarian Feast for 8

O Sole Mio Ravioli, page 81

Three-Cheese-Stuffed Red and Yellow Peppers, page 141

Chef John Coletta's Calabrian Fennel Salad with Raisins and Red Finger Chiles, page 33

Truffled Mushrooms, page 165

Lemon Crostata, page 201

Big Night In: Dinner Buffet for a Crowd

Stuffed Olives, page 27

Italian Cheese Platter, page 39

Gabriella's Lasagne Verde alla Bolognese, page 91, or Eggplant Parmigiana Deluxe, page 138

Pasta Timballo, page 99

Mixed Grilled Platter of Steaks, Chops, Thighs, and Sausages, page 113, or Beef Tenderloin alla Bandiera Italiana, page 133

Red, White, and Green Salad with Lemon-Balsamic Dressing, page 58

Frank's Garlic Bread, page 45

Cheesecake Sundaes, page 187

Sources

For imported Rizzoli anchovies, chestnut products, farro,
Pandoro cake, and other Italian specialties:
A. G. Ferrari Foods
877-878-2783
www.agferrari.com

For almond flour, almond meal, and pearl sugar:
King Arthur Flour
800-827-6836
www.kingarthurflour.com

For fennel pollen and marrons glacés:
Market Hall Foods
888-952-4005
www.markethallfoods.com

Index

Table of Equivalents

The exact equivalents in the following tables have been rounded for convenience.

LIQUID/DRY MEASUREMENTS

U.S	METRIC
¼ teaspoon	1.25 milliliters
½ teaspoon	2.5 milliliters
1 teaspoon	5 milliliters
1 tablespoon (3 teaspoons)	15 milliliters
1 fluid ounce (2 tablespoons)	30 milliliters
¼ cup	60 milliliters
⅓ cup	80 milliliters
½ cup	120 milliliters
1 cup	240 milliliters
1 pint (2 cups)	480 milliliters
1 quart (4 cups; 32 ounces)	960 milliliters
1 gallon (4 quarts)	3.84 liters

U.S	METRIC
1 ounce (by weight)	28 grams
1 pound	448 grams
2.2 pounds	1 kilogram

LENGTHS

U.S.	METRIC
⅛ inch	3 millimeters
¼ inch	6 millimeters
½ inch	12 millimeters
1 inch	2.5 centimeters

OVEN TEMPERATURES

FAHRENHEIT	CELSIUS	GAS
250	120	½
275	140	1
300	150	2
325	160	3
350	180	4
375	190	5
400	200	6
425	220	7
450	230	8
475	240	9
500	260	10